THE
SAN FRANCISCO
CHRONICLE
COOK BOOK

THE
SAN FRANCISCO
CHRONICLE
COOK BOOK

by JANE BENÉT

CHRONICLE BOOKS

For readers who enjoy food and cooking as much as I do.

Designed and illustrated by Wolfgang Lederer.

Library of Congress Catalog Card Number: 73-84521
ISBN O-87701-046-3

Published by Chronicle Books
54 Mint Street
San Francisco, California 94103

Contents

Introduction

Over the years, *The Chronicle* has printed literally thousands of recipes in its sections called *Food*. Many of these have been in response to readers' requests, others have dealt with national food promotions and a very large number of them have resulted from our own interests in food and cooking.

This volume, then, is a collection of what we consider to be the best and most popular of those recipes—the ones that have stood the test of time and have been used again and again, and the ones most often requested by readers.

It is not meant to be a big basic cookbook—there are more than enough of those in print already. But it is meant to replace the many unsorted, unclassified and, consequently, unused loose recipes clipped from publications over the years, and stowed in boxes and drawers.

We hope, too, that it will be useful and enjoyable for cooks all over the land. It is, after all, the best of *Food*.

Jane Benét
San Francisco
June 1973

Appetizers

More and more, we note happily, the fare at cocktail parties is inclined to be on the hearty side. It's a nice change from a bowl of plain potato chips and a few olives. This appetizer is on the hot side. It is served hot and it is seasoned hot—or to taste.

Corned Beef con Queso

1 T. butter
1 medium onion, minced
1 12-oz. can corned beef,
    unchilled

1 c. drained, canned tomatoes
½ lb. American cheese, cubed
1 roasted, peeled green chili
Corn chips

Sauté onion in butter until tender but not browned. Add corned beef and flake with a fork while heating. Stir in tomatoes and mix well to break into small pieces. Add cheese and green chili (or a few drops of hot pepper sauce). Cook, stirring, over low heat until cheese melts and blends in. Serve hot with corn chips as "dippers."

Stuffed Grape Leaves (Dolmadakia)

1 jar vine leaves (about 36)
¾ c. raw rice
¼ c. pine nuts
1 bunch scallions,
    finely chopped
1 T. parsley,
    finely chopped

1 T. fresh chopped dill
¼ c. seedless currants,
    soaked in white wine
2 lemons
1 can beef bouillon
¾ c. olive oil
Salt, pepper

Remove leaves from jar, scald with hot water and drain. Cut off stems carefully, pat each leaf dry and place on paper towels with shiny surface down. Sauté onions and parsley in 2 tablespoons hot olive oil in a skillet; add rice, dill, pine nuts and currants with wine; salt and pepper to taste. Cover and simmer for 15 minutes, set aside to cool. When cool, place 1 teaspoon of the rice mixture in the center of each leaf; fold end of leaf over to cover filling; fold up sides of leaf and roll over carefully until a cylinder, about 2 inches long, is formed. Arrange the leaves in layers in a pot; sprinkle each layer with lemon juice and 2 tablespoons olive oil. Pour bouillon, 1 cup water and the remaining olive oil over all; place a plate on top to weight them down; simmer over very low heat for 40 to 50 minutes. Remove, drain and cool before serving.

To serve, arrange stuffed leaves on a platter garnished with lemon wedges and accompanied by a bowl of chilled yoghurt.

Raclette, taken from the French word racler, meaning to scrape, is prepared by exposing the cut edge of a half wheel of Bagne cheese (exported to the U.S. as "raclette") to an open fire. The surface of the cheese is allowed to melt, then quickly scraped off to a hot serving plate with a small boiled potato and gherkin pickle.

Although traditionally served by a roaring fire, this dish may be prepared more "conveniently," but far less flamboyantly, using the recipe that follows.

Raclette

½ lb. imported Swiss raclette, cut into 12 slices about ⅛ inch thick, 5 x 2 inches	4 freshly boiled small new potatoes, peeled
	4-8 small sour gherkins
	4-8 pickled onions

Preheat oven to 500 degrees. Heat four 10-inch oven-proof plates.

When ready to serve, remove the plates from the oven, holding them with potholders, and, as quickly as you can, arrange three slices of the cheese in the center of each plate, overlapping slightly. The cheese should begin to sizzle immediately. Quickly place the plates on the rack, by source of heat. The cheese should melt to a creamy, bubbly mass; do not let it turn the slightest bit brown. Serve immediately with potatoes, gherkins and onions. Serves 4.

Bagna Cauda is a traditional dunking sauce for a good selection of raw fresh vegetables. It is served hot in its cooking pot.

Bagna Cauda

½ c. butter
¼ c. olive oil
4 small cloves garlic, mashed

1 2-oz. flat tin
anchovy filets
Raw vegetables

Choose a heatproof container that will be only about half filled by the quantity of sauce. In it, combine butter, olive oil and garlic. Drain anchovy filets well on paper towels; chop them finely and add to sauce. Stir over moderate heat until mixture bubbles.

To serve, set over candle or low alcohol flame. Mixture must not get hot enough to brown or burn. Accompany with raw vegetables—pepper strips, celery sticks, carrots, cauliflowerettes, cherry tomatoes, drained marinated artichoke hearts, raw mushrooms, etc. Makes enough for 8 to 10 servings.

Steak Tartare Gaulois

6 oz. lean beef sirloin,
  freshly ground
1 T. capers
1 T. chopped cornichons
1 T. chopped champignons
  de Paris

1 T. chopped onion
1 T. chopped parsley
1 raw egg yolk
  (optional)
Dijon mustard
Salt and pepper

The meat must be used the same day it is purchased. Serve it well-chilled and shaped into a patty. If desired, cradle a raw egg yolk in the center (use the egg shell as a tiny cup), or serve separately. The other ingredients are placed around the meat and each diner seasons his portion to suit his taste.

Some of the better, but often lesser known, recipes of Italy come from Tuscany, the picturesque area surrounding Florence. This part of Italy combines fine oils, tender meats and excellent wines in its cuisine.

One of the region's famed recipes, for Florentine Crostini, comes from the family of Barone Bettino Ricasoli, whose ancestors began making fine wines at Castle Brolio in the 12th Century. The Crostini may be served as an appetizer, a first course or, even, a simple supper entrée.

Florentine Crostini

½ lb. chicken livers,
rinsed, dried
4 T. minced green onion
(white only)
6 T. fine olive oil, about
2 T. rinsed, drained
capers, about
4 tsp. Brolio Chianti Classico

1½ T. minced fresh parsley
Dash Tabasco
Salt, freshly-ground
black pepper
6 thin slices French-style
bread, each about 2 x 4
inches, toasted on one side,
brushed with oil on the other

Sauté chicken livers and onions in 2 tablespoons of the olive oil in a frying pan over medium heat for about 5 minutes. Add capers. Roughly mash livers and capers with a fork. Add Chianti and 1 tablespoon of the parsley and cook for about 3 minutes more, until liquid has disappeared. Season generously to taste with Tabasco, salt, pepper and olive oil. Spread on untoasted side of bread. Sprinkle with remaining parsley. Serve with some of the same wine used in its preparation. Serves 6 as a first course.

Cucumber Dip

1 pt. sour cream
1 medium cucumber,
pared, seeded, chopped
¼ c. chopped scallions *or*
2 T. chopped chives
2 T. salad oil

2 T. lemon juice
1 tsp. salt
¼ tsp. pepper
6 artichokes, cooked,
trimmed, chilled

Combine sour cream, cucumber, scallions, oil, lemon juice, salt and pepper; chill. Serve as a dip with artichokes. Makes about 3 cups.

Note: This dip may be heated slowly and served with warm artichokes.

Herbed Cheese Crock

1 10-oz. pkg. Muenster cheese
½ lb. aged cheddar cheese
3 T. brandy
⅛ tsp. sweet basil, crushed

1/16 tsp. dried dill weed
1 tsp. Dijon-style mustard
½ tsp. paprika
2 T. soft butter

Grate cheeses into mixing bowl. Add all remaining ingredients. Beat until well blended. Cover and refrigerate until an hour before serving. Makes 3 cups.

If you haven't yet tried those wonderful Japanese forest mushrooms, called shii-ta-ke, here's an unusual recipe to start with. It is for a relish that is excellent served with cooked prawns—or with baked ham, corned pork or cold turkey or luncheon meats.

Mushroom Relish

1 c. shii-ta-ke
3 T. brown sugar
½ tsp. ground ginger
⅔ c. tarragon wine vinegar
1 T. oil
2 T. finely-chopped parsley

1 onion, sliced
1 c. green pepper strips
2 T. chopped pimiento
1 c. thin cucumber slices
½ c. thin radish slices
½ c. stuffed green olives

Pour hot water over mushrooms to cover; let stand 15 to 45 minutes. Drain well; clip and discard stems. Leave small mushrooms whole, cut larger ones in strips. Combine brown sugar, ginger, oil, vinegar and parsley in small jar. Cover and shake until well blended; pour over mushrooms. Cover and marinate 1 hour or longer. Combine with all remaining ingredients. Serve as a relish or as a salad with hot or cold cooked prawns, crab or other seafood. Serves 6 to 8.

Sauterne Ham Spread

1 12-oz. can chopped ham
1 T. plain gelatin
¼ c. cold water
⅔ c. Calif. Sauterne *or*
    other white dinner wine
1 c. cottage cheese

1 8-oz. pkg. cream cheese
¼ c. mayonnaise
1 tsp. prepared mustard
½ tsp. onion powder
Dash Tabasco

Grind chopped ham, using medium blade of food chopper. Soften gelatin in cold water. Heat wine just to simmering; add softened gelatin and stir until it is completely dissolved. Cool to room temperature. Place in blender jar with cottage cheese and blend until smooth (or force cottage cheese through a sieve, then blend into cooled gelatin). Soften cream cheese with a fork and gradually blend in gelatin-cottage cheese mixture, beating until smooth. Blend in mayonnaise, mustard, onion powder and Tabasco. Add ground ham and mix well. Turn into a 4½-cup mold and chill until firm.

Swingin' Party Squares

2 9½-oz. pkgs. pie crust mix
Sour Cream Topping
2 large tomatoes
Salt

2 4-oz. pkgs. thin sliced
cooked ham *or* 2 c. thin
pieces cooked ham,
turkey or chicken

Prepare pastry mix as package directs. Roll each ball of pastry to a rectangle about 9 x 12 inches. Place the two rectangles on baking sheets; prick top surface with a fork. Bake in a preheated 475-degree oven until crisp and golden brown, about 8 to 10 minutes. Mix topping. When ready to serve, arrange very thin tomato slices over pastry; sprinkle lightly with salt. Cover with ham, turkey or chicken. Spoon topping over meat, spreading gently to cover. Broil about 3 inches from heat until bubbly and flecked with brown. Watch carefully to keep from burning. Trim off edges, then cut each rectangle into 2-inch squares. Makes about 4 dozen squares.

Sour Cream Topping: Beat 1 egg, stir in 1 cup sour cream, 1 cup grated cheddar cheese, 1 teaspoon prepared mustard, ½ teaspoon salt and 2 teaspoons toasted instant minced onion. Use as directed.

Sherried Cheese Ball

2 8-oz. pkgs. cream cheese
1 c. grated sharp
cheddar cheese
½ c. mashed blue cheese

¼ c. California dry
sherry wine
¼ c. toasted sesame seeds
2 T. paprika

Soften cream cheese. Combine all cheese and sherry and beat until smooth. Chill until mixture handles easily, then shape into a ball. Cut triangles of waxed paper and press against sides of ball to mark wedges. Sprinkle toasted sesame seeds between paper strips. Move strips to cover seeds and sprinkle paprika thickly to make red wedges between. Or, simply roll the whole ball in toasted sesame seeds and forget the paprika.

Shrimp Paste

¼ lb. cheddar cheese
¼ c. butter
1 4½-oz. can small
  wet-pack shrimp
1 T. finely-grated onion pulp

¼ tsp. paprika
⅛ tsp. curry powder
½ tsp. Worcestershire
2 T. lemon juice
2 T. chili sauce (optional)

If cheese is not soft enough to cream with butter, put it through a food chopper or grate it fine. Drain shrimp and rinse with cold water; drain again well; mash fine or put through food chopper with cheese. Mix creamed cheese and butter with shrimp and remaining ingredients; chill. Spread on thin slices of rye or pumpernickel for an appetizer.

King Crab Puffs

1 7½-oz. can Alaska king crab
  or ½ lb. frozen crab
3 green onions, chopped
½ c. grated sharp
  cheddar cheese
1 tsp. Worcestershire

½ tsp. dry mustard
1 c. water
½ c. butter
¼ tsp. salt
1 c. flour
4 eggs

Drain and finely slice canned crab. Or, defrost, drain and finely slice frozen crab. Combine crab with onion, cheese, Worcestershire sauce and dry mustard. Combine water, butter and salt in saucepan and bring to boil. Remove from heat. Add flour all at once, beating until mixture forms a ball and leaves sides of pan. Add eggs, one at a time, beating thoroughly after each addition. Blend in crab mixture. Drop by small teaspoonfuls on ungreased baking sheet. Bake in a preheated 400-degree oven 15 minutes. Reduce heat to 350 degrees and bake an additional 10 minutes. Serve hot. Makes 4 to 5 dozen puffs.

Marinated Shrimp

⅓ c. salad oil
¼ c. California white
   dinner wine
¾ tsp. seasoned salt
¼ tsp. basil

⅛ tsp. seasoned pepper
1 T. lemon juice
2 c. cooked shrimp
Mayonnaise

Combine all ingredients except shrimp and dressing in small covered jar and shake well. Pour over shrimp, cover and chill for an hour or longer. Drain shrimp just before serving. Serve on lettuce leaves with a little mayonnaise. Serves 4 to 6.

This spread keeps very well in the refrigerator.

Gypsy Caviar

2 T. olive oil
1 medium onion, diced
1 medium green pepper, diced
1 large carrot, pared,
   coarsely grated
1 medium eggplant, peeled,
   cut in ½-inch cubes

1 8-oz. can tomato sauce
Salt, pepper to taste
½ tsp. oregano
½ tsp. basil
1 clove garlic, crushed

Heat olive oil in large skillet; add onion and cook, covered, over low heat until wilted and golden. Add pepper, carrot and eggplant, cover and continue cooking, stirring occasionally, until eggplant is cooked through, about 20 minutes. Add remaining ingredients and cook, uncovered, until thick. Serve hot or cold as a spread with sesame seed crackers.

Note: Some prefer to omit the carrot in this recipe.

Chili con Queso

¼ c. corn oil
1¼ c. finely-chopped onion
1 clove garlic, crushed
1 1-lb. can tomatoes
2 T. cornstarch
⅓ c. diced canned
    chili peppers

1 T. Worcestershire
2 c. shredded
    cheddar cheese
1½ c. pasteurized process
    cheese spread

Heat oil in skillet over medium heat. Sauté onion and garlic in it and cook until tender and transparent. Drain ⅓ cup liquid from tomatoes; mash tomatoes, if necessary. Mix cornstarch and reserved tomato liquid. Add to onion mixture with tomatoes, chili peppers and Worcestershire sauce; mix well. Heat mixture to boiling and boil 1 minute, or until it thickens. Reduce heat and stir in cheese. Heat until cheese is completely melted. Serve hot with chips or crackers. Makes about 4 cups.

Rumàki

⅓ c. soy sauce
¼ tsp. ground ginger
¼ tsp. curry powder

½ lb. chicken livers
Bacon slices
Water chestnuts

Combine soy sauce, ginger and curry powder in a bowl. Halve chicken livers and add. Allow ½ bacon slice for each half liver and add to marinade. Marinate about 4 hours. Remove and drain. Hold each piece of liver and a thin slice of water chestnut together and wrap with a bacon piece; secure with a food pick. Place on foil-lined shallow baking pan. Broil, turning once, until bacon is cooked and crisp. Makes about 1½ dozen.

Sesame Log

1 3-oz. package cream cheese
¼ c. California white
    dinner wine
¼ tsp. nutmeg

¼ tsp. salt
¾ lb. Jack or Swiss
    cheese, grated
⅓ c. toasted sesame seeds

Beat cream cheese until soft; blend in wine, nutmeg and salt. Stir in grated cheese. Shape into log about 10 inches long and 2 inches in diameter. Toast sesame seeds in shallow pan in 400-degree oven until they are golden brown—about 5 minutes. Sprinkle seeds on waxed paper. Roll cheese log in seeds, pressing them gently into the log. Chill in refrigerator until firm enough to slice—about 2 hours.

This French twist on crackers and cheese goes equally well as an hors d'oeuvre, an accompaniment to soup or a partner to fresh fruit.

Croûtes au Fromage

½ c. butter or margarine	6 T. heavy cream
2 c. unsifted flour	1 egg, beaten
¼ tsp. salt	1½ c. grated Gruyère
Dash cayenne	or Swiss cheese
2 c. grated cheddar cheese	

Cut 6 tablespoons butter into flour, salt and cayenne pepper. Cut in cheddar cheese. Stir in heavy cream until mixture leaves sides of bowl and forms a ball.

Roll dough out to ⅛-inch thickness. Cut into rounds, using 2-inch cookie cutter. Brush with beaten egg and place on ungreased baking sheets. Bake in a 425-degree oven about 8 minutes, or until lightly browned.

Just before serving, cream remaining 2 tablespoons butter into Gruyère or Swiss cheese. Spread mixture on half the rounds and top with remaining rounds. Bake in a 425-degree oven about 2 minutes, or until cheese is melted. Makes about 32 appetizers.

Oeufs a la Chimay, Sauce Aurore

12 hard-cooked eggs	2 T. butter
5 large mushrooms	Salt and pepper
1 medium onion	Nutmeg

Cut eggs in half, remove yolks and sieve. Chop mushrooms and onions very fine. Sauté onion in butter for about a minute without browning. Add mushrooms, stir and cook about 4 minutes. Set aside to cool slightly. Mix this duxelles with egg yolks; season to taste with salt, pepper and nutmeg. Use to fill the egg white halves.

Spoon about half an inch of the sauce (below) into the bottom of a shallow oven-proof baking dish. Place eggs, filling up, in rows over the sauce. Spoon remainder of sauce over eggs, covering well. Sprinkle top with grated Swiss cheese. Place under broiler until hot and cheese is brown. Serve at once. Serves 12.

Sauce Aurore

3 c. Béchamel sauce	Salt and pepper
3 T. tomato paste, about	

Make a medium thick Béchamel (white) sauce. When thick, add salt and pepper to taste and then enough tomato paste to make the sauce a pale salmon color.

Terrine

½ lb. chicken livers, ground	1 egg
2 lbs. ground veal	1 lb. thin-sliced bacon
1 lb. ground fresh pork	1 whole chicken breast
4 shallots, minced (divided)	2 ½-inch thick ham steaks
½ c. chopped fresh parsley	¼ c. Madeira
¼ tsp. Spice Parisienne	¼ c. Cognac
Salt and pepper	1 bay leaf

Have livers, veal and pork ground together; add half the shallots, the parsley, spice, egg and salt and pepper and mix well (this is the farce). Blanch bacon; spread on paper toweling to cool. Bone and remove nerves from chicken breast; cut in ½-inch lardons (or strips). Trim ham and cut meat into ½-inch lardons. Put chicken and ham in a shallow dish; sprinkle remaining shallots and the Madeira and Cognac over them; let marinate for 15 minutes, turning a couple of times. Drain marinade into ground meat mixture and mix in lightly.

Place a layer of overlapping bacon slices on bottom of 2-quart terrine mold. Pat a ¾-inch thick layer of farce into mold. Place a layer of chicken on that, add a thin layer of farce to cover well, add a layer of ham, cover with farce; continue until mold is full, ending with farce. Cover with a layer of overlapping bacon slices (as on the bottom); top with a single bay leaf. Cover tightly (being sure lid has a steam hole in it) and seal with thick flour and water paste. Bake in a pan of boiling water (water should be two or three inches deep in pan) in a 375-degree oven for 1½ to 2 hours. Cool and refrigerate until ready to use.

To serve, cut in squares, skewer with toothpicks and accompany with tiny sour pickles and Dijon mustard for dunking, if desired.

Note: If seal is not broken, terrine should keep in the refrigerator for up to two weeks. It freezes well, but should be removed from the mold and wrapped properly for this.

*R*ock *lobster tails should be kept on hand in the freezer, for they are ideal for last-minute preparation.*

Potted Lobster Tails

6 4½-oz. frozen rock
    lobster tails
¼ c. butter or margarine
    Juice ½ lemon
3 T. catsup
¼ c. dry sherry

½ clove garlic, minced
½ tsp. salt
    Pinch basil
    Pinch tarragon
1 T. minced parsley

Cook still-frozen lobster tails in boiling salted water to cover for 7 to 8 minutes, or until shells are bright red. Cut away underside of tails and remove meat in one piece. Set aside. Melt butter in large skillet; add lemon juice, catsup, sherry, garlic, salt, basil and tarragon. Place lobster tails in sauce and bring slowly just to boiling, occasionally spooning sauce over lobster meat. Remove lobster tails from sauce and arrange on serving platter. Pour remaining sauce into sauce boat or bowl, sprinkle with minced parsley and serve as a dip. Makes 6 appetizer servings.

Parmesan Cheese Fingers

½ c. butter

1 clove garlic, sliced

10 slices white bread

1 c. grated Parmesan cheese

Melt butter; add garlic and let stand 5 minutes. Remove garlic. Trim crusts from bread and cut each slice into 4 strips. Brush bread on both sides with butter. Roll in Parmesan cheese. Place on baking sheet. Sprinkle any remaining cheese over bread strips. Bake in a 350-degree oven 10 to 12 minutes, or until lightly browned. Makes 40 fingers.

Toasty hot cheese tidbits are delightful served either as snacks or appetizers.

Cheese Puffs

¼ c. butter

1 egg, separated

¼ lb. processed American
  cheese, shredded

½ tsp. salt

½ tsp. dry mustard

½ tsp. paprika

¼ c. mayonnaise

30 1-inch rounds thin
  day-old bread

Cream butter; add beaten egg yolk and beat well. Combine cheese, salt, mustard, paprika and mayonnaise with egg mixture. Fold in stiffly beaten egg white. Spread mixture on bread rounds. Place on cookie sheet. Bake in a 350-degree oven 12 to 15 minutes, or until lightly browned. Makes 30 puffs.

Tiropeta

12 eggs

1 lb. Ricotta

1 lb. Feta
  (Greek goat's milk cheese)

½ lb. butter,
  melted, cooled

½ lb. phyllo pastry sheets

½ lb. butter, melted

Beat eggs until thick. In another bowl, mix cheese with the melted and cooled butter. Add eggs to cheese mixture. Line an 11 x 14 x 2-inch pan with 10 buttered sheets of phyllo. Add egg-cheese mixture. Top with eight buttered sheets of phyllo. Do not cut. Bake in a 350-degree oven for about 30 minutes, or until golden brown. Cut in small rectangles or squares. Serve warm.

Spanakopeta

2 lbs. spinach
1 onion, finely chopped
4 T. butter
1 c. cream sauce
1 c. finely-crumbled Feta
(Greek goat's milk cheese)

Salt and pepper
Dash nutmeg
½ lb. phyllo pastry sheets
Melted butter

Wash spinach and discard stems. Dry as thoroughly as possible on absorbent paper and cut in pieces. Sauté onion in butter until soft. Add spinach and saute a few minutes longer. Cool. Add cream sauce, cheese, salt, pepper and nutmeg. Mix well.

Place six or seven layers of phyllo in an 11 x 14 x 2-inch pan, brushing each sheet well with melted butter. Add spinach mixture, then place seven or eight layers of phyllo on filling, again buttering each sheet.

Bake in a 350-degree oven for about 30 minutes, or until crust is golden brown. Cut into rectangles or squares, which should be small and may be speared with toothpicks to keep pastry and filling together.

Huîtres en Couquille au Sylvaner Riesling

24 fresh oysters on shell
1 tsp. finely-chopped shallots
¼ c. Sylvaner Riesling
2 oz. butter
1 peanut-size Beurre Manie
¾ c. whipping cream
¼ c. Hollandaise sauce

Salt
Freshly-ground pepper
1 c. finely-chopped
mushrooms, cooked in a little
butter and a few drops
lemon juice until dry

Remove oysters from shells without discarding oyster water. Cook the oysters in their water, along with the wine, shallots and butter, over moderate heat in a covered saucepan for 4 to 5 minutes. Remove oysters from cooking liquid and keep warm. Add cream to pan and let evaporate until only half of liquid is left. Using a soft whip, thicken liquid with Beurre Manie. Bring to a boil. Remove pan from heat; stir in Hollandaise sauce and season to taste.

Select the deepest shells; wash them well with hot water; place side by side on a fireproof platter and warm platter in hot oven for a minute or two. Then fill each shell's cavity with the chopped mushrooms, which should be very warm, and top with an oyster. Coat with sauce. Place under preheated grill until nice and brown. Serve at once. Serves 4 to 6.

Seviche with Avocado

1 lb. boneless fish filets
(white fish, sole, halibut,
snapper or bass)
½ c. lime juice
2 tsp. salt
2-inch piece bay leaf
1 large red onion
¼ c. white wine vinegar

¼ c. salad oil
¼ tsp. crushed red
chili pepper
1 clove garlic, crushed
1 tomato
1 California avocado
1 T. chopped parsley
Watercress

Remove all skin and bones from fish and cut into 1-inch pieces. Place in glass bowl; cover with lime juice. Add 1 teaspoon salt and bay leaf. Marinate 5 or 6 hours, or overnight. Several hours before serving, peel and cut onion into thin slices; separate into rings or cut into quarters. Combine vinegar, oil, chili pepper, garlic and remaining salt. Pour over onion and add to fish. Peel tomato; cut into wedges. Cut avocado into halves, lengthwise; remove seed and skin. Cut avocado crosswise into crescents, then add, with tomato, to fish mixture. Mix carefully. To serve, spoon onto platter and sprinkle with parsley. Garnish with watercress. Serves 8 to 10.

This clam dip is best made ahead, then chilled for several hours so the flavors blend and mellow.

Western Clam Dip

2 8-oz. pkgs. cream cheese
1 c. commercial sour cream
1 7-oz. can minced clams,
drained

2 T. instant minced onion
1 T. lime or lemon juice
½ tsp. salt
¼ tsp. paprika

Cream cheese until soft. Blend in remaining ingredients. Refrigerate several hours before using. Makes about 3 cups.

Note: Some of the drained clam liquor may be used to thin the mixture, if desired.

Eggs and Ripe Olives Indienne

3 hard-cooked eggs
¼ c. chopped ripe olives
3 T. mayonnaise
½ tsp. salt

¼ tsp. curry powder
Sliced bread
Thin cucumber slices
Sliced ripe olives

Chop eggs fine. Add chopped ripe olives, mayonnaise, salt and curry powder and mix well. Cut 2-inch rounds of bread with a cookie cutter. Place a cucumber slice on each bread round and cover with egg-olive mixture. Top each with an olive slice. Cover with a damp towel and refrigerate until serving time. Makes 1 cup filling, or enough for about 20 sandwiches.

Chicken livers are favored at our house, no matter how they're got up. Here they are with chopped mushrooms, hard-cooked eggs and California sherry in a mixture that will be favored anywhere.

Chicken Livers Supreme

1 c. (½ lb.) chopped or mashed
cooked chicken livers
¼ c. chopped cooked
mushrooms (4-oz. can)
2 hard-cooked eggs,
chopped

3 T. chopped parsley
2 tsp. instant minced onion
½ tsp. seasoned salt
¼ c. California sherry

Combine all ingredients. Let stand several hours to blend flavors. Makes about 2 cups. Serve with crackers or Melba toast.

Porcupine Cheese Log

1 T. instant minced onion
⅛ tsp. garlic powder
½ tsp. dry mustard
¼ tsp. dried dill
¼ c. California dry sherry

1 lb. soft cheddar
cheese spread
¼ lb. Roquefort cheese
1 8-oz. package cream cheese
Slivered almonds

Measure onion, garlic powder, mustard and dill into sherry. Blend until well mixed. Add cheeses and beat until smooth. Shape into a log, roll in foil and chill until firm. Stud top and sides of roll with almonds. Serve with assorted crackers.

Coconut Chips

First, as they say, catch your coconut. Poke holes in the "eyes" with an icepick (or something equally sharp) and drain off the liquid. (Incidentally, when buying a coconut, be sure to shake it and listen for the gurgle of the liquid. If it is dried out, you don't want it.) Now crack the nut and remove the white meat, trimming off the thick brown skin. Use a vegetable peeler to "shave" the meat into thin strips. Arrange these in a shallow pan or on a cookie sheet, sprinkle lightly with salt and toast in a preheated 250- to 300-degree oven for half an hour, or until evenly golden. Stir from time to time and don't brown too much. Serve hot, or store in airtight containers.

Soups

Nothing, it seems at times, says "home" better than the great smells coming from the kitchen on baking day. But it isn't just the baking—that's the day you make a big pot of soup for supper.

Why? Well, if you're in the kitchen anyway, making bread, rolls, a cake, a pie or two and some cookies, why not have a kettle of soup simmering on the back of the stove? That way you can give it all the attention it needs, you probably won't forget it and let the kettle go dry, and you'll have some lovely freshly-baked bread to serve with it.

Next time you plan a baking day, make it a soup day, too.

Hearty Beef-Vegetable Soup

3 lbs. soup meat with bones	1 c. sliced celery *or* ¼ c. celery flakes
1½ lbs. soup bones	2 T. parsley flakes
Water	1 bay leaf
1 1-lb., 12-oz. can tomatoes, broken up	¼ tsp. whole peppercorns
1 c. cut onion *or* ⅓ c. onion flakes	3 c. diced cabbage
	2 c. sliced carrots
4 tsp. salt, divided	3 medium potatoes, peeled, diced

Combine soup meat, bones and water to cover (approximately 10 cups) in a large kettle. Bring to boiling point, skimming off all foam. Add tomatoes, onion and 2 teaspoons of the salt. Tie celery and parsley flakes, bay leaf and peppercorns in a cheesecloth bag; add to soup. Cover and simmer 2 to 2½ hours or longer, if desired. Add remaining vegetables and cook 30 to 40 minutes longer, or until vegetables are tender. Remove and discard cheesecloth bag. Remove meat and bones. Cut meat into chunks and return to soup along with marrow from remaining bones. Taste. Add remaining 2 teaspoons salt, if needed. Serves 6 to 8.

All anyone has to do is mention French onion soup and I'm off to the kitchen like a shot, peeling and slicing onions (crying a lot), getting down the lidded bowls with their baskets, making French bread toast and grating Parmesan cheese. And that's really just about all there is to making this simple but good version of the greatest of all soups, as a matter of fact.

French Onion Soup

5 c. thinly-sliced sweet Spanish onions	½ tsp. salt Freshly-ground black
¼ tsp. sugar	pepper to taste
¼ c. butter	2 T. brandy
3 10½-oz. cans condensed beef broth	6 slices buttered French bread, toasted
3 soup cans water	½ c. grated Parmesan cheese

Sprinkle onions with sugar. Sauté slowly in butter until they turn a delicate gold. Add beef broth and water. Cover and simmer gently for 45 minutes. Add salt, pepper and brandy. Place in large ovenproof soup tureen or individual ovenproof bowls. Top with toasted French bread and sprinkle with grated Parmesan cheese. Bake in a 400-degree oven 8 minutes. Serves 6.

Fresh Onion Soup

¼ c. butter or margarine	1 tsp. salt
5 c. thinly-sliced onion	6-8 slices French bread, 1 inch thick
4 10½-oz. cans undiluted beef bouillon	¼ c. grated Parmesan cheese
1 soup can water	

Heat butter in large skillet. Add onions; sauté over moderate heat 30 minutes, stirring often. In a medium-sized saucepan, combine onions, bouillon, water, salt and pepper. Bring to boiling point. Reduce heat; cover and simmer 1 hour. Toast bread. Place toast in one large or in individual casseroles. Add soup; sprinkle toast with cheese. Serve with additional cheese, if desired. Serves 6 to 8.

Gazpacho, the cold raw-vegetable soup that originated in Spain many years ago, is said to be made from as many recipes as there are people making it. This one is simple, but good, highlighted just to perfection with a bit of Tabasco, and whizzed together in a blender.

Gazpacho

2 ripe tomatoes	⅛ tsp. Tabasco
¼ large green pepper	½ tsp. salt
¼ small onion	1 T. olive oil
½ cucumber	4½ tsp. wine vinegar
½ garlic clove	¼ c. ice water

Quarter tomatoes; seed and slice green pepper; peel and slice onion and cucumber; peel garlic clove. Place in blender. Add Tabasco and remaining ingredients. Cover and blend 3 seconds, or until of serving consistency. Chill. To serve, pour into soup plates with an ice cube in the center of each. If desired, garnish with sour cream and avocado slices. Serves 3.

Hearty soups make wonderful meals. Whether made with canned or dried mixes or by the long, slow-cooking method, a little wine added to the broth puts them in a special class.

Vegetable-Meat Ball Soup

1 large beef soup bone
2 or 3 marrow bones
½ c. pearl barley
2½ qts. water
1 c. California red
  dinner wine
2 c. diced fresh tomatoes
1 lb. ground chuck
½ c. cracker crumbs
1 egg, beaten
2 tsp. salt
½ tsp. pepper
4 medium carrots,
  cut in slices
3 stalks celery, with tops,
  sliced crosswise
1 medium onion, chopped
1 minced clove garlic
2 small zucchini,
  thinly sliced
½ c. frozen peas
  (or fresh in season)

Cover bones and barley with water and wine. Simmer, covered, 3 hours. Discard bones. Measure broth and add water to make total liquid 2 quarts. Add tomatoes; simmer slowly while preparing meat balls. Mix together beef chuck, cracker crumbs, egg, 1 teaspoon salt and ¼ teaspoon pepper. Shape into tiny meat balls about 1-inch diameter. Drop into simmering broth. Add carrots, celery, onion, garlic and remaining salt and pepper. Simmer slowly 45 minutes. Add zucchini and peas and cook 10 minutes longer. Lace each serving with an additional tablespoon of wine, if desired. Serves 8.

Zuppa Pasta Fagiola

¾ lb. dried white
  kidney beans
Water
2 lbs. ham shank
  or ham bone
2 cloves garlic, minced
2 medium-firm tomatoes,
  peeled, chopped
½ tsp. coarsely-ground
  black pepper
¼ tsp. rubbed sage
¼ tsp. thyme leaves
1½ qts. water
¼ c. olive oil
2 medium-firm tomatoes,
  peeled, chopped
1 c. dry white wine
1 tsp. salt
¼ tsp. coarsely-ground
  black pepper
1 c. macaroni or small
  macaroni shapes

Soak beans in water overnight; drain. Remove skin and excess fat from ham shank. In a large kettle, combine beans, ham shank, garlic, 2 chopped tomatoes, ½ teaspoon pepper, sage, thyme and

1½ quarts water. Bring to a boil; cover and simmer gently 2 hours, or until beans are tender. Remove shank from kettle; dice meat and return to stock.

Meanwhile, in medium saucepan, combine olive oil, 2 chopped tomatoes, wine, 1 teaspoon salt and ¼ teaspoon pepper. Simmer, uncovered, 20 minutes. Pour into stock. Bring to a boil; add macaroni and continue to cook 10 minutes, or until tender. Serve in large soup bowls. Serves 8.

Bouillabaisse

12-24 fresh clams or mussels,
    in shells
  1 lb. shrimp
1½ lbs. fish filets
    (halibut, cod, sole)
  2 T. oil
  1 medium onion, chopped
  1 clove garlic, crushed

1 6-oz. can tomato paste
1 1-lb. can stewed
  whole tomatoes
½ tsp. salt
½ tsp. sugar
½ tsp. Tabasco
1 c. water
½ c. dry white wine

Scrub clam shells well. Shell and devein shrimp. Cut fish into pieces. Heat oil in skillet; add onion and garlic and sauté until tender, about 5 minutes. Add remaining ingredients. Bring sauce to boil in large kettle. Add fish and clams, cover and boil for 2 minutes. Add shrimp; boil 4 to 6 minutes, or until fish flakes easily with a fork. Serves 6 to 8.

Note: Two pounds cleaned lobster or crab meat (with or without shells) may be added, if desired, with clams.

Split Pea Sipping Soup

1 lb. green or yellow
  split peas
7 c. water
1 tsp. salt

2 T. butter
1 c. ham or chicken stock
½ c. cream
1-3 T. dry sherry

Combine washed split peas with water, salt and butter in a 3- to 4-quart Dutch oven. Bring to boil rapidly over high heat, uncovered. Reduce heat to simmer and cook until split peas are soft enough to sieve, about 1 hour. Stir occasionally to avoid sticking. Remove from heat and while still hot put through sieve, food mill or blender. Purée should be of canned pumpkin consistency; add water if it is not.

Mix 3 cups puree with 1 cup ham or chicken broth; heat over medium heat. Just before serving, stir in cream and sherry. Garnish with grated Parmesan cheese, chopped chives or parsley, a sprinkle of dill weed or a dollop of sour cream. Serves 4.

Avocado Soup

4 ripe avocados	1 tsp. salt
1 qt. half and half	1 tsp. monosodium glutamate
¾ c. dry sherry wine	1 tsp. grated onion

Peel, seed and sieve avocado; add remaining ingredients and whip all together well. Strain and serve cold. Serves 6.

Note: This may be prepared in a blender, of course.

Beautiful to look at and absolutely marvelous to eat—that's Borscht. It's a good hearty soup, and you need only serve a fresh crusty bread with it and a dessert to make a whole meal.

Ukranian Borscht

1½-2 lbs. round steak, bone in	1 bunch medium beets, pared,
6 c. water	cut in narrow strips
2 beef bouillon cubes	2 c. chopped cabbage
1½ tsp. salt	1 c. chopped onion
1 bay leaf	1 c. sliced carrots
1 6-oz. can tomato paste	Dairy sour cream

Trim all fat from beef. Place beef and bone in deep kettle (about 4½-quart size); add water, bouillon cubes, salt and bay leaf. Bring to a full boil, skim. Cover, simmer 1 hour, or until beef is almost tender. Remove beef, bone and bay leaf. Cut beef into bite-sized pieces, return to simmering stock. Stir in tomato paste. Add vegetables, bring to a full boil; cover and simmer 1 hour longer. Serve in large soup bowls topped with dollops of sour cream. Makes about 3 quarts soup.

Scotch Broth with Barley

Meaty bones and pieces
   from lamb shoulder
   or 2 lbs. lamb
2 qts. water, about
1 T. salt
1 onion stuck with 4 whole cloves
8 peppercorns

½ bay leaf
2 T. butter
¼ c. finely-cut carrot
¼ c. finely-cut celery
¼ c. finely-cut turnip
½ tsp. marjoram
½ c. barley

Place meaty lamb bones in deep kettle wide enough to hold them with room to spare. Add cold water to come an inch above meat. Add salt, peppercorns, onion and bay. Bring quickly to a boil. Skim off any foam. Cover and simmer 1½ hours. Cool. Skim off top fat (if rushed, drop ice cubes into soup and fat will collect around them). Remove bone and dice meat clinging to it. Strain broth, discarding onion and peppercorns. Heat butter in saucepan, add chopped vegetables and cook, stirring for 5 to 6 minutes. Add marjoram, broth, diced meat and barley. Simmer about an hour, or until vegetables and barley are very tender and soup has thickened. Serves 6.

Potato Soup with Artichoke Crowns

2 jars marinated artichoke
   crowns (bottoms)
6 slices bacon
8 medium potatoes,
   peeled, diced
1 c. chopped onion

1 tsp. salt
Water
¼ c. snipped parsley
4 c. milk
½ c. butter
Pepper to taste

Drain crowns well, reserving marinade to use as a base for salad dressing. Cook bacon until crisp; set aside until cool; crumble. Put potatoes, onions and salt in a large saucepan or kettle with just enough water to cover. Cook, covered, about 15 minutes, or until potatoes are tender. Add the artichoke crowns, which have been cut into small chunks, and parsley. Cook another 5 minutes. Blend in butter and milk. Add pepper to taste and heat through, but do not boil. Serve in bowls, garnished with crumbled bacon. Serves 6.

Homemade Tomato Soup

2 lbs. tomatoes, about 5 medium to large
1½ c. homemade chicken stock *or* 1 can condensed chicken broth
1 c. medium white sauce, unseasoned (2 T. butter, 2 T. flour, 1 c. milk)
½ tsp. salt
Freshly-ground pepper to taste
½ tsp. Worcestershire (or less)
1 T. minced chives

Wash and quarter tomatoes and place in a saucepan; add chicken stock. Cover and cook over medium heat 10 minutes. Turn through fine grater or food mill to remove skins and seeds and purée pulp. Gradually stir tomato broth into white sauce; add seasonings. Heat until hot. Ladle into soup bowls and sprinkle with chives. Makes about 5 cups.

Philippe's Tomato Soup

6 medium tomatoes
2 medium potatoes
1 medium onion
1 bay leaf
Thyme, salt and pepper
Thick cream

Core the tomatoes and smash them up a little in a soup pot. Peel the potatoes, cut them in chunks and add them to the pot. Slice the onion and add it with the bay leaf and seasonings to taste. Add water to the pot to cover the ingredients, bring to a boil and then simmer, uncovered, until tender. Put through a food mill, using the coarse blade (or put through a colander or very coarse strainer), reheat and pour into bowls. Swirl a couple of tablespoons of thick cream through each portion. Serves 4.

Salads

S alade Nicoise, though there is often quite a bit of controversy about the authenticity of any one recipe, is quite simply a combination salad in the Mediterranean manner.

It starts out as a potato salad made with olive oil and wine vinegar dressing. Marinated stringbeans are added, along with anchovies, tuna chunks, hard-cooked eggs, tomato wedges, ripe olives (always), a bit of crisp lettuce and fresh herbs, if possible.

It's hearty, and if you serve it with hot French bread, you can make a pretty good meal of it.

Salade Nicoise

6 c. sliced cooked potatoes	4 medium tomatoes
2-3 c. cooked cut green beans	4 hard-cooked eggs
1 c. oil-wine vinegar dressing	Anchovy filets
	Pitted large ripe olives
½ c. chopped sweet Spanish onions	Crisp salad greens
	1 or 2 7-oz. cans light tuna

Scrub 8 or 9 medium-sized potatoes, about 3 pounds. Place in heavy saucepan or Dutch oven. Add cold water about 2 inches up on sides of pan. Sprinkle lightly with salt. Bring water to boiling point. Reduce heat. Cover tightly and simmer until tender when stuck with a thin skewer, about 40 minutes. Drain off water. Return to low heat to dry off.

Just as soon as they can be handled, peel and cut in ⅛-inch thick slices. Put in warm bowl and drizzle over them about ¼ cup oil-wine vinegar dressing or dry white wine, or white wine vinegar. Add the chopped onion and toss very gently. Cover.

Pour a small amount of the same dressing over the hot drained beans. Cover. Let both stand at room temperature until cool. Then refrigerate both at least 2 hours. This may be done the day before.

To serve, toss together the potatoes and beans, using a gentle touch, and adding more dressing as needed. Place in a mound in the center of a chilled chop plate or large shallow bowl. Arrange lettuce or other crisp greens around edge of plate. (Butter lettuce is excellent.)

Place peeled tomatoes, cut in wedges, and the egg quarters alternately around potato salad. Add olives. Garnish top of salad with anchovy strips. Sprinkle with 2 tablespoons capers or snipped parsley or fresh green herbs, such as basil, savory or marjoram. Cover with foil or clear wrap and chill until serving time. Turn the tuna onto a chilled plate and garnish with watercress and lemon slices. Serve with the salad, along with a cruet of the dressing and a bowl of mayonnaise—and hot French bread, of course.

Oil-Wine Vinegar Dressing: Shake together in a covered jar ¾ cup salad oil (traditionally olive oil), ¼ cup red wine vinegar, ¼ teaspoon each, salt, coarsely-ground black pepper and mustard. Makes 1 cup.

Continental Potato Salad

8-10 medium potatoes	¼ tsp. dry mustard
¼ c. dry white wine	½ c. olive oil
3 T. white wine vinegar	1 tsp. dried tarragon
1 tsp. salt	leaves
¼ tsp. freshly-ground	6 green onions, sliced
black pepper	2 tsp. minced parsley

Cook potatoes in their jackets until tender but still firm. Peel potatoes while still warm. Slice in ⅛-inch rounds and layer in a large mixing bowl, sprinkling each layer with some of the wine. Beat vinegar, salt, pepper and mustard together in a small bowl. Slowly beat in oil until mixture is creamy. Add tarragon. Sprinkle potatoes with sliced green onions and parsley. Add dressing and mix gently, being careful not to break slices of potatoes.

Sour Cream Potato Salad

4 c. diced cold	4 hard-cooked eggs
cooked potatoes	1 c. sour cream
½ c. diced cucumbers	¼ c. mayonnaise
1 T. instant minced onion	1 T. cider vinegar
½ tsp. celery seed	½ tsp. dry mustard
2 tsp. salt	
½ tsp. coarsely-ground	
black pepper	

Mix together lightly potatoes, cucumbers, onion, celery seed, salt, pepper and diced egg whites. Mash 3 of the egg yolks and combine with sour cream, mayonnaise, vinegar and mustard. Add to potatoes and mix lightly. Chill. Serve on lettuce. Put remaining egg yolk through a sieve and sprinkle a little over each salad as a garnish. Makes 6 cups.

Pineapple Pepper Slaw

1 large head crisp	1 tsp. salt
green cabbage	⅓ c. mayonnaise
1 crisp green pepper	½ c. canned pineapple
1 tsp. dry mustard	chunks or tidbits
2 T. vinegar	½ tsp. caraway seed
4 T. sugar	Thin strips baked ham

Shred cabbage finely and set to crisp in ice water. Drain. (You should have 4 to 6 cups of shredded cabbage.) Slice half of green pepper into rings, dice rest. Mix mustard, vinegar, sugar and salt into mayonnaise. In a large bowl, mix the drained cabbage, diced green pepper and most of the pineapple. Toss with dressing. Stir in caraway seed. Chill. Serve in a salad bowl lined with lettuce leaves or leaves of curly cabbage. Decorate top with green pepper rings filled with pineapple and bundles of thin ham strips. Serves 6.

Favorite Tuna Salad

½ c. ripe olives	1 T. lemon juice
1 6½- or 7-oz. can tuna	¼ tsp. salt
2 hard-cooked eggs	⅛ tsp. pepper
¾ c. chopped celery	½ tsp. prepared mustard
2 T. chopped green pepper	Salad greens
¼ c. mayonnaise	

Cut olives into large pieces, flake tuna and dice eggs. Combine olives, tuna, eggs, celery and green pepper. Blend together mayonnaise, lemon juice, salt, pepper and mustard. Pour over salad ingredients and toss lightly. Serve on salad greens. Serves 4 or 5.

Stringbeans with Dill Vinaigrette Sauce

½ c. oil-and-vinegar
French dressing
1 T. chopped parsley
1 T. finely-chopped
green pepper

2 T. finely-chopped pickle
1 tsp. chopped chives or onion
1 tsp. dill seed
1 lb. cooked fresh
stringbeans

Combine French dressing, parsley, green pepper, pickle, onion and dill seed. Beat with a hand or electric beater. Serve on hot beans as a vegetable or on chilled cooked beans as a salad. Serves 6.

Elegant Chicken Salad

1 c. diced cooked chicken
1 c. sliced celery
½ c. halved seeded grapes
⅓ c. chopped or ready-diced
almonds

⅓ c. mayonnaise
1 tsp. lemon juice
½ tsp. grated onion
Salt to taste
Salad greens

Combine chicken, celery, grapes and almonds. Blend mayonnaise, lemon juice, onion and salt and mix lightly with chicken mixture. Serve on crisp salad greens. Serves 4.

Fresh Tomato Aspic

3 T. plain gelatin
½ c. cold water
8 large tomatoes
1 tsp. sugar
1 bay leaf
1 tsp. salt
2 small onions,
coarsely chopped

1 tsp. peppercorns
1 stalk celery,
coarsely chopped
3 T. lemon juice
⅛ tsp. Tabasco

Sprinkle gelatin in water to soften. Quarter tomatoes, cutting away white core and stem end. Prepare about 2 quarts of quartered tomatoes. Place them in a saucepan and add sugar, bay leaf, salt, onions, celery and peppercorns. Cook over low heat until tomatoes are soft, about 10 minutes. Strain through a food mill and measure 5 cups of tomato juice. If measure is less than 5 cups, add enough water, canned tomato juice, consomme or bouillon to make 5 cups. Add softened gelatin to hot tomato juice and stir to dissolve, then add lemon juice, salt, pepper and Tabasco. Turn into lightly greased mold and chill in refrigerator until firm.

To remove aspic, loosen edges with a knife and dip mold in a bowl of warm water. Place platter on top of mold and turn upside down. Aspic may be made in a loaf pan and then cut into squares. Serve on lettuce with mayonnaise, cottage cheese, French or Thousand Island dressing. Serves 10.

Spanish Salad

1 c. ripe olives	1 T. inst. minced onion
2 tomatoes	1 tsp. salt
1 cucumber	¼ tsp. dried basil
1 green pepper, cubed	⅛ tsp. pepper
½ c. chopped parsley	⅛ tsp. garlic powder
3 T. lemon juice	Lettuce cups
2 T. olive oil	

Cut ripe olives in large pieces. Slice tomatoes vertically; cut slices into quarters. Pare and chop cucumber. Combine all ingredients except lettuce and toss to blend. Chill. Serve in lettuce cups.

Avocado Salad Mexicano

½ c. diced tomato	1-2 T. crumbled blue cheese
½ c. chopped green pepper	¼ c. French dressing
¼ c. chopped celery	3-4 avocados
3 T. chopped green onion	Lime or lemon juice
½ c. cooked vegetables	Salad greens
(green beans, peas, etc.)	Whole ripe olives for garnish

Gently mix vegetables, sliced olives, blue cheese and French dressing. Season to taste and chill thoroughly. Cut avocados in halves lengthwise; remove seeds and skin. Sprinkle with lime or lemon juice. Arrange on salad greens and heap marinated vegetables into halves. Top each portion with a whole ripe olive. Serves 6 to 8.

Marinated Tomatoes with Artichoke Bottoms

¼ c. vinegar
¾ c. salad oil
1 sm. clove garlic, crushed
¾ tsp. salt
¼ tsp. pepper
½ tsp. paprika
¼ tsp. basil
⅛ tsp. oregano

⅛ tsp. tarragon
6 slices tomato,
  about ½-inch thick
6 large artichokes
3 T. lemon juice
1½ tsp. salt
3 pimiento-stuffed green
  olives, cut in half

Combine vinegar, oil, garlic, ¾ teaspoon salt, pepper, paprika, basil, oregano and tarragon; blend or shake well. Add tomatoes. Chill 3 hours, turning tomato slices occasionally.

Meanwhile, wash artichokes, cut off stems, pull off tough outer leaves. Trim bases until smooth. Cook artichokes in 1 inch boiling water to which 3 tablespoons lemon juice have been added. Sprinkle ¼ teaspoon salt over each artichoke. Cover tightly and cook 30 to 45 minutes, or until bottoms can be easily pierced with a fork.

Remove artichokes and turn upside down immediately to drain. Remove leaves and scrape fleshy pulp from leaves with a metal spoon; discard leaves. Remove hearts and discard chokes. Force pulp and hearts through food mill. Cool artichoke bottoms. Drain tomato slices; reserve oil mixture. Top tomato slices with artichoke bottoms and olive halves. Combine oil mixture and artichoke pulp; blend or shake. Serve artichoke-tomato salad topped with fresh basil, with assorted cold cuts and the oil-pulp mixture. Serves 6.

24-Hour Salad

Cooked Fruit Dressing

1 egg	⅓ c. pineapple juice *or* syrup
½ c. sugar or honey	from canned pineapple tidbits
1 T. cornstarch	⅓ c. lemon juice
⅛ tsp. salt	¼ tsp. grated orange rind
⅓ c. orange juice	1 c. whipping cream

Using top of double boiler or a heavy saucepan, beat the egg until thick and lemon-colored. Gradually beat in the combined sugar, cornstarch and salt. Then stir in the fruit juices and grated peel. Cook over hot water or very low heat, stirring constantly until thickened. Remove from heat. Cover. Chill. Then fold in the cream, which has been whipped until fairly stiff. In the meantime, prepare fruit.

Salad Mixture

2 c. cut fresh purple prune plums	1 c. orange segments cut in pieces
2 c. seedless grapes	2 c. tiny marshmallows *or*
2 c. pineapple tidbits, drained	16 large marshmallows
1 c. sliced banana	cut in eighths

Prepare plums by cutting in half lengthwise, zipping out the seed with the point of the paring knife. Cut each half once lengthwise, then once crosswise for neat even pieces. Using the salad bowl from which you plan to serve, lightly combine all of the fruit and the marshmallows. Carefully fold in a liberal amount of the salad dressing so that each piece of fruit and the marshmallows are well coated. Any dressing that is left may be served with the salad, though it really does not need it. (It's good with other fruit salads, though.)

Cover the salad bowl with a bowl cover, foil, waxed paper or clear wrap. Place in refrigerator to chill at least 24 hours. Just before serving, pretty up the top of the salad with thin slices of plums and drained maraschino cherries. Tuck in sprigs of mint or watercress. Chill the salad plates. Serves 8.

Asparagus Vinaigrette

½ tsp. salt	1 small clove garlic
½ tsp. sugar	(optional)
½ tsp. dry mustard	1 lb. fresh asparagus, cooked
½ tsp. paprika	1 tomato, sliced
⅓ c. wine vinegar	4 ripe olives
⅛ tsp. Tabasco	2 fresh mushrooms, sliced
⅔ c. salad oil	1 hard-cooked egg, quartered

Combine salt, sugar, mustard and paprika; add vinegar, Tabasco, oil and garlic, if used. Shake or beat well. Pour into a flat dish. Place asparagus, sliced tomato, olives and mushrooms in marinade. Let stand for about an hour. Remove from marinade; drain and arrange on serving plate. Garnish with hard-cooked egg. Serves 2 or 4.

Palace Court Salad

Prepare a bed of finely-shredded lettuce ½ inch deep and about 4 inches in diameter as a base for each salad. Around this put a border of very finely-chopped hard-cooked egg. Center a thick slice of tomato on the lettuce and top with a large heart of artichoke, "cup" side up.

Add some diced celery to diced crab (shrimp, tuna or chicken may be substituted) along with just enough mayonnaise to hold the mixture together. Fill the cup of the artichoke with the crab mixture and build up a tower, spoonful by spoonful. Garnish with sliced pimiento. Serve with either Thousand Island or French dressing.

Bacon and Egg Salad

1 head western iceberg lettuce	¼ c. dairy sour cream
4 hard-cooked eggs	2 T. finely-chopped
6 strips bacon	green onion
1 c. mayonnaise	1 tsp. prepared mustard

Core, rinse and thoroughly drain lettuce. Refrigerate in crisper. Cook bacon crisp; break into medium-large pieces. Slice 2 eggs.

Coarsely chop remaining eggs and combine with mayonnaise, sour cream, onion and mustard. When ready to serve, cut or tear lettuce into bite-size chunks. Layer in chilled salad bowl with crisp bacon and sliced eggs. Toss with dressing and serve at once. Serves 6 to 8.

Note: If thinner dressing is desired, add a tablespoon of milk.

Tossed Salad with Roquefort Dressing

2 c. torn lettuce	2 T. salad oil
2 c. torn chicory	1 T. fresh lemon juice
1 small cucumber, sliced	⅓ c. sour cream
½ c. sliced green onions	2 tsp. snipped fresh chives
1 T. crumbled Roquefort	½ tsp. salt
or blue cheese	⅛ tsp. pepper

Combine lettuce, chicory, cucumber and green onions in a salad bowl. Mash cheese; mix in oil and lemon juice until smooth. Blend cheese mixture with sour cream, chives, salt and pepper. Serve dressing with salad. Serves 4.

Even people on the east coast and in the middle west, it is rumored, are eating more salads the year around now. Supposedly, it's the California influence that's brought this about, but more likely it's the availability of western lettuce and other salad ingredients the year around as produce is shipped from everywhere to everywhere these days.

Crab Louis, Scoma

Louis Dressing	8 slices hard-cooked egg
1 large head western	8 slices pickled beets
iceberg lettuce	8 ripe olives
1¼ lb. cooked crab meat	4 lemon wedges
8 tomato quarters	

Make up dressing and chill. Core, rinse and thoroughly drain lettuce. Refrigerate in crisper. When ready to serve, arrange large outer leaves on chilled salad plates. Shred remaining lettuce and mound on plates. Top with crab meat. Arrange remaining ingredients on salads. Serve Louis Dressing separately. Serves 4.

Louis Dressing: Combine 1 cup mayonnaise, 2 tablespoons catsup, 1 tablespoon each, sweet pickle relish, chili sauce and chopped parsley, 2 teaspoons finely-chopped green onion and ¼ teaspoon Worcestershire sauce. Makes 1⅓ cups dressing.

If you'd prefer crab with Green Goddess Dressing, which is quite rich, here is a recipe:

Green Goddess Dressing

1 c. mayonnaise	3 T. chopped parsley
½ c. dairy sour cream	1 T. chopped green onion
3 T. tarragon wine vinegar	1 T. anchovy paste
¼ c. chopped chives	1 tsp. Dijon-type mustard

Combine all ingredients in a small bowl and mix well. Chill an hour or so to blend flavors before serving. Makes 2 cups dressing.

Fresh Mexican Lettuce Salad

1 small head iceberg lettuce	1 c. shredded Monterey
1 avocado, peeled, pitted	Jack cheese
2 T. fresh lime juice	2 tomatoes, peeled,
½ tsp. salt	cut in 8 wedges each
⅛ tsp. Tabasco	Chili Sauce

Remove 4 whole leaves from head of lettuce; with sharp knife, cut remaining lettuce into long thin shreds. Mash avocado in medium bowl; add lime juice, salt and Tabasco. Place whole lettuce leaf on each of 4 individual plates; top with layers of shredded lettuce and cheese. Arrange 4 tomato wedges in circles on top and spoon ¼ avocado mixture into center of each serving. Divide ¼ of the Chili Sauce over each portion. Serves 4.

Chili Sauce

½ lb. ground beef	½ c. beef broth
2 T. chopped fresh onion	¼ c. dry red wine
¼ clove garlic, mashed	⅛ tsp. ground cumin
3 tomatoes, peeled, chopped	⅛ tsp. Tabasco
	1 tsp. chili powder
½ c. water	1 tsp. salt

Brown beef in a large skillet over medium heat; add onion and garlic and cook until tender. Add remaining ingredients and simmer, uncovered, for 20 minutes. Cool at room temperature for 10 minutes.

Western Bean Salad

1 16-oz. can pinto or red beans, drained	1 small onion, sliced in rings
1 11-oz. can mandarin orange segments, drained	1 medium avocado, sliced
1 c. sliced celery	1 T. lemon juice
1 medium-sized green pepper, cut in strips	¼ c. mayonnaise
	½ tsp. chili powder
½ c. sliced pitted ripe olives, drained	½ tsp. salt
	½ tsp. basil
	2-3 drops Tabasco

Combine beans, orange segments, celery, green pepper, olives and onion rings. Dip avocado slices in lemon juice and reserve. Mix 1 teaspoon lemon juice with mayonnaise, chili powder, salt, basil and Tabasco. Pour over vegetables and toss. Fold in avocado slices. Chill 1 hour or longer. Serves 6.

Meat

Clay pot cookery has really taken hold in the last few years. However, it has been used primarily for poultry.

The clay pot, which has been new to many of us, actually is the old — ancient — way to roast anything. And it turns out to be ideal for beef. The meat goes in the cooker with seasonings, is covered and put in a cold oven, then cooked at a fairly high temperature. The result is a moist and juicy piece of meat with good flavor throughout.

Decorative clay pots come in many sizes and shapes, but the simple oval ones are best for a beef roast. Be sure to follow the manufacturer's instructions for seasoning before using for the first time (also on cleaning and storing).

Have your roast as nearly the same size as the cooker as possible. It may be rolled and tied to make it fit snugly. Good fit insures good brown color for the meat when it's done.

California Beef Round

1 4- to 5-lb. eye	¼ tsp. pepper
of round roast	4 green onions, sliced
1 tsp. salt	3 T. undiluted frozen
1 tsp. dry mustard	orange juice concentrate

Trim all but a very thin layer of fat from meat. Rub with salt, mustard and pepper. Place in clay cooker. Sprinkle with green onion and orange juice concentrate. Cover. Place in cold oven. Set thermostat at 400 degrees. Cook for 2½ hours, or until meat is tender. Cut into thin slices to serve. Pan juices may be thickened with a little cornstarch and served with the meat. Serves 8 to 10.

Oriental Meat Balls

1 lb. ground beef
½ tsp. ground ginger
Soy sauce
4 T. salad oil
1½ c. diagonally sliced celery
½ c. whole blanched almonds
1 10½-oz. can undiluted
beef broth

⅓ c. dry sherry
2 T. cornstarch
2 T. sugar
2 T. vinegar
1 c. drained canned or fresh
sliced tomatoes
Hot steamed rice

Mix ground beef, ginger and 2 tablespoons soy sauce; shape into 1- to 1½-inch balls. Heat 2 tablespoons oil in a skillet, add meat balls about 6 at a time and saute until browned, turning carefully. Remove all meat balls from skillet. Add 2 more tablespoons oil to pan and add celery and almonds and saute until celery is tender-crisp.

Mix 1 tablespoon soy sauce, the beef broth, sherry, cornstarch, sugar and vinegar; pour into pan and cook, stirring, over medium heat until sauce comes to a boil and is thickened. Gently drop meat balls into sauce and cook, covered, for 10 minutes. Taste and correct seasoning. Gently stir in tomatoes and heat through. Serve immediately over hot steamed rice. Serves 4.

Beef Stroganoff Filling for Crêpes

1½ lbs. cooked beef, cut in
¼- to ½-inch cubes
½ lb. mushrooms, sliced
1 c. onion, finely chopped
2 T. butter or margarine
2 T. flour
⅓ c. cold water

2 beef bouillon cubes
⅓ c. boiling water
2 T. Worcestershire
1 tsp. prepared mustard
2 tsp. salt
⅛ tsp. pepper
1 c. dairy sour cream

Lightly brown mushrooms and onion in butter. Blend flour with ⅓ cup cold water. Dissolve bouillon cubes in ⅓ cup boiling water, stir into flour paste to blend and add to vegetables in skillet. Stir in Worcestershire sauce, mustard, salt and pepper and heat, stirring constantly, until thickened. Add beef cubes, cover and cook slowly 10 to 15 minutes, until heated through. Remove from heat and stir in sour cream.

Place about ½ cup hot filling across center of each prepared crêpe; overlap opposite sides on top to form roll. Place in baking pan. Sprinkle each with 1 tablespoon shredded mild cheddar cheese. Bake in a 350-degree oven for 3 to 5 minutes. Makes about 12 filled crêpes.

Hamburgers Fondue

2 lbs. ground lean beef	¼ tsp. thyme
2 T. instant minced onion	¼ tsp. pepper
6 T. fine dry bread crumbs	6 slices tomato
⅔ c. red dinner wine	6 thin slices onion
2 tsp. salt	Fondue Sauce

Combine beef, onion, crumbs, wine, salt, thyme and pepper and mix well. Shape into 6 thick patties. Grill until browned on one side. Turn and place tomato and onion slice (break up rings) on top of each. Cook to desired degree of doneness. Serve with Fondue Sauce to spoon over. Serves 6.

Fondue Sauce: Rub a small saucepan with a cut clove of garlic. Discard garlic. Add 8 ounces process Swiss cheese, shredded, 2 teaspoons cornstarch, 1 teaspoon Dijon-style mustard, ½ cup California white dinner wine and a dash each, nutmeg and white pepper. Cook on back of grill (or over very low heat of range), stirring frequently, until cheese is melted and sauce is smooth and thick.

Tofelspitz

2 medium carrots	1 leek
1 medium parsnip	5 c. water
½ small celery root	2 tsp. salt
(optional)	6 medium Idaho potatoes,
3 lbs. beef brisket	peeled, cut in half
¼ lb. cubed beef liver	½ c. light cream
1 celery heart, including leaves	Paprika
1 med. onion, finely chopped	Parsley sprigs

Peel and cut carrots, parsnip and celery root into 2-inch strips. Put in large pot and add brisket, liver, celery, heart, onion, leek, water and 1 teaspoon salt. Bring to a boil, reduce heat to a simmer, cover and simmer 2½ hours, skimming any foam that rises from time to time. Add potatoes. Simmer for 30 minutes, or until meat is tender. Remove brisket and potatoes. Strain liquid, setting aside 2½ cups broth. Return meat and potatoes to pot, cover with remaining broth and keep hot until ready to serve. Purée vegetables, liver and reserved broth in blender. Pour into a pan and stir in 1 teaspoon salt, paprika and light cream. Simmer 5 minutes and serve with parsley sprigs. Slice meat and arrange on a platter surrounded by potatoes. Serves 6.

Easy California Beef Chili

2 lbs. lean boneless beef chuck or stew
1 10-oz. can Spanish red chili sauce (enchilada or taco sauce)
1 10½-oz. can beef bouillon or broth

Cut beef into ½-inch pieces, trimming off any fat. Simmer beef, chili sauce and bouillon in covered pan about 45 minutes, or until good and tender. If desired, thicken sauce with 2 tablespoons cornstarch mixed with a little cold water. Serves 6 to 8.

One Way: Serve beef chili with beans or rice.

Other Way: Wrap beef chili in flour tortillas. Cover bottom of shallow baking dish with sauce from chili. Place rolled tortillas in sauce. Sprinkle with grated cheddar cheese and chopped green onions. Heat in a 350-degree oven 10 to 15 minutes, until piping hot and cheese melts.

Beef and Vegetables, California

1 lb. ground lean beef
2 T. fine dry bread crumbs
⅓ c. milk
1 egg yolk
2 T. chopped parsley
1 minced clove garlic
1 tsp. salt
2 tsp. chopped pine nuts

¼ c. olive oil
1 9-oz. package frozen artichoke hearts (or fresh)
¼ lb. small mushrooms
½ tsp. crumbled oregano
Freshly-ground pepper
2 T. lemon juice

Combine beef with bread crumbs, milk, egg yolk, parsley, garlic, salt and nuts. Shape into 1-inch balls. Brown in hot olive oil.

Meanwhile, blanch frozen artichoke hearts in boiling water about 2 minutes. Drain.

Remove browned beef balls from skillet or push to one side. Add mushrooms and cook until heated through. Add artichoke hearts and beef balls; sprinkle with pepper, oregano and lemon juice. Toss lightly to mix. Serve at once. Serves 4.

Danish Blue Steak

1 top round or "London Broil" steak, cut 1½ in. thick
¼ lb. Danish blue cheese, crumbled
  Salt, pepper

Make slit along center of one long side of steak and cut through to within 1 inch of other long side, forming a pocket. Fill pocket with cheese, pushing toward closed side. Insert picks or small skewers to close open side of steak.

Broil about 10 minutes on a side for medium rare. Sprinkle with salt and pepper, let stand a couple of minutes before carving. Remove picks and cut steak in thin slices on the diagonal (across the grain) as for London Broil. Serves 6.

Baroque Beef Steak

1 3½- to 4-lb. New York steak
  (or enough steak of your
  choice to serve 8)
½ c. butter
1 minced clove garlic
1½-2 lbs. whole med. mushrooms
½ c. chopped shallots
  Few drops Worcestershire
  Salt and pepper to taste
½ c. Baroque (dry red) wine

Sear steak a few minutes on either side close to a large bed of coals, then raise up 5 or 6 inches above the coals and cook until done to your liking. If you have a hood for the grill, use it. If not, make a hood of heavy-duty foil. The cooking time is about 30 to 40 minutes in all.

Meanwhile, melt butter. Add garlic and shallots and sauté very slowly just until beginning to soften but not brown. Add mushrooms, increase heat slightly and stir until mushrooms begin to brown ever so slightly. Add Worcestershire sauce, salt and pepper and wine and simmer gently for about 10 minutes. Serve in a sauce dish as an accompaniment for the meat. Serves 8.

California Beef Pot Roast

1 4-lb. rolled beef sirloin butt or rolled rump	3 T. oil or drippings
Veal Forcemeat	4 thick slices bacon
3 T. flour	1 10½-oz. can beef broth
1 tsp. salt	1 c. red table wine
¼ tsp. pepper	4 mushrooms, sliced
	1 T. butter

Make slits in beef with long sharp knife and push forcemeat into them. Combine 2 tablespoons flour with salt and pepper. Rub into beef. Sear on all sides in hot oil or drippings in Dutch oven. Lay bacon strips over top of beef. Add broth and wine. Cover closely and simmer until tender, about 1½ to 2 hours. Discard bacon. Remove beef and keep warm. Skim fat from cooking liquid. Add mushrooms to remaining liquid. Stir in butter kneaded with remaining 1 tablespoon flour. Simmer 5 minutes. Serve with beef. Serves 8.

Veal Forcemeat: Grind ½ pound veal and 1 ounce beef suet together twice, using fine blade of food chopper. Mix with ½ teaspoon onion salt and a dash each, pepper, cloves and nutmeg. Blend in 1 egg white and use as directed.

Beef and Pea Pods

1 lb. sirloin steak, cut 1 inch thick	1 tsp. sugar
¼ c. soy sauce	2 T. cooking oil
2 T. sherry	8 green onions, sliced
4 tsp. cornstarch	½ to 1 lb. pea pods (or 6-oz.
1 tsp. monosodium glutamate	package frozen, thawed)

Cut meat into strips about 1½ inches long and ¼ inch thick. Combine soy sauce, sherry, cornstarch, monosodium glutamate and sugar in a medium bowl. Stir in meat and let marinate for 10 minutes.

Remove meat from marinade, reserving marinade. Heat oil in a large skillet and brown meat until it has lost almost all its red color. Add onions and cook until tender-crisp. Stir in pea pods and cook about 2 minutes, stirring. Stir in reserved marinade and heat through. Serve with steamed or boiled rice. Serves 4.

Beef on the Rocks

1 4- to 5-lb. beef chuck roast, bone in
1 c. prepared mustard, about
3 c. rock salt, about

Trim fat from edges of beef. Spread roast with mustard to coat top and sides completely. Pack rock salt into mustard as thick as it will stick. Let stand a few minutes, adding more salt if any mustard starts to show through. Turn roast over. Coat reverse side with mustard and rock salt. Again let stand as above. Place beef directly on bed of glowing coals. Cook about 20 to 30 minutes, depending on thickness of roast. Turn meat, using a small baking sheet and a broad spatula. Continue cooking for another 20 to 30 minutes. To determine degree of doneness, make a small deep cut into roast near bone. Remove beef from coals. Knock off any salt coating that remains and slice meat diagonally to the grain. Serves 6 to 8.

Sauce Bordelaise is a three-part sauce to be served with steak.

Entrecôtes Sauce Bordelaise

I—Demi Glace

2 T. shortening
1 onion, chopped fine
1 carrot, chopped fine
2 T. flour
2 shallots, finely chopped

2 cloves garlic, finely chopped
   Bouquet garni with celery
1 T. tomato paste
1½ c. beef bouillon
   Salt, pepper

Heat shortening in heavy-bottomed saucepan. Add onion and carrot and brown, stirring once in a while. When well browned, add flour and cook until nut brown. Add remaining ingredients in order given and simmer slowly, uncovered, for 30 minutes. Strain and set aside.

II—*Réduction*

¾ c. red wine
3 chopped shallots

Place wine and shallots in small saucepan. Reduce liquid over high heat until there is only about 1 tablespoon. Add to strained sauce.

III—*Garniture*

About 6 inches of fresh marrow

Remove marrow from bones. Cut into ½-inch slices. Place in a saucepan with a little cold water; bring to a light simmer (do not let boil) and cook until marrow has lost its pink color, about 5 minutes. Remove to a plate and set aside. Dice all but 6 slices.

Assembly: Heat sauce slowly, add diced marrow and a tablespoon each, Madeira and Cognac. Do not overheat or marrow will disintegrate. Place 6 grilled steaks (not peppered) on a large serving platter. Put a slice of marrow on each and spoon some of the sauce over all. Sprinkle with chopped parsley and pass remaining sauce in a sauce boat. (One large steak may be used, if desired.) Serves 6.

Bitoks à la Russe

1 medium onion,
    very finely chopped
    Butter
1½ lbs. very lean beef,
    ground twice
    Salt, pepper
1 c. whipping cream,
    divided

¾ lb. medium mushrooms
    Juice ½ lemon
1 T. butter
    Flour
8 croutons
2 tsp. cornstarch
2 T. Cognac
    Chopped parsley

Cook onion in a little butter without letting it brown. Set aside to cool.

Place ground meat on a cool flat surface. Begin mashing beef with a large stiff knife, pushing little bits away from the bulk. Add a little salt and pepper and begin incorporating ⅓ cup of the cream, a tablespoon at a time (add more cream only after the previous bit has been well worked into meat). Add the onion and continue working until mixture is stiff and not granular. Place in a bowl and refrigerate 3 hours or more.

Place mushrooms in saucepan and add water to come ⅓ way up. Add lemon juice, salt, pepper and the 1 tablespoon butter. Bring to a boil and cook 2 minutes only. Cool in juice. When cool, drain, cut in quarters and set aside, reserving cooking liquid.

Sprinkle a little flour on work surface. Put meat mixture on it and shape in a roll about 3 inches in diameter, being sure the roll is dusted with flour. Cut into 8 equal portions; pat down a bit to the size of a tournedo; dust cut surfaces with a little flour.

Heat 4 tablespoons butter in a large saute pan. Cook bitoks 2 or 3 minutes on each side. Salt and pepper lightly. Place on croutons (pieces of sauteed bread) that have been cut to fit bitoks. Place in a slow oven to keep warm. Remove grease from pan and add mushroom liquid and remaining cream and bring to a boil. Mix cornstarch with a little water and use to thicken slightly. Add mushrooms and heat. Add Cognac. Spoon sauce over meat, sprinkle with parsley and serve hot. Serves 4.

Galley Beef Chunks

3 lbs. boneless beef chuck	¼ tsp. oregano
1½ c. dry white wine	¼ tsp. thyme
1 T. wine vinegar	¼ tsp. pepper
	1 sliced onion

Cut beef into 1½-inch cubes. Combine all remaining ingredients and pour over meat. Cover and refrigerate 2 to 3 days.

Drain beef. Grill over charcoal or broil until well browned on all sides. Serves 6 to 8.

Rond de Gîte à la Noix Garni

¼ lb. fresh pork fat
   in one long piece
¼ c. Cognac
¼ c. Madeira
1 shallot, minced
3 to 4 lbs. eye of round roast
   Oil and butter for browning
2 c. dry red wine
1 c. beef bouillon

1 finely-chopped onion
1 finely-chopped carrot
   Bouquet garni
   Salt, pepper
1 T. tomato paste
1 T. chopped shallot
   Braised vegetables for
   garnish (tiny carrots,
   onions, baby turnips)

Combine Cognac, Madeira and minced shallots in a flat utensil. Cut the fat into lardons (long strips, ¼ inch square) and marinate them in the mixture for a few minutes. Use these to "lard" the roast (below).

Dry the roast carefully with paper toweling and brown well on all sides in hot butter and oil (about half and half). Add remaining ingredients (except braised vegetables) in order given, including the lardon marinade. Cover and cook gently about 1 hour per pound.

Remove meat to hot platter; strain sauce, return to low heat and thicken with beurre manie. Slice meat and surround with braised vegetables; spoon a little of the sauce over the meat on the platter and pass the rest. Serves 6 to 8.

Beurre Manie: Equal parts of butter and flour rubbed together. Break off pea-size pieces and add to sauce, stirring with a whisk, until thickened as you like it.

Larding: Twist a larding needle through the meat, place the lardon in it and press down to fit, then pull the needle back, pushing the lardon with it to come out the other end. The needle then comes out and the lardon remains in the meat. Trim off scraggly ends.

Gourmet Steak

4 boneless club steaks,
   1 inch thick
1 clove garlic, mashed
½ tsp. salt
¼ tsp. black pepper
½ tsp. crumbled marjoram
1 4¾-oz. can smoked
   liver pâté

½ lb. Port Salut or Bonbel
   cheese, cut in 8 slices
¼ c. butter
2 T. chopped parsley
½ c. dry red wine
1 beef bouillon cube

Using a sharp knife, cut a pocket in one side of each steak, leaving the fatty edge joined. Rub steak inside and out with garlic, salt, pepper and marjoram. Cut open both ends of can of pâté and push the contents out by using one of the ends. Cut pâté into 4 slices. Put 1 slice of pâté and 1 slice of cheese into each pocket. Close openings with toothpicks. Heat butter and brown meat quickly on both sides, about 5 minutes on each. Remove from heat and top each with a cheese slice. Cover and reheat for 1 minute, until cheese melts. Place meat on a heated platter and keep warm. Add remaining ingredients to pan drippings and simmer until liquid has thickened slightly. Spoon pan juices over meat. Serve hot. Serves 4.

Steak on a Stick

1½ lbs. beef sirloin
½ c. dry sherry
2 T. soy sauce
1 T. honey

1 T. catsup
1 T. garlic-flavored
  wine vinegar

Cut sirloin into one-inch chunks. Combine remaining ingredients, mixing well. Pour over beef chunks and let marinate ½ hour. Thread beef on skewers. Grill on hibachi or barbecue, or broil to desired degree of doneness. Serves 6 to 8 as an appetizer, 3 or 4 as a main course.

Barbecued Beef Filet

1 3-lb. beef filet
1 c. hot water
2 oz. dried mushrooms
1 tsp. sugar
1 lb. fresh mushrooms,
  sliced thickly

1 bunch green onions, diced
2 cloves garlic, crushed
1 c. butter
1 tsp. salt
2 T. brandy

Have butcher tie beef with thin layer of fat. Barbecue slowly over hot coals, turning often, about 1 hour for rare, or to desired degree of doneness.

Meanwhile, pour water over dried mushrooms (we used the Japanese shii-ta-ke and found them excellent) and sprinkle with sugar; let stand ½ hour. Cook fresh mushrooms, onion and garlic in butter until mushrooms are just tender. Drain dried mushrooms. Chop coarsely and add to fresh mushroom mixture along with salt. Heat brandy, flame and pour over sauce.

Remove strings and any burned fat from beef. Slice thickly and serve with mushrooms. Serves 6 to 8.

Note: Tapered ends of filet usually are less expensive. See if your butcher won't put two end pieces together and tie with fat to make a roast.

Stuffed South American Flank Steak

1 3-lb. flank steak	½ c. soft bread crumbs
2¼ tsp. salt	½ c. cooked chopped spinach
½ tsp. pepper	½ c. cooked corn
6 T. instant minced onion	1 hard-cooked egg, chopped
½ c. bottled oil and vinegar dressing	3 crisp bacon slices, crumbled
	2 T. shortening
½ c. mixed vegetable flakes	2 c. beef bouillon

Score one side of steak in diamond pattern. Sprinkle both sides with 1½ teaspoons of the salt and ¼ teaspoon of the pepper. Place in a large bowl. Combine 4 tablespoons of the minced onion with oil and vinegar dressing; pour over meat. Cover and refrigerate 6 hours or overnight.

In another bowl, combine remaining minced onion, vegetable flakes and ½ cup water. Let stand 8 minutes for vegetables to soften. Add bread crumbs, spinach, corn, egg, bacon and remaining salt and pepper.

Remove meat from marinade; reserve marinade. Spoon filling onto scored side of steak, spreading so it almost extends to edge. Roll jelly roll fashion; tie securely with string. Heat shortening in large skillet. Brown steak on all sides, 15 to 20 minutes. Pour reserved marinade and bouillon over steak. Cover and simmer about 1 hour, or until fork tender. Place steak on warm platter; remove strings, serve with strained pan juices. Serves 6.

Boeuf en Croûte

¾ c. finely-chopped onion
2 T. butter
½ bay leaf
2 whole cloves
⅓ c. white dinner wine
2 beaten eggs
Milk
¾ lb. ground lean beef

¾ lb. ground veal
1 c. fine soft bread crumbs
1½ tsp. salt
¼ tsp. pepper
Pastry
Dill pickle strips
Cooked carrot strips
4 hard-cooked eggs

Cook onion slowly in butter with bay leaf and cloves about 5 minutes, until onion is transparent but not browned. Add wine and simmer until liquid is reduced to about 2 tablespoons. Remove from heat, discard bay leaf and cloves. Cool. Combine 1 teaspoon of beaten egg with 1 teaspoon milk. Set aside for egg wash.

Combine remaining beaten eggs with beef, veal, crumbs, salt, pepper and onion mixture. Beat with a fork until well mixed.

Roll ¾ of the pastry to a 9½ x 13½-inch rectangle. Fit carefully into an 8½ x 4½ x 2½-inch loaf pan, allowing edges to overhang slightly. Put a thin layer of beef mixture in pan. Place dill pickle and carrot strips lengthwise over it. Add a little more meat, then hard-cooked eggs, then more pickle strips at sides. Cover with more meat, pickle and carrot strips and smooth remaining meat over top.

Roll remaining pastry to fit top of pan. Brush edges with cold water; fit top pastry in place. Pinch edges firmly together and flute. Cut two small holes in top to allow steam to escape. Roll pastry trimmings and cut in narrow strips. Arrange lattice fashion over top of loaf. Brush with egg wash; insert small foil funnels in holes. Set loaf on baking sheet. Bake in a preheated 375-degree oven 1½ hours. Remove from oven and allow to cool 10 to 15 minutes. Carefully remove from pan and cut into slices to serve.

Pastry: Combine 2½ cups sifted flour and 1 teaspoon salt. Cut in ½ cup butter and ⅓ cup shortening. Beat 1 egg lightly with ⅓ cup milk. Stir into flour mixture to make stiff dough. Chill about ½ hour before rolling out.

Burgundy Meat Balls

3 slices French bread
1 c. California burgundy
2 lbs. ground beef chuck
1 egg, beaten
1 T. instant minced onion

1 tsp. garlic salt
1 tsp. seasoned pepper
½ tsp. dry basil
2 T. cooking oil

Place French bread slices in mixing bowl; pour on ¾ cup wine. Let stand ½ hour, until bread has absorbed wine and is very soft. Beat with egg, onion, salt, pepper and basil until well blended. Combine with meat lightly but thoroughly. Divide into 18 equal-size portions; shape each one into a ball. Brown meat balls slowly in heated oil on all sides. Add remaining wine to pan. Cover tightly and cook over low heat until meat is done, about 15 minutes longer. If liquid in pan is completely absorbed before cooking is completed, add ¼ cup water. Pile meat balls on top of hot cooked spaghetti to serve. Serves 6.

Spaghetti: Cook 8 ounces spaghetti until just tender in boiling salted water, then drain and toss with ¼ cup butter, ½ cup shredded Parmesan cheese and 2 tablespoons chopped parsley.

Flank steak is the traditional cut used for this old favorite.

London Broil

1 flank steak
½ c. salad oil
½ c. wine or wine vinegar
Juice 1 lemon

½ c. soy sauce
1 clove garlic, minced
Salt
Pepper

Prepare a marinade by blending together oil, wine, lemon juice, soy sauce, garlic and salt and pepper to taste. Pour over flank steak and place in refrigerator overnight, or let stand a minimum of 6 hours at room temperature. Turn steak several times. Before broiling, let meat stand at room temperature for at least an hour. Slash edges of steak with a sharp knife to keep them from curling under the broiler. Broil steak 3 inches from heat source for 5 to 6 minutes. Turn and broil other side 5 minutes. To serve, carve in very thin slices diagonally across the grain. Serves 4 to 6.

Baked Short Ribs Mount Vernon

4 T. flour	1 T. vinegar
1 tsp. salt	½ tsp. dry mustard
¼ tsp. pepper	½ c. catsup
4 lbs. beef short ribs	½ c. beer or ale
2 T. butter or margarine	1 c. beef bouillon
2 medium onions, chopped	6 whole carrots,
2 T. brown sugar	scraped, halved

Combine flour, salt and pepper; roll short ribs in mixture. Brown ribs on all sides in hot butter in skillet; reduce heat and add onion and cook until tender, but not brown. Combine brown sugar, vinegar, dry mustard, catsup, beer and bouillon. Turn all into a 2-quart casserole and bake in a preheated 350-degree oven 1½ hours. Add carrots and bake 1 hour longer. Serves 8.

Salt Roasted Beef is a barbecue favorite. It is charred on the outside and juicy red inside.

Salt Roasted Beef

1 3-lb. eye roast of beef	1 T. cracked black pepper
1-2 cloves garlic	1 tsp. cloves
1½ T. prepared mustard	½ c. salt
1 T. chili sauce	Heavy foil

Have meat at room temperature before cooking. Quarter garlic; place in deep slits cut into meat. Combine mustard, chili sauce, pepper and cloves; spread over meat. Let stand ½ hour. By rubbing and patting, pat salt onto meat until surface is thickly coated. Let stand 1 hour.

Line grill with foil. Add briquets to make a 2-inch bed of coals. Let burn until coals are covered with fine ash.

Join 2 strips of 14-inch foil with interlock fold, to accommodate two turns of the meat so that it will be cooked all around. Place meat on one side of the piece of foil and lower onto coals. Cook about 10 minutes. Roll meat over; cook 8 to 10 minutes. Repeat. Cut beef diagonally in thin slices. Serves 6 to 8.

The long slow method for cooking a beef roast has caught on in recent years—here is how it's done.

'Perfect' Cross Rib Roast

5-lb. rolled cross rib beef roast
Salt and pepper

Sprinkle beef with salt and pepper. Insert meat thermometer into center of roast. Let stand at room temperature for 30 minutes. Preheat oven to 375 degrees. Place roast on rack in shallow open pan and roast in oven one hour. Turn off heat. Do *not* open oven door for one hour (very important).

During this resting period the beef continues to cook slowly and the heat is distributed evenly throughout the meat. Turn oven regulator to 300 degrees. Allow roast to reheat about 30 minutes, until beef has reached desired internal temperature. It will be pink and juicy all the way through when the thermometer registers 130 degrees.

If you want it very rare, remove from the oven a few minutes earlier. If you prefer it well done, continue cooking until it is just the way you like it.

Meat Loaf en Croûte

1 onion, finely chopped	¼ c. flour
1 clove garlic, mashed	2 eggs
3 T. butter	¼ tsp. white pepper
¼ lb. chicken livers, halved	¼ tsp. ground cloves
⅓ c. brandy	½ tsp. ginger
2 lbs. ground meats	½ tsp. nutmeg
(beef, pork, veal, mixed)	½ tsp. dry mustard
for meat loaf	1½ tsp. salt
2 bay leaves	Buttery Pastry

Cook onion and garlic in butter until soft. Add chicken livers and cook until lightly browned. Remove livers from pan and reserve. Add brandy to onions and cook, stirring, until most of liquid has evaporated. Combine onion mixture in a large bowl with ground meats, flour, 1 whole egg and 1 egg yolk (save the white), and all seasonings *but* bay leaves. Mix well until smooth.

Roll out about half the pastry on a floured board to make a strip about 28 inches long and 4 inches wide. Place this pastry around inside of a 9 x 5-inch loaf pan, pressing it firmly against the sides and letting a little pastry overlap at both the top and bottom edges. Roll half the remaining pastry to a 9 x 5-inch rectangle. Press it into the bottom of the pan, sealing it to the pastry lining the sides.

Fill the pastry-lined pan with half the ground meat mixture. Top with chicken livers. Cover with remaining ground meat. Place bay leaves on ground meat. Roll out remaining pastry to an 11 x 7-inch rectangle for top crust. Crimp edges to seal top crust to pastry lining the sides. Beat reserved egg white with 1 teaspoon water; brush over pastry. Slash top pastry in several places to enable steam to escape. Decorate with pastry cutouts, if desired; brush them with egg white wash, too.

Bake in a preheated 375-degree oven for 1¼ to 1½ hours, until pastry is well browned and a long skewer inserted into center of meat mixture comes out clean. If necessary, during baking, place another pan below rack on which meat loaf is baking to catch any drippings. Cool the loaf on a rack, then chill overnight or for up to 48 hours before serving. Serves 8 to 10.

Note: This may be served hot, but is devilish to cut. And, the flavor is better if it is chilled.

Buttery Pastry: Cut ½ cup firm butter and ¼ cup lard into a mixture of 3½ cups unsifted all-purpose flour and ¾ teaspoon salt in a large bowl, using a pastry blender, until mixture is crumbly and forms very small particles. Beat 1 egg yolk in a measuring cup, then add cold water to make ½ cup. Gradually add egg mixture to flour mixture, about a tablespoon at a time, tossing the mixture lightly with a fork after each addition, until the pastry clings together. If necessary, add 2 to 3 tablespoons more water. Using your hands, work the pastry until smooth, shape it into a roll and wrap it in plastic wrap. Chill for 1 hour, or longer.

Son-of-a-Gun Stew

1½ lbs. stew meat (beef)　　　　6 T. chopped parsley
½ lb. beef heart　　　　　　　　6 med. cloves garlic, chopped
1 lb. beef tongue　　　　　　　　¼ tsp. thyme
1 set brains　　　　　　　　　　1 tsp. sweet basil
2 T. suet　　　　　　　　　　　Salt to taste
¾ lb. onions　　　　　　　　　　4 chili tepines
¼ lb. celery root　　　　　　　　1 c. dry red wine

Trim and chop heart into 1- or 1½-inch pieces and start cooking, as it needs more time than the stew meat. Also, partially precook the tongue enough so you can skin and chop it into bits. Brown the stew meat in the rendered suet and add the heart and tongue, garlic, herbs, onion and celery root, salt and chili tepines. Add enough water to keep it from burning and let simmer 2 to 2½ hours. About ½ hour before it is done, prepare brains, chop into bite-size pieces and add to stew along with parsley and wine.

Flank Steak Teriyaki

1 flank steak,　　　　　　　　⅛ tsp. powdered garlic
　　about 1½ lbs.　　　　　　　1 tsp. salt
1 c. beef bouillon　　　　　　　½ c. soy sauce
1 tsp. seasoned salt　　　　　　2 T. fresh lemon juice
⅓ c. finely-chopped onion　　　2 T. honey

Have membrane removed from steak, but do not have it scored. Remove fat and gristle. Cut meat into diagonal strips about an inch wide. Combine bouillon, salt, onion, garlic, salt, soy sauce, lemon juice and honey. Pour over strips of meat and marinate about 24 hours. Remove meat from marinade, drain and thread on skewers; cap each with a whole mushroom, if desired. Broil 4 to 5 minutes, turning once. Serves 4 to 6.

Western-Style Flank Steaks

2 flank steaks, about
  1½ lbs. each
1 c. chili sauce
½ c. red wine vinegar
1 c. dry red wine
2 T. Worcestershire
1 T. instant minced onion
¼ tsp. garlic powder

2 tsp. prepared mustard
1 T. salt
¼ c. salad oil
1 10½-oz. can condensed
  consommé
3 T. cornstarch
3 T. water

Combine chili sauce, vinegar, wine, Worcestershire sauce, onion, garlic powder, mustard, salt and oil; mix well and pour over steaks in a mixing bowl. Cover closely and let stand 2 hours, or longer. Drain steaks, saving marinade. Broil steaks about 3 inches from heat over charcoal or in range broiler. For medium rare, allow 5 to 7 minutes on each side over charcoal. While meat is cooking, heat marinade to boiling. Add consommé and thicken with the cornstarch dissolved in the water. When steaks are done, transfer to a cutting board and slice diagonally across the grain. Serve with sauce. Serves 8.

Lamb

We eat lots of lamb in Northern California. We curry it, stew it, broil and roast it and we barbecue it. One of our favorites is:

Barbecued Butterflied Leg of Lamb

Have a 5- to 6-pound leg of lamb boned. Spread it flat (butterfly) and sprinkle with a mixture of minced garlic, powdered rosemary, salad oil, salt, coarsely-ground pepper and dry red or white wine. Place, seasoned side down, over glowing coals, about 6 inches from them, and season other side. Cook for from 30 to 40 minutes, or until done to your liking, turning once. Slice thinly to serve.

Irish Stew

2 lbs. lamb shoulder
  meat, cubed
½ lb. sliced bacon,
  cut in 1-inch pieces
6 cubed potatoes
8 sliced onions

6 thinly-sliced carrots
2 tsp. salt
¼ tsp. pepper
¼ tsp. thyme
¼ tsp. rosemary
1 c. cold water

Combine all ingredients in a large heavy pot or casserole. Cover tightly and simmer over low heat 1½ hours, or until meat is tender and potatoes and carrots are soft. Serves 6.

New Zealand Lamb Curry

2 medium onions
2 cloves garlic
1 green pepper
2 tart apples
3 T. butter or oil
2 T. curry powder

½ tsp. powdered ginger
2 lbs. lamb cubes
2 T. flour
2 tsp. salt
1½ c. chicken broth or water
1 T. lemon juice

Peel and chop onions, garlic, seeded pepper and apples. Heat butter or oil (half and half is best), add chopped material and curry powder and ginger. Cook slowly until onions and apple are smooth pulp, curry bright golden. Trim meat of fat, toss with flour and add to pan; cook about 10 minutes, stirring often to brown meat. Add salt and broth. Cover and simmer until sauce is smooth and thickened and lamb very tender, about 45 minutes. Add lemon juice and stir until smooth, then serve with boiled rice and condiments. Serves 6 to 8.

Condiments: Chopped peanuts, raisins, grated coconut, chutney, minced onion, chopped mint, chopped hard-cooked egg (yolk and white separated). Serve at least four of these.

Stuffed Lamb Breast Florentine

2½-3 lbs. lamb breast
1 tsp. salt
¼ tsp. pepper
½ lb. fresh pork sausage,
   casings removed
3 T. chopped onion
1 3-oz. can chopped
   broiled mushrooms

1 10-oz. package frozen
   chopped spinach,
   thawed, drained
2 eggs, beaten
½ c. cornflake crumbs
¼ tsp. thyme

Lay meat flat. With sharp knife, and starting at narrow end of ribs, make a large pocket between top layer of meat and ribs, leaving meat attached on three edges of breast. Season meat with half the salt and pepper. Fry sausage until done, stirring to crumble. Drain off fat. Add onion and cook until tender. Drain mushrooms reserving broth for some other use. Combine sausage, onion, spinach, mushrooms, eggs, cornflake crumbs, thyme and remaining salt and pepper. Mix well and spoon into pocket. Skewer or sew closed. Place meat, ribs down, in a shallow baking pan. Roast in a preheated 325-degree oven for 2 hours, or until tender. Serves 3 or 4.

Satay Kambing
(Indonesian Lamb)

3 lbs. lean lamb cut in
   ½-inch cubes (leg best)
1 c. cider vinegar
½ c. minced onion
2 tsp. salt

2 tsp. ground coriander
1 tsp. ground ginger
4 cloves garlic, minced
½ tsp. ground chili pepper
1 tsp. ground cumin

Marinate cubed lamb in vinegar for 30 minutes. Then roll it in a mixture of the remaining ingredients and marinate one hour.

Heat 4 tablespoons peanut oil and brown lamb in it; add ½ cup water and cook, covered, over low heat for 30 minutes, or until tender.

Spring Lamb Steaks

2 lamb sirloin steaks,
  each about ½ lb.,
  1 inch thick
Olive oil, butter
Salt, freshly-ground
  black pepper
1 large banana, cut in
  ½-inch diagonal slices,
  dipped in lemon juice

3 T. minced green onions
  with some tops
¼ c. dry red dinner wine
½ c. beef bouillon
1 small clove garlic,
  minced or mashed
½ tsp. crumbled dried oregano

Put about ½ tablespoon each, olive oil and butter, in a heavy frying pan and place over medium-high heat; brown steaks well on one side, then turn and brown second side. If necessary, reduce heat and cook until done to your liking. Remove meat to a warm platter; season generously with salt and pepper; keep warm.

Add 1 tablespoon butter to frying pan; add banana slices and turn just to coat with butter and heat through; arrange on platter with meat. Add 2 tablespoons of the onions and the remaining ingredients to the pan and cook over high heat, stirring, until reduced at least by half—to a thin glaze consistency. Pour over steaks. Sprinkle with remaining onions. Serves 2.

Lamb Roast, Greek Style

1 leg of lamb,
  chops removed
2 cloves garlic
¼ c. olive oil
¼ c. fresh lemon juice

1½ tsp. salt
½ tsp. pepper
3 tsp. oregano leaves
Lemon slices
Fresh mint

Place lamb on rack in shallow roasting pan. Cut 5 slits ½ inch wide and 2 inches deep at intervals over top of meat. Slice 1 clove garlic into 5 pieces; insert 1 in each slit.

Mince remaining clove garlic and combine with oil, lemon juice, ½ teaspoon salt, ¼ teaspoon pepper and 2 teaspoons oregano in small saucepan. Heat and stir until blended. Brush lamb with some of oil mixture. Mix remaining 1 teaspoon salt, ¼ teaspoon pepper and 1 teaspoon oregano; sprinkle over surface of lamb.

Roast in a 325-degree oven 30 minutes per pound, or until meat thermometer registers 175 degrees. Baste meat occasionally with oil mixture. Remove lamb to heated platter and remove garlic. Garnish with lemon and mint. Serves 5 or 6.

Indian Lamb Curry

2 lbs. boneless leg of lamb, cut in 1-inch pieces
1 c. yoghurt
2½ tsp. salt
1 tsp. ground cumin
1½ tsp. ground turmeric
½ tsp. ground cardamom
¼ c. peanut oil or clarified butter
1½ c. chopped onion
1 clove garlic, crushed

1 tsp. dry mustard
1 tsp. ground ginger
½ tsp. ground cinnamon
½ tsp. freshly-ground black pepper
¼-½ tsp. cayenne
⅛ tsp. ground cloves
1 c. water
1 tsp. lemon juice
2 T. grated fresh coconut

Combine meat, yoghurt, salt, cumin, turmeric and cardamom in a mixing bowl; marinate two hours. Heat 1 tablespoon oil in a skillet and brown meat. Pour off excess fat. Cook onion and garlic in remaining oil in another skillet until golden. Add spices and cook, stirring, two minutes. Add lamb, cover and cook 20 minutes. Add 1 cup water and mix. Cover and simmer 30 minutes, adding more water only to keep from burning.

Just before serving, add lemon juice and coconut. Serve with plain rice and curry condiments. Serves 6 to 8.

Crown of Lamb Istanbul

16-rib crown of lamb
2 T. oil

1 tsp. bouquet garni for lamb Stuffing

Stuffing

2 T. butter
1 c. bulghar wheat
2 c. water
2 T. instant minced onion
2 T. chicken seasoned stock base

½ tsp. spearmint
¼ tsp. bouquet garni for lamb
4 thin lemon slices
¼ c. toasted pine nuts

Have butcher tie crown and leave it unfilled. Combine oil and crushed bouquet garni. Rub mixture over meat. Place in a shallow roasting pan, ribs down, covering crown bones with a strip of aluminum foil so they won't char. Roast in a 350-degree oven 2½ to 3 hours, until cooked through. Lift roast onto a heated serving platter. Fill center with Stuffing and serve at once. Serves 8.

Stuffing: Melt butter in a 1½-quart saucepan. Stir in wheat until lightly toasted. Remove from heat. Add water, onions, chicken stock base, spearmint, bouquet garni for lamb and lemon slices. Mix well, return to heat, bring to boil. Cover and simmer 25 minutes. Stir in toasted pine nuts just before serving.

Lamb and Peppers

2 T. butter or margarine
1½ lbs. boneless lamb
   shoulder, diced
3 med. green peppers, diced

1 small onion,
   coarsely chopped
2 canned pimientos, diced
   Salt, pepper to taste

Melt butter, add lamb and cook until lightly browned on all sides. Add green peppers, onion and pimientos; cover and cook over low heat 45 minutes, or until lamb is tender. Season with salt and pepper. Serve over rice, as desired. Serves 4.

Lamb Curry

¼ c. salad oil
2 large onions,
   coarsely chopped
1½ c. coarsely-chopped celery
1 c. seedless raisins
1 c. water

4 c. diced cooked lamb
1½ c. lamb stock or
   chicken bouillon
1½ c. chopped green apples
¼ c. curry powder
   Hot cooked rice

Heat oil; add onions and celery and cook until tender. Add raisins, 1 cup water, diced lamb and 1 cup lamb stock or bouillon. Cook, covered, over low heat 35 minutes. Add apples, curry powder and remaining stock. Mix well and cook, covered, 10 minutes, or until apples are tender. Serve over hot cooked rice with condiments as desired.

A variety of condiments might include chutney, chopped green onion, chopped green pepper, chopped peanuts, grated egg, toasted flaked coconut and preserved kumquats.

Lamb Spareribs with Barbecue Sauce

2 T. salad oil	1 tsp. salt
1 c. finely-chopped onion	1 tsp. garlic salt
½ c. finely-chopped green pepper	1 tsp. celery seed
	¼ tsp. pepper
½ c. brown sugar	2 lbs. lamb spareribs
1 8-oz. can tomato sauce	4 medium potatoes, pared,
3 T. vinegar	sliced ¼ inch thick

Heat oil. Add onions and green pepper. Cook over low heat until onions are tender. Add sugar, tomato sauce, vinegar, salt, garlic salt, celery seed and pepper; mix. Cover and cook over low heat 15 minutes, stirring occasionally.

Meanwhile, arrange lamb and potatoes on broiler pan. Brush lamb and potatoes with half of sauce. Broil 3 or 4 inches from heat source for 5 to 6 minutes. Turn and brush with remaining sauce. Broil an additional 5 to 6 minutes, or until lamb and potatoes are tender. Serves 4.

Pork

When pork is on the menu, it's usual to give it interesting and unusual treatment.

Serve sasaties with steamed rice, small rolls brushed with peanut butter and crisped on the grill and a cool frozen fruit salad.

Javanese Pork Sasaties

3 lbs. pork shoulder, boned, cubed, tenderized
18 small tart plums or prunes, pitted, stuffed with chutney
1 No. 2 can pineapple juice
¼ c. vinegar
¼ c. honey
1 large clove garlic, crushed
2 T. ground ginger *or* 1-inch piece fresh ginger, grated
1 to 2 T. curry powder

Combine pineapple juice, vinegar, honey, garlic, ginger and curry; pour over pork cubes in bowl and refrigerate overnight. Skewer pork and fruit alternately and broil until thoroughly done, at least 20 to 25 minutes. Turn frequently and baste with marinade. Serves 6.

Pork Sate

2 lbs. lean pork cut in 1-inch cubes
¼ c. peanut butter
1-2 T. coriander
½ tsp. crushed chili peppers
3 T. soy sauce
1½ tsp. ground cumin
1 T. lemon juice
1 clove garlic, crushed
1 c. soy sauce
¼ c. sherry
2 T. pineapple juice
½ tsp. grated ginger root
1 clove garlic, minced

Skewer pork on wooden sate sticks. Make a paste of peanut butter, coriander, chili, 3 tablespoons soy sauce, cumin, lemon juice and garlic. Rub the meat on each skewer with the paste (you might wear rubber gloves while doing this). Marinate 20 minutes or more.

Broil meat 20 to 30 minutes, turning often. Serve with steamed rice and a sauce made by boiling together the last five ingredients (soy, sherry, etc.). Strain and cool before using.

Polynesian Pork Loin

½ c. pineapple juice
¼ c. oil
2 T. soy sauce
2 T. lemon juice
1 tsp. dry mustard
1 tsp. ginger
½ tsp. monosodium glutamate
1 tsp. Bon Appétit seasoning
⅛ tsp. mace
1 3-lb. pork loin roast

Combine pineapple juice, oil, soy sauce, lemon juice and next five ingredients thoroughly. Place roast on rack in roasting pan; baste with sauce. Roast in a 325-degree oven 1½ to 2 hours, or until meat thermometer registers 185 degrees. Baste frequently with sauce, using all of it. Serves 4.

Note: This roast may be cooked over charcoal, turning and basting frequently with the sauce.

Stuffed Pork Chops

1 c. cooked noodles	⅛ tsp. rubbed sage
¼ c. chopped celery	¼ tsp. pepper
¼ c. chopped onion	1 tsp. salt
2 T. vegetable oil	4 double pork chops
1 3-oz. can chopped	2 tsp. bottled browning sauce
broiled mushrooms	1 8-oz. can tomato sauce
1 T. minced parsley	½ c. water

Cook celery and onion in 1 tablespoon oil until tender. Add broth from mushrooms and cook until liquid is reduced by half. Stir in mushrooms, parsley, sage, pepper and ½ teaspoon salt. Mix with cooked and drained noodles.

Trim excess fat from chops and cut a deep pocket in the edge of each one almost through to the bone. Stuff chops with mushroom-noodle mixture. Fasten with wooden picks and lace with string. Brush with bottled browning sauce. Brown on both sides in remaining oil. Sprinkle with remaining salt and add tomato sauce and water. Bring to a boil, cover and continue cooking over low heat until chops are tender, about 1 hour. Baste with sauce now and then. Serves 4.

Sherried Creamy Ham

3 T. butter	¼ tsp. salt
¼ c. flour	¼ tsp. rosemary, crushed
1 2-oz. can mushrooms	1 tsp. lemon juice
1 c. half and half	¼ tsp. Worcestershire
⅓ c. dry sherry	1 T. chopped pimiento
⅓ c. milk	1 T. chopped parsley
1 tsp. chicken stock base	2 c. diced cooked ham

Melt butter and blend in flour. Drain mushrooms, reserving liquid. Gradually stir into flour-butter mixture the half and half, milk, mushroom liquid and sherry. Add chicken stock base, salt and rosemary. Cook, stirring constantly, over moderate heat until sauce boils and thickens. Add remaining ingredients and heat through. Serve in patty shells or over hot rice or hot biscuits. Serves 6.

Hawaiian Barbecued Ribs

2 racks spareribs	¼ c. sherry
½ c. soy sauce	1½ c. consommé or bouillon
½ c. honey	1 clove garlic, chopped
½ c. vinegar	¼ tsp. powdered ginger

Cut ribs apart. Combine remaining ingredients and marinate ribs in mixture for three hours. Spoon sauce over often. Grill or roast in a 350-degree oven for 1½ hours, basting frequently. Serve with mustard and Chinese duck sauce (from a jar). Makes appetizers for 6 or a main dish for 2 or 3.

Good veal seems to get harder to find and more expensive almost on a weekly basis. However, when available it is one of the very best and most delicate of all meats.

Riesling Veal

1½ lbs. boneless veal cutlet, pounded very thin	1½ c. dairy sour cream
2 T. flour	1 tsp. Worcestershire, or to taste
Salt, freshly-ground black pepper	Egg noodles, cooked al dente, drained, browned in butter
5 T. butter, about	¼ c. finely-chopped toasted almonds
4 T. minced green onion, white only	2 tsp. finely-chopped fresh parsley
2 tsp. paprika	
⅓ c. Johannesberg Riesling	

Slice veal in strips about 3 x ¼ inch. Combine flour, ¾ teaspoon salt and ½ teaspoon pepper in a clean paper bag. Add veal and shake to coat. Sauté veal in 4 tablespoons of the butter in a large, heavy frying pan over medium-high heat just until tender and lightly browned. (Butter will brown.) Remove from pan and keep warm.

Melt remaining butter in frying pan, add onions and sauté until limp. Stir in paprika. Add wine and cook and stir until liquid reduces to about 2 tablespoons. Reduce heat to low. Stir in sour cream and Worcestershire. Season well with salt. Fold veal into sour cream. Serve immediately over or with noodles. Sprinkle meat with toasted almonds and parsley. Serves 4.

Veal Farci à la Périgourdine

3 c. cooked rice
1 4½-oz. can smoked
  goose pâté
2 T. chopped truffle
1 c. chopped raw mushrooms
1 T. dehydrated beef stock
2 T. butter

2 T. flour
½ c. milk
  Salt, pepper
1 3- to 4-lb. breast of veal
  with pocket
2 T. butter
1 c. chicken broth

Combine rice, pâté, truffle, mushrooms and beef stock in a bowl. Melt butter in a saucepan and stir in flour. Gradually stir in milk. Cook while stirring, over low heat, until sauce bubbles and is very thick. Add to rice mixture and blend. Season to taste with salt and pepper.

Sprinkle veal inside and out with salt and pepper. Stuff with rice mixture. Skewer or sew opening together. Brush top with melted butter. Place in a shallow roasting pan, add chicken broth, cover pan with foil and bake in a 350-degree oven 2 hours, or until veal is almost tender. Uncover and roast another 30 minutes, until top of meat is brown.

To serve cold, cool meat and then chill. Remove bones to simplify slicing and serve with a side dish of vinaigrette sauce. Serves 6 to 8.

Escalopes de Veau Chasseur

½ lb. mushrooms, cut
    in small wedges
Butter
1 T. finely-chopped shallots
1 clove garlic,
    finely chopped

1½ lbs. veal scallops,
    pounded tissue thin
Flour
White wine

Saute mushrooms in about 2 tablespoons butter over high heat until lightly browned. Remove from pan and set aside.

Dust veal lightly with flour. Add more butter to the pan the mushrooms were cooked in and saute veal quickly—about 4 or 5 minutes. Set aside on a platter and keep warm.

Deglaze pan with about ½ cup white wine. When all brown bits are loose, add shallots, garlic and mushrooms. Simmer about 2 minutes, then pour over veal. Serve immediately. Serves 4.

Variation: Pork chops are excellent prepared this same way. *But*, have them cut ½ inch thick, allow two per person and cook them, after browning, about 30 minutes, reducing heat and covering saute pan.

Blanquette de Veal au Riz

2 lbs. cubed veal
¼ c. butter
2 lge. onions
⅓ c. flour
½ c. dry white wine
⅓ c. dry vermouth
    Salt, pepper

Bouquet garni
2 c. water
½ lb. mushrooms, chopped
1 egg yolk
1 tsp. lemon juice
½ c. fresh cream

Cut veal into 1-inch cubes, wipe dry with paper towels and brown in the butter in a deep sauté pan. When brown, add onions, which have been chopped, and brown them slightly. Add the flour to make a roux, then pour in white wine. Stir and cook for a couple of minutes, then add vermouth. Mix well, add salt and pepper to taste and the bouquet garni (below). Stir in the water, cover pan and simmer about 1¼ hours. Add mushrooms and cook another 15 or 20 minutes.

Shortly before serving, remove pan from heat and correct seasoning, if necessary. Remove and discard bouquet garni. Whisk the egg yolk in the lemon juice and add to the pan. Pour in the cream and mix well. Keep hot but do *not* let the mixture boil, for it will curdle quite easily.

Serve with steamed fluffy rice that has been dressed with melted sweet butter and grated Parmesan cheese.

A bouquet garni consists of a branch or two of parsley, a bay leaf, ½ teaspoon thyme and, sometimes, a piece of celery. These are all tied together in a cheesecloth "bag" and secured so they cannot come loose in the pan.

Veal in Wine

1¼ lbs. thinly sliced veal round steak	1 c. sliced mushrooms
Salt	⅔ c. white table wine
⅓ c. grated Parmesan cheese	⅛ tsp. rosemary
2 T. cooking oil	½ c. frozen peas
1 small onion, minced	2 tsp. cornstarch
1 clove garlic, minced	1 T. cold water

Sprinkle veal with salt and coat both sides with cheese. Brown slowly in hot oil. Add onion, garlic, and mushrooms. Cook until onion is lightly browned; add wine and rosemary. Cover and simmer 25 minutes. Add peas. Cover and cook 5 minutes longer. Stir in cornstarch blended with water. Cook a minute longer, stirring until sauce thickens. Serves 4.

Veal in Wine-Cheese Sauce

1½ lbs. veal stew meat	1 tsp. salt
2 T. oil	½ c. dry white dinner wine
1 clove garlic, finely chopped	Cheese Sauce
½ tsp. mixed Italian herbs	Hot cooked noodles

Dice or cube veal and brown slowly in oil. Add garlic and herbs and sauté a minute longer, stirring. Add salt and wine. Cover and simmer about 45 minutes, until veal is tender and liquid is almost gone.

Meanwhile, prepare Cheese Sauce and cook noodles. Add veal, including any remaining liquid, to sauce. Serve over hot noodles. Serves 4.

Cheese Sauce

2 T. butter
2½ T. flour
1¼ c. milk

¾ tsp. salt
¼ c. grated Parmesan cheese
⅓ c. dry white dinner wine

Melt butter, add flour and cook until mixture bubbles thoroughly but is not browned. Remove from heat; stir in milk and salt. Return to heat and cook, stirring constantly, until mixture bubbles and is thickened. Stir in cheese and wine and heat, but do not boil.

Veal Parmesan

1½ lbs. veal scallops,
pounded thin
1-2 eggs, slightly beaten
¼-½ c. fine dry bread crumbs
½ c. freshly-grated
Parmesan cheese

Olive oil
½ lb. Mozzarella cheese,
sliced thin
Tomato sauce, below

Dip veal in egg, then in bread crumbs mixed with ¼ cup Parmesan cheese. Coat a large skillet lightly with olive oil and cook the veal in single layers, quickly, until lightly browned on both sides.

Layer the veal in a 9 x 9 x 2-inch baking dish alternately with tomato sauce and slices of Mozzarella cheese. Sprinkle with the remaining Parmesan. Bake in a preheated 350-degree oven about 40 minutes. Serves 5 or 6.

Tomato Sauce: Saute 2 medium onions, finely diced, and 3 cloves garlic, crushed, in a small amount of olive oil. Add a 1-pound can Italian tomatoes, breaking up with a spoon. Simmer 10 minutes. Then add an 8-ounce can tomato sauce, ½ teaspoon oregano, ¼ teaspoon thyme, salt and pepper to taste. Simmer 1 hour.

Veal Parmigiana

2 lbs. veal cutlets,
 about ½ inch thick
1¼ c. fine, dry bread crumbs
½ c. Parmesan cheese
2 eggs, well beaten
1 T. water

1 tsp. salt
¼ tsp. pepper
⅓ c. vegetable oil
2 8-oz. cans tomato sauce
 with mushrooms
6 slices Mozzarella cheese

Have meat cut in 6 equal pieces. Pound with mallet or edge of saucer. Combine bread crumbs and grated Parmesan cheese. Set aside. Mix together eggs, water, salt and pepper. Heat oil in large heavy skillet. Dip cutlets into egg mixture and then in crumb mixture. Brown cutlets in skillet; pour tomato sauce over cutlets, top each with a Mozzarella cheese slice. Cover and simmer 10 minutes, or until cheese is melted and slightly golden. Serves 6.

Breast of veal is one of, if not the, least expensive veal cuts. It is perfect for stuffing. Just cut a pocket in the breast, or ask your butcher to do it for you.

Stuffed Breast of Veal

3-4 lbs. breast of veal
1 c. seedless raisins
½ c. cooked rice
3 slices rye bread,
 soaked in milk
¼ lb. finely-diced salt pork
2 egg yolks

1 10-oz. package chopped
 spinach, thawed, drained
1 tsp. basil
Salt, pepper
Nutmeg
1 c. white wine
2 bay leaves

Cut pocket in veal. Mix raisins, rice, bread, salt pork, spinach, egg yolks and seasonings in bowl; stuff the pocket and skewer opening. Brown on both sides in a little oil in a roasting pan. Sprinkle with salt and pepper and top with bay leaves. Add wine, cover and bake at 350 degrees about 2 hours, until tender. Serve hot or cold with a sauce of sour cream mixed with raisins. Serves 6.

Variety

W hat one can create from the remains of a roast can be pure genius. This meat loaf, or "pantin" as named by the French, begins with leftover meat—ham, beef, pork, lamb or veal—and ends by being a perfectly delicious one-dish meal.

Pantin en Croûte

2 packages pie crust mix or
  pastry for 2-crust pie
3 lbs. (6 c.) ground smoked ham,
  beef, lamb, pork or veal
2 4-oz. cans pate de foie

½ c. parsley
½ c. chopped shallots
⅓ c. sliced cornichons
3 eggs, well beaten
1 c. biscotte crumbs

Prepare pastry according to package directions, or in the usual manner. Roll out ⅔ of the crust on a floured board to a large oval, 14 x 20 inches. Place crust on cookie sheet.

Mix ham (or other meat), pate, parsley, shallots, cornichons, eggs (reserving ¼ cup for glazing top) and biscotte crumbs. Mix well and shape into loaf 5 x 9 inches. Place meat loaf in center of crust.

Brush edges with some of the reserved egg. Roll crust up and over the loaf and enclose it completely. Roll out remaining crust to ¼-inch thickness and into an oblong large enough to cover top of loaf. Brush loaf with egg. Use remaining pastry trimmings to make decorations. Place decorations on crust and brush with egg. Bake in a preheated 350-degree oven for 1 hour, or until richly browned. Serve with Mustard Sauce. Serves 6 to 8.

Mustard Sauce: Melt ¼ cup butter and stir in ¼ cup flour. Gradually stir in 2 cups milk. Cook over low heat, stirring constantly until sauce bubbles and thickens. Stir in ⅓ cup Dijon mustard, 1 teaspoon wine vinegar and salt and pepper to taste.

Sweetbreads Amandine

1½ lbs. sweetbreads
Water
2-3 T. lemon juice
1½ tsp. salt
¼ c. butter or margarine
¼ c. flour

1½ c. milk
⅔ c. cream
¼-½ tsp. white pepper
½ c. minced parsley
⅔ c. toasted slivered almonds
Toast triangles

Rinse sweetbreads in cold water; combine with water to cover, 1 tablespoon lemon juice and 1 teaspoon salt in large saucepan. Simmer 15 minutes; drain and plunge into cold water. Cut away any tough membrane or tubes, then cut sweetbreads into bite-size pieces. Melt butter in saucepan; add sweetbreads and brown lightly; remove from pan. Blend flour into remaining butter; stir in milk, cream, pepper and remaining lemon juice and salt. Stir over medium heat until mixture thickens and comes to a boil. Stir in sweetbreads, parsley and ½ cup almonds; heat through. Place in serving dish and sprinkle with remaining almonds. Serve at once on toast triangles. Serves 4 to 6.

Viaggio di Quatro Sapori

1½ lbs. Italian sausage,
   cut in 1-inch slices
2 large cans Italian
   artichoke hearts
1½ lbs. fresh mushrooms

3 cloves garlic, peeled
¼ c. fresh parsley, chopped
Olive oil
Salt, pepper

Preheat oven to 350 degrees. Blanch mushrooms for about a minute in rapidly boiling water, drain well.

Place garlic cloves in the bottom of a large, shallow baking dish. Line up sausage chunks in rows across center of dish. Arrange artichoke hearts (drained) on one side of the sausage; mushrooms, tops up, on the other. Remember to keep the sausage in the center. There should be a garlic clove under each section.

Sprinkle about 2 tablespoons olive oil over artichoke hearts and about 2 tablespoons over the mushrooms. Add salt and pepper to taste and then distribute fresh chopped parsley over all.

Cover the casserole and bake for a half hour. Remove foil and bake a half hour longer.

Rognons de Veau, Sauce Bearnaise

Sauce

1 T. chopped fresh tarragon	2 T. water
1 shallot, finely chopped	¼ lb. sweet butter, melted
2 T. white wine vinegar	Salt, pepper
2 egg yolks	2 T. chopped fresh parsley

Combine tarragon, shallot and vinegar in a small saucepan and cook (reduce) until liquid has evaporated. Set aside.

Beat egg yolks and water into reduced shallots and tarragon. Beat constantly over very, very low heat (you should be able to touch the bottom of the pan for 3 seconds without burning your hand). Continue stirring until eggs have thickened quite a bit (the mixture should be the consistency of homemade mayonnaise). Off the heat, add the melted butter by drops, stirring the while, until all butter is used.

Caution: The butter should never be any hotter than the egg mixture to which it is added.

When the Bearnaise is completed, add chopped parsley and salt and pepper to taste.

Kidneys: Remove casings and fat from 3 or 4 veal kidneys. Cut each into 4 "scallops," cutting on the diagonal. Grill or sauté them in butter about 3 minutes. (They cook very quickly, so take care not to let them get tough.)

Serve the kidneys with the Bearnaise sauce and thin French fried potatoes. Serves 4.

Contrary to common belief, Cocido, not Paella, is the national dish of Spain—we are told. It is a stew, made with chick peas and various kinds of available meats. Sometimes it yields rabbit, lamb, veal and garlic-flavored sausages all in one pot. This is but one version.

Cocido

½ c. Spanish olive oil
3 garlic cloves, minced
1 4-oz. jar pimientos, drained, diced
2 large onions, chopped
½ c. chopped parsley
½ lb. chorizo or other garlic-flavored sausage, sliced
1 c. diced cooked ham
1 lb. chicken parts

1 lb. stewing beef, cubed
3 sweet or white potatoes, peeled, quartered
2 carrots, cubed
1 1-lb. can tomatoes
2 1-lb. cans chick peas (garbanzos)
½ tsp. saffron
2 qts. boiling water
Salt to taste

Place ¼ cup olive oil in a large heavy pot or Dutch oven and add the garlic, chopped onion, parsley and pimiento. Simmer until vegetables are tender. Place remaining oil in a skillet and add beef, cut in 1-inch cubes, ham and sausage and cook until lightly browned on all sides. Spoon meat into onion mixture; add chicken, carrots, tomatoes, potatoes, water, saffron and 1 tablespoon salt. Cover, bring just to a boil, lower heat and simmer 1 to 1½ hours. Add canned chick peas and, if needed, additional salt. Cook ½ hour longer. Serves 8 to 10.

Coulibiac is a famous Russian dish that is often misspelled and misrepresented. Basically, it consists of a meat or fish filling baked in a casing of yeast-risen dough (not pastry). The filling may be ground meat or strips of filet—or it may be a salmon mixture or whole salmon. Both the dough and filling may be prepared days ahead, then combined for the final rising and baking.

Coulibiac

Brioche Dough

1½ c. corn oil margarine
4 c. flour
1 T. sugar
1 tsp. salt

6 eggs
2 pkgs. or cakes dry or compressed yeast
½ c. lukewarm water

Cream margarine in a mixer. Remove from bowl and, without washing bowl, put in 3 cups flour, the salt, sugar and eggs. Beat until well mixed. Dissolve yeast in lukewarm water. Add to remaining 1 cup flour and stir with a wooden spoon until well mixed. Turn out onto a lightly floured board and knead until a smooth surface forms on top. Cut a cross on top as for a hot cross bun and drop into a bowl of lukewarm water. Leave until it rises to the surface. Add creamed margarine and then the yeast mixture to egg mixture in bowl. Mix well and turn into a lightly floured bowl. Cover with plastic wrap and put in a warm place until doubled in bulk. Stir down to break the rise. Cover and place in the refrigerator overnight or for several days. To store longer, put in the freezer.

Meat Loaf

1 lb. ground beef	1 T. finely-chopped
½ lb. ground veal	parsley
¼ lb. ground pork	2 tsp. salt
1 small onion, finely chopped	1 tsp. freshly-ground
½ tsp. finely-chopped garlic	black pepper
2 T. finely-chopped celery	⅛ tsp. nutmeg
3 small eggs	½ lb. bacon

Put all ingredients except bacon in a bowl. Mix well. With wet hands, form into a 9-inch loaf. Punch a few holes in a double sheet of aluminum foil. Place meat loaf on top. Arrange bacon strips crosswise on loaf, covering it completely. Place on a roasting rack in a pan. Turn back foil so that meat loaf is uncovered during cooking. Bake in a preheated 375-degree oven 50 to 55 minutes without basting. Remove and chill.

Line a well-greased 9 x 5 x 4-inch bread pan with brioche dough rolled to ¼ inch thickness. Place meat loaf in the center. Cover with another layer of dough. Cover with a cloth. Allow to rise in a warm place about ¾ hour. Brush with beaten egg. Bake in a preheated 425-degree oven 35 to 40 minutes. Serve hot or cold.

Good soy sauce adds to ordinary home-cooked dishes quite as much as it does to traditional Oriental dishes, and it is especially popular for outdoor barbecue cookery.

Kikkoman Shish Delish

1 c. soy sauce	¼ c. salad oil
1 c. dry white wine	1 tsp. powdered ginger
1 c. chopped onion	1 clove garlic, chopped

Combine all ingredients; marinate meat or fowl in the mixture for an hour or so before skewering. Baste all contents of skewers with the marinade as you grill over hot coals.

Bacon, Mushrooms, Chicken Livers: Weave bacon between alternating mushrooms and livers. Grill slowly.

Green Pepper Strips: Weave with whole small white onions, bacon slices cut to small squares and round steak strips rolled loosely so meat cooks in center. Grill slowly.

Round Steak Strips: Cut meat fairly thin and weave around small green onion bulbs on skewers, working close to skewer points. Grill quickly.

Poultry

Chicken

Chicken is wonderful—there's almost no way it can't be prepared.

Pot Roasted Chicken

1 5- to 6-lb. roasting chicken	1 T. flour
2 tsp. salt	¼ tsp. marjoram
1 T. instant minced onion	¼ tsp. crushed rosemary
⅔ c. California white dinner wine	¼ tsp. white pepper
	¼ tsp. paprika
3 T. butter	2 T. cornstarch
	1 10½-oz. can chicken broth

Remove any pinfeathers from chicken. Rinse chicken in cold water, drain and pat dry. Rub body cavity with 1 teaspoon salt. Combine instant onion with 2 tablespoons wine and let stand until softened. Pour remaining wine into body cavity and skewer shut. Tie legs.

Cream butter with flour, herbs, pepper and paprika. Mix in the onions and wine. Spread over skin of chicken. Place on a large sheet of heavy-duty foil and fold over with a double fold to enclose chicken completely (*or* place chicken in Dutch oven with a tight cover, or in a clay baker). Bake in a preheated 400-degree oven for 1½ hours. Open foil and pour all liquid into saucepan. Blend cornstarch with 1 tablespoon cold water. Skim any excess fat from cooking liquid, then stir cornstarch mixture and chicken broth into pan contents, stirring and cooking until sauce boils and thickens. Makes about 2½ cups sauce. Chicken serves 6.

Sherried Mushroom Chicken

2 c. sliced fresh mushrooms	1 tsp. paprika
½ c. butter or margarine	½ tsp. crushed rosemary
8 large chicken breasts	1½ c. dry sherry
2 tsp. salt	½ c. water
¼ tsp. pepper	2 tsp. cornstarch
¼ tsp. garlic powder	½ c. sliced green onion

Lightly brown mushrooms in 4 tablespoons heated butter; remove from pan and set aside. Wipe chicken pieces dry; brown in remaining butter. Sprinkle with salt, pepper, garlic powder, paprika and rosemary. Add sherry; cover and simmer until tender, about 30 to 40 minutes. Blend water and cornstarch; stir into pan liquid. Cook, stirring until thickened. Add mushrooms and green onion. Heat a few minutes longer before serving. Serves 8.

California Chicken

1 c. dry white dinner wine	1 clove garlic, crushed
½ c. soy sauce	1 tsp. powdered ginger

Shake all ingredients together in a covered jar until blended. Pour over chicken halves or pieces; refrigerate several hours or overnight. Remove chicken from refrigerator about 1 hour before grilling.

When ready to cook, drain chicken, reserving marinade. Spread coals to distribute heat evenly. Rub grill with fat to keep chicken from sticking. Place chicken halves, bone side down, on grill (if using pieces, start legs and thighs 10 minutes before breasts). Have chicken 6 to 8 inches from coals. Turn often during cooking, basting frequently with reserved marinade. Grill 45 minutes to 1 hour, depending on size of chicken.

Note: For glazed chicken, add ½ cup honey to marinade after removing chicken.

This is a California version of the French classic, Coq au Vin.

Classic Chicken in Wine

1 5- or 6-lb. roasting chicken, cut in large pieces
Salt, pepper
¼ c. chicken fat
½ c. butter or margarine
⅓ c. California brandy
1 c. chicken broth
3 c. California dry white dinner wine
1 tsp. marjoram
12 small white onions
12 tiny new carrots
12 small new potatoes
Chopped parsley

Wipe chicken with a damp cloth; sprinkle with salt and pepper. Melt chicken fat and ¼ cup butter in a large heavy skillet or Dutch oven; brown chicken slowly on all sides. Pour brandy over it and ignite. When flames die down, add wine, broth and marjoram. Cover and place in a 250- to 300-degree oven for about 3 hours, or until chicken is nearly tender. (Add a little more wine during cooking, if necessary.) Meanwhile, brown onions, carrots and potatoes in remaining butter. Add to chicken; continue cooking about 30 minutes, or until vegetables are tender. Sprinkle with chopped parsley. Serves 6.

Chicken-Asparagus Yolanda

3 chicken breasts, boned, split
¼ c. flour
2 eggs, beaten
Salt, pepper
½ c. butter or margarine
1 3-oz. package cream cheese, diced
18 asparagus stalks, cooked
1 c. sour cream
⅓ c. grated Parmesan cheese

Have butcher bone chicken breasts. Pound them out flat. Dip each into flour and then into beaten egg. Season with salt and pepper. Fry in butter until golden and cooked through, about 20 minutes. Arrange in heatproof shallow dish. Cover with diced cream cheese. Place 3 asparagus spears on each. Top with sour cream and sprinkle with grated Parmesan cheese. Place under broiler about 4 or 5 inches from heat source and cook until cheese browns, about 3 to 5 minutes. Watch closely. Serves 6.

Cara Mia Chicken Cacciatore

1 jar marinated artichoke hearts	½ tsp. oregano
1 large frying chicken, cut up	½ tsp. basil
2 T. olive oil	½ tsp. pepper
1 No. 2 can tomatoes	½ lb. fresh mushrooms, sliced
2 cloves garlic, minced	½ c. dry sherry
1¼ tsp. salt	Chopped parsley
1 tsp. monosodium glutamate	Flour for dredging chicken

Drain marinade from artichoke hearts into large skillet and add olive oil. Dredge chicken in flour and brown in oil until golden. Transfer chicken pieces from skillet to large casserole. Combine tomatoes, artichoke hearts, garlic, mushrooms and seasonings in hot skillet and stir. When thoroughly mixed, pour over chicken. Cover and bake in a 350-degree oven for one hour, or until tender. During the last few minutes, add sherry. Serve garnished with chopped parsley. Serves 4 to 6.

Chicken and Mushrooms Oriental Style

1 c. Japanese forest mushrooms	2 T. oil
1 c. chicken broth	2 c. cooked chicken pieces
1 medium onion, quartered	1½ T. cornstarch
1 medium green pepper	2 T. soy sauce
2 c. diagonally-sliced celery	Hot cooked rice

Cover mushrooms with warm water and let stand 15 minutes. Drain and clip off stems. Quarter or slice large mushrooms. Add broth, cover and simmer 10 minutes.

Meanwhile, separate onion into flakes and core, seed and slice green pepper. Sauté onion, pepper and celery in oil about 5 minutes, stirring constantly. Add mushrooms with broth, and chicken, and cook 5 to 10 minutes longer, just until vegetables are crisp-tender. Stir cornstarch into soy sauce. Add to vegetable mixture and simmer 2 or 3 minutes, until clear and slightly thickened. Serve over rice. Serves 4.

Chicken, Mushrooms and Artichokes

6 medium artichokes	6 T. butter or margarine
Boiling salted water	½ lb. mushrooms, sliced
2 frying chickens,	2 T. flour
cut up	⅔ c. chicken stock or broth
½ tsp. paprika	⅔ c. dry sherry
¼ tsp. pepper	Salt

Remove 2 or 3 layers of outer artichoke leaves, cut off stems and trim off ⅔ from top of each. Cut in half; cook in 2 to 3 inches boiling salted water 15 to 20 minutes, until tender. Drain and remove chokes.

Sprinkle chicken with paprika and pepper. Brown in 4 table-spoons butter in large skillet. Arrange chicken and artichokes in large shallow roasting pan. Add remaining butter and mushrooms to skillet; sauté mushrooms until browned. Stir in flour; gradually add stock and wine. Bring to boil, stirring constantly. Add salt to taste. Pour over artichokes and chicken. Bake, covered, in a 375-degree oven for 1 hour, basting occasionally. Serves 6.

Coq au Vin

24 small onions	3 T. flour
½ lb. bacon or salt pork	Bouquet garni
¾ lb. fresh whole	3 cloves garlic,
small mushrooms	finely minced
Oil and butter	¾ bottle dry red wine
————	1 10½-oz. can beef bouillon
1 3-lb. chicken, cut up	2 T. tomato paste
2 medium onions, diced	Salt, pepper to taste
2 shallots, finely cut	

Peel and boil onions; set aside. Blanch bacon, which has been cut in ¼-inch dice; set aside. Sauté onions, bacon and mushrooms separately in half oil and half butter until golden; set aside.

Brown chicken in same pan, adding oil and butter as needed. Add diced onions and when brown, stir in flour. Add remaining ingredients, cover and simmer about 20 minutes. Remove chicken pieces to hot platter. Strain sauce and return to saute pan. Remove any grease from sauce. Add reserved onions, bacon and mushrooms and heat through. Spoon over chicken on platter. Sprinkle all with chopped fresh parsley. Serves 4.

Poulet Farci à l'Italienne

¼ lb. spaghetti
3 chicken livers
1 truffle

Salt, pepper
1 3- or 3½-lb. frying chicken
Sauce Mornay

Cook spaghetti as package directs. Rinse in cold water, drain and set aside. Chop chicken livers in small pieces and saute for a few seconds in a little butter in a small pan; add salt and pepper to taste; set aside. Chop the truffle into small dice and add to chicken livers.

Sauce Mornay

3 T. butter
3 T. flour
1½ c. milk

Salt, pepper
3 egg yolks
2-4 T. grated Parmesan cheese

Melt butter in a heavy-bottomed saucepan; add flour, stirring until mixture becomes white. Add milk, stirring constantly, until sauce thickens; continue cooking and stirring 2 minutes. Off heat, add salt and pepper to taste, egg yolks and Parmesan cheese, blending well. Place on heat and cook about ½ minute.

Assembly: Cut spaghetti into 1-inch pieces. Stir in the Sauce Mornay and the truffle-chicken liver mixture; stir to blend well. The mixture should be very loose. Taste and correct seasoning if necessary.

Stuff chicken with this mixture, being sure not to pack tightly. Sew up opening and truss bird. Spread with butter and sprinkle lightly with salt and pepper. Roast, first on one side, then on the other (never on back or breast), in a 375-degree oven for about 45 minutes to an hour, basting frequently. Serves 4.

Note: Never cook a chicken (or other poultry) on its bones.

Nautical Barbecued Chicken

2 small fryers, cut up
¾ c. soy sauce
½ c. olive oil
1 c. white wine
1 crushed clove garlic

½ c. chopped scallions
1 T. prepared mustard
¼ c. chili sauce
1 large lemon, grated,
   squeezed

Combine ingredients and pour over chicken; marinate over-night in a plastic container, turning several times. Drain. Grill until golden brown, basting with remainder of marinade. Serves 4 to 8.

Coq au Riesling

1 2½- to 3-lb. chicken
  Flour
  Butter
  Salt, pepper
1 small onion

1 c. white wine
2 shallots, finely chopped
½ c. thick cream
1 T. cognac
  Chopped parsley

Cut chicken in quarters (or in smaller pieces, if desired). Place on a plate and flour well on all sides. Heat butter in a large flat casserole. Add chicken and brown on both (or all) sides (cook bone side first). Salt and pepper to taste and add the uncut onion. Turn the heat low, cover and cook about 30 to 35 minutes, or until chick-en is just tender.

Remove chicken to a hot platter. Discard onion and most of the fat in the pan. Replace chicken, add wine and bring to a simmer. Turn chicken once or twice in wine and cook about 5 minutes. Remove chicken and keep warm in a low oven.

Now, over high heat, add chopped shallot and cook to reduce wine to about half. Correct seasoning. Add cream, boil for 10 sec-onds and then add about 1 tablespoon Cognac. Place chicken in a serving dish and spoon sauce over it. Garnish with a bit of chopped fresh parsley and serve immediately. Serves 4.

Poulet Sauté Marengo

1 3-lb. chicken, cut in
   8 pieces
Butter
1 onion, cut in chunks
3 T. flour
1½ c. bouillon
2 shallots, chopped
2-3 cloves garlic, chopped

¾ c. dry white wine
1 tsp. tomato paste
Bouquet garni
Salt, pepper
½ lb. mushrooms, quartered
2 tomatoes, peeled, seeded,
   quartered
Fresh chopped parsley

Melt butter and saute chicken pieces in it in a large shallow skillet. When well browned on all sides, add onion; mix well and cook until onion is lightly browned. Sprinkle on flour and stir to blend well. Add bouillon, shallots, garlic, wine, tomato paste, bouquet garni and salt and pepper to taste. Cover and simmer about 20 minutes, or until chicken is tender.

Saute mushrooms and prepare tomatoes. Add these to chicken about five minutes before cooking time is completed.

Remove chicken to a serving platter. Correct seasoning of sauce and distribute tomatoes and mushrooms over chicken. Spoon sauce over all and sprinkle generously with chopped parsley. Serves 4.

Lemon Grilled Chicken

¾ c. salad oil
½ c. fresh lemon juice
1 T. grated onion
½ tsp. salt
½ tsp. paprika

¼ tsp. pepper
Dash powdered thyme
Dash poultry seasoning
1 3-lb. frying chicken,
   quartered

Blend together the oil, lemon juice and seasonings. Pour over the chicken pieces in a shallow dish. Cover and marinate several hours or overnight, turning once. Remove chicken from marinade, reserving marinade.

Using highest position of grill rack, grill chicken until brown and tender, basting frequently with reserved marinade. Top each chicken quarter with a lemon slice during last few minutes of grilling. Serves 4.

Chicken Primavera

2 broiler-fryer chickens
(2 lbs. each), halved,
rib cages removed

½ tsp. salt

Stuffing

3 T. butter or margarine
3 T. chopped onion
1½ c. chopped fresh mushrooms
⅓ c. chopped green pepper
Chicken livers (from
chickens), chopped

½ c. uncooked rice
1 c. water
½ tsp. salt
⅛ tsp. pepper
2 T. chopped parsley
¾ tsp. dried leaf thyme

Either have your butcher remove rib bones from chickens or do it yourself as follows: Use a very sharp knife to cut meat away from bones, while gently pulling away the bones. The halves, with the breast bone remaining to give shape to each piece, are then stuffed and folded over to look like tiny whole chickens.

Sprinkle salt on inside of chicken halves; set aside.

Stuffing: Melt butter over low heat. Add onion, mushrooms, green pepper and livers and cook 10 minutes, stirring occasionally. Add remaining stuffing ingredients, mix well and bring to a boil. Turn heat as low as possible, cover tightly and steam 20 minutes. Turn off heat and let stand 20 minutes. Fluff mixture with a fork.

Place ½ cup stuffing on each chicken half. Fold the breast section over thigh section and hook wing over thigh. Place each folded chicken half on a 9 x 10-inch sheet of aluminum foil. Fold the foil up around the chicken about 2 inches all around. This keeps in the juices but leaves the top of the chicken exposed to brown. Place chickens in a shallow pan and bake in a preheated 375-degree oven for 50 to 60 minutes, until tender. Serves 4.

Chicken Maricado

6 whole chicken breasts
Salt and pepper
1 can cream of mushroom
soup
½ c. dry sherry
Juice 1 lemon

1 c. sour cream
2 ripe avocados, in
large chunks
1 clove garlic, mashed
¼ tsp. salt
⅛ tsp. pepper

Season chicken with salt and pepper. Place skin side down in baking dish. Bake 45 minutes at 350 degrees.

Meanwhile, combine remaining ingredients in blender and whir until smooth. Turn chicken, cover with sauce and continue baking 30 to 45 minutes. Serves 6.

Mediterranean Chicken

2 or 3 fresh nectarines
2 c. hot cooked rice
Butter
½ c. dark seedless raisins

¾ c. lemon juice
2 2½- to 3-lb. chickens
Salt, pepper
Parsley

Dice nectarines to get about 1½ cups, packed. Mix hot rice with ¼ cup butter and then add diced nectarines, the raisins and ¼ cup lemon juice. Stuff into chickens; skewer or sew up openings.

Sprinkle chickens with salt and pepper and place in large roasting pan. Pour remaining ½ cup lemon juice over. Add ¼ cup butter to bottom of pan. Roast in a preheated 375-degree oven 1 hour, or until tender, basting with pan liquids every 15 minutes. Serve with a garnish of parsley. Serves 8.

Chicken Florentine

1 2½- to 3-lb. broiler-fryer,
cut up
Salt, pepper
2 T. oil
1 15-oz. can tomato
herb sauce
½ c. dry red wine or water
1 c. uncooked rice
1½ c. boiling water

1 2¼-oz. can sliced ripe
olives, drained
2 10-oz. packages frozen
chopped spinach, thawed
1 c. ricotta or cottage cheese
1 egg
½ tsp. marjoram, crumbled
¼ tsp. nutmeg
¼ c. grated Parmesan cheese

Season chicken with salt and pepper; brown in skillet in oil. Combine tomato sauce and wine. Lightly oil a 3-quart baking dish, then combine 1 cup tomato sauce mixture with rice, olives, 1 teaspoon salt and boiling water in the dish; arrange chicken over all. Cover dish tightly and bake in a preheated 350-degree oven 45 minutes.

Meanwhile, press spinach very dry; combine with ricotta, egg, marjoram, nutmeg and ½ teaspoon salt. Uncover pan, spoon spinach mixture over center and pour over remaining herb tomato mixture. Sprinkle with Parmesan cheese. Continue baking, uncovered, another 10 to 15 minutes. Serves 6.

Suprêmes de Volaille à la Gasconne

3 large whole chicken breasts	Dash each, nutmeg,
1 c. dry white wine	cinnamon, cloves
½ c. Armagnac (or Cognac)	1 6- to 7-oz. can pâté
1 tsp. salt	de foie d'oie
¼ tsp. pepper	2 T. minced truffles

Skin and bone chicken breasts. Flatten breasts by pounding between two pieces of waxed paper. Place breasts in a shallow bowl and add wine, Armagnac, salt, pepper and spices. Cut pâté into six finger-length pieces and place them in the marinade—gently. Let stand at room temperature for an hour.

Drain chicken and pâté and reserve marinade. Roll pâté in truffles and place 1 piece on each chicken breast. Roll up, turning in ends, and fasten with string or toothpicks. Place rolls in heatproof boilable plastic bag. Pour in reserved marinade. Tie bag tightly and place in boiling water. Cook for 30 minutes, or until chicken is done. Remove chicken from marinade and serve on rice. If desired, marinade may be thickened with flour mixed with a little water, and then spooned over chicken. Serves 6.

Stuffed Chicken Breasts

4 large half breasts of chicken	2 T. flour
2 c. finely-chopped fresh mushrooms	2 T. chopped parsley
	4 thin slices boiled ham,
¼ c. finely-chopped onion	4 inches square
3 T. butter	1 egg
¼ c. white dinner wine	1 T. milk
½ tsp. salt	¾ c. soft bread crumbs
¼ tsp. sage	2 T. oil
⅛ tsp. pepper	Creamy Sauce

Remove bones and skin from chicken breasts. Pound out thin between two sheets of waxed paper.

Sauté mushrooms and onion in 1 tablespoon butter. Add wine, salt, sage, pepper and 1 teaspoon flour and cook until mixture is thickened. Remove from heat, stir in parsley and cool.

Place a rounded tablespoonful of the mushroom mixture on each slice of ham. Place on chicken and fold over to cover. Fasten with picks. Chill.

Shortly before serving, dust with remaining flour. Beat egg with milk, dip floured rolls in egg, then in crumbs. Heat remaining 2 tablespoons butter with oil and brown chicken rolls slowly on all sides, turning carefully with two spatulas.

Place in pan in preheated 350-degree oven and bake about 20 minutes, until cooked through. Remove picks and serve with Creamy Sauce. Serves 4.

Creamy Sauce: Melt 2 tablespoons butter and blend in 2 tablespoons flour. Add 1 cup half and half, 1 chicken bouillon cube, ¼ cup dry white dinner wine, ¼ teaspoon salt, ¼ teaspoon onion powder and a dash each, nutmeg and white pepper. Cook, stirring, until sauce boils and thickens. Stir in 1 tablespoon chopped parsley. Makes about 1 cup sauce.

Split Pea-Chicken Casserole

1 lb. green or yellow split peas	6-8 pieces broiler-fryer
5 c. water	chicken parts
1 large garlic clove crushed	½ tsp. crushed dried thyme
with 1½ tsp. salt	¼ tsp. crushed dried rosemary
¾ c. chopped onion	1 10½-oz. can condensed
2 T. butter	cream of mushroom soup
2 T. salad oil	⅔ c. milk

Bring water to boil and add split peas. Bring again to boil, boil 2 minutes and remove from heat. Stir in garlic, which has been crushed with salt. Cover and let stand ½ hour. This helps to keep the shape of the split peas and gives you a chance to prepare the rest of the ingredients.

Cook onion in butter over low heat until soft and clear. Lift from skillet and set aside. Add oil to pan and brown chicken carefully, turning with tongs or two wooden spoons. Turn split peas into a wide shallow casserole or baking dish (2-quart size) and spread onions over top. Half bury chicken pieces in split peas. Sprinkle mixed herbs over top. Mix the mushroom soup and the milk and stir into the chicken drippings (over low heat) until smooth. Pour over chicken. Cover loosely and bake in a preheated 350-degree oven 1 hour, removing cover last 10 minutes to brown a bit. Serves 6 to 8.

Mushroom-Chicken Liver Sauté

½ c. butter or margarine	¼ tsp. crushed basil
1 onion, minced	¼ c. sherry
1 garlic clove, minced	1 T. flour
1½ lbs. chicken livers	4 c. cooked rice
1 lb. mushrooms, sliced	Minced parsley
¼ tsp. Tabasco	

Melt butter in large skillet; sauté onion and garlic until onion is tender. Add chicken livers, mushrooms, Tabasco and basil. Sauté, stirring occasionally until livers are browned on each side. Pour in sherry. Move ingredients to one side of pan; stir flour into liquid until smooth. Bring just to the boil, stirring. Spoon mushrooms and chicken livers around rice mound on serving platter; pour sauce over meat mixture. Garnish with parsley. Serves 6.

Turkey

In most American homes, the turkey continues to be the choice for Thanksgiving dinner. Whether you've been cooking turkeys for years or this will be your first, we think you'll enjoy this method for making the bird buttery and brown and crisp and good. It is called butter roasting.

Butter Roasting

To prepare a turkey for butter roasting, first thaw (if purchased frozen), using the chart for Thawing Frozen Turkeys.

Meanwhile, prepare plain or flavored butter for basting, following instructions below. One-fourth cup is sufficient for a 12-pound turkey. When turkey is thawed, remove neck and giblets from neck and body cavities. Reserve turkey liver for use in dressing.

While turkey roasts, butter-brown the remaining giblets and neck in a saucepan; cover with water or chicken broth and simmer on top of the range. This produces a delicious liquid for the gravy, and the chopped cooked giblets are a good addition to it, too.

Rinse turkey with cool running water, inside and out. Pat dry with a clean towel or paper towels. Starting from the body cavity of the bird, use fingers to separate the skin from the flesh. Loosen it over the breast, down the sides and over the drumsticks. Then slip butter slices into all these areas. This allows the turkey to baste itself, saving you the trouble, all through the roasting period.

Now stuff the turkey. You may make the dressing ahead and refrigerate it, but whatever you do—*do not* stuff the bird until it is ready to go in the oven. Allow about ⅔ cup dressing per pound of turkey. Spoon the stuffing in lightly—do not pack. Use skewers and string to close the cavities and tie the legs and tail together with string.

Before placing it in the oven, rub the turkey all over with 2 to 3 tablespoons of butter. This helps to brown it and crisps the skin. Place it on a rack in an open pan and roast in a preheated 325-degree oven according to the Chart for Roasting Turkeys.

During roasting you may brush the turkey with pan drippings. However, if you've used the butter-under-the-skin treatment, this probably won't be necessary. If the bird seems to be getting too brown, put a loose tent of foil over it to prevent further browning.

When done, transfer the turkey to a platter and cover it lightly with foil to keep it warm and let the meat and juices settle while you make the gravy.

Pour drippings out of roasting pan and skim off fat. (Reserve fat for gravy.) Add warm water or giblet broth to roasting pan to loosen good brown bits; add this to the skimmed drippings.

Allow 1 to 2 tablespoons flour per cup of liquid for a thin to medium gravy. If you are using chopped giblets, remember they tend to thicken it.

Heat skimmed fat, 1 tablespoon for each tablespoon of flour to be used in gravy, in a saucepan. Add flour and cook until bubbly. Gradually add liquid, stirring with a wire whisk and cooking until thickened. Taste and correct seasoning and stir in giblets, if used, at the last.

Flavored Basting Butter

For a 12-pound turkey, soften ¼ cup butter and blend in ¼ teaspoon onion powder and ⅛ teaspoon sage or poultry seasoning. Or, blend in 1 teaspoon each, grated lemon rind and lemon juice; or 2 teaspoons sherry and a dash of nutmeg; or ⅛ teaspoon each, cumin and coriander and a dash of cayenne. Shape flavored butter into a roll, wrap in waxed paper and chill until firm. Slice thinly and follow instructions for inserting between skin and meat of turkey.

Thawing Frozen Turkeys

On Shelf in Refrigerator

4 to 12 lbs.	1 to 2 days
12 to 20 lbs.	2 to 3 days
20 to 24 lbs.	3 to 4 days

To speed thawing, remove giblets from body as soon as bird is pliable enough.

Roasting Turkeys in Foil

Ready-to-Cook Weight	Oven Temperature	Total Cooking Time
7 to 9 lbs.	450 deg.	2¼ to 2½ hrs.
10 to 13 lbs.	450 deg.	2¾ to 3 hrs.
14 to 17 lbs.	450 deg.	3 to 3¼ hrs.
18 to 21 lbs.	450 deg.	3¼ to 3½ hrs.
22 to 24 lbs.	450 deg.	3½ to 3¾ hrs.

Chart for Roasting Turkeys

Ready-to-Cook Weight	Oven Temperature	Approximate Cooking Time
6 to 8 lbs.	325 deg.	2 to 2½ hrs.
8 to 12 lbs.	325 deg.	2½ to 3 hrs.
12 to 16 lbs.	325 deg.	3 to 3¾ hrs.
16 to 20 lbs.	325 deg.	3¾ to 4½ hrs.
20 to 24 lbs.	325 deg.	4½ to 5½ hrs.
Over 24 lbs.	300 deg.	14 min. per lb.

Differences in the shape and tenderness of individual birds, as well as temperature when put in oven, may necessitate increasing or decreasing cooking time slightly. This chart is only a guide to total roasting time. For best results, use a roasting thermometer, which should read 185 deg. when bird is done.

Roasting Other Poultry

Oven temperature is 325 deg. for all the following:

CHICKEN

2 to 2¾ lbs.	66 to 63 min. per lb.
2¾ to 3½ lbs.	55 to 51 min. per lb.
3½ to 4½ lbs.	49 to 45 min. per lb.
4½ lbs.	43 min. per lb.

CAPON

6 to 7 lbs.	35 min. per lb.

DUCK

3 to 4¼ lbs.	45 min. per lb.
4¼ to 5 lbs.	40 min. per lb.

GOOSE

7 to 8 lbs.	30 min. per lb.
11 lbs.	25 min. per lb.

Rich Chestnut Stuffing

1½ lbs. chestnuts	1 lb. sausage meat
½ c. diced celery	4 c. dry bread crumbs
¼ c. diced onion	2 T. minced parsley
½ c. butter	Salt and pepper

Make crosscut in chestnuts and drop them into rapidly boiling water. Allow to simmer 15 minutes. Remove a few nuts at a time with a slotted spoon and, protecting your hands with kitchen gloves or paper toweling, slip off outer and inner skin (if inner skin doesn't come off easily, return to hot water for a few moments). Chop peeled chestnuts very coarsely.

Melt half the butter in a small skillet and saute the celery and onion in it for 5 minutes without browning.

Cook the sausage meat in a larger skillet until nicely browned, breaking it into small pieces with a wooden spoon. When sufficiently cooked, pour off all fat. Combine sausage meat and vegetables with the bread crumbs; add chopped chestnuts and parsley and moisten with the remaining butter, which has been melted. Add salt and pepper, if needed. Sufficient dressing for two 10-pound geese or a 12- to 15-pound turkey.

Baked Turkey Sandwiches

¼ c. butter or margarine	Salt and pepper
¼ c. flour	8 slices crisp toast,
1⅔ c. milk	crusts removed
⅓ c. sherry	4 servings sliced cooked turkey
1 4-oz. can mushroom stems	8 slices crisp cooked bacon
and pieces, drained	½ c. grated cheddar cheese
Dash mace	Paprika

Melt butter and stir in flour; add milk and cook, stirring constantly, until mixture boils and thickens. Add wine, mushrooms, mace, salt and pepper. Place 2 slices toast side by side in each of 4 shallow, oval, individual baking dishes. Spread toast with some of the mushroom sauce; top with sliced turkey, then with bacon strips. Pour remaining sauce over all; sprinkle with grated cheese and paprika. Bake in a preheated 450-degree oven 10 minutes, or until bubbly. Serve at once. Serves 4.

Turkey and Ham Pie

1 10-oz. package frozen	2 tsp. chicken stock
patty shells	base
½ c. coarsely-chopped onion	½ tsp. salt
¼ c. butter	¼ tsp. thyme
¼ c. flour	Pepper to taste
1 4-oz. can button mushrooms	1 tsp. Worcestershire
⅔ c. Chablis or other white	2 c. diced cooked turkey
dinner wine	1 c. diced cooked ham
1 c. milk	1 c. thawed frozen peas

Thaw patty shells, then stack together. Roll out on lightly floured board, turning over frequently, to a thin sheet to fit the top of a shallow 1½-quart baking dish. Trim edges neatly. Roll trimmings and cut strips to decorate top of pastry, if desired. Place on ungreased baking sheet and prick top. Place in a preheated 450-degree oven and bake 15 to 20 minutes, until golden brown.

Meanwhile, prepare filling. Sauté onion in butter until soft but not browned. Blend in flour. Drain mushrooms and add liquid from can, wine and milk to butter-flour mixture. Stir in chicken stock base, salt, thyme, pepper and Worcestershire sauce. Sauce may look slightly curdled as it heats, but will smooth out when it boils. Stir continuously. Add turkey, ham and peas and cook over very low heat about 5 minutes. Turn into heated baking dish and top with baked pastry top. Serve at once. Serves 6.

Other

Game hens, domestic ducklings and rabbits all are runners-up in the poultry popularity contest. (Rabbits end up in this category simply because they are sold by poulterers in this part of the country—most places they would be considered game, surely.

Sherried Game Hens with Grapes

2 T. butter
3 1½-lb. game hens
2 tsp. salt
½ tsp. freshly-ground
  black pepper
½ c. dry white table wine

½ c. chicken stock
¼ c. dry sherry
½ c. halved seedless
  white grapes (whole
  canned grapes, drained)

Melt butter in a large casserole. Rub hens with salt and pepper and place, breast down, in casserole. Bake, uncovered, in a preheated 450-degree oven for 10 minutes. Turn hens breast side up and continue roasting for 20 minutes more.

In the meantime, heat the white wine and chicken stock together. Reduce the oven temperature to 350 degrees and bake hens another 20 minutes, basting with stock and wine. Remove hens to a warm platter and split each lengthwise. Add sherry to casserole; place over direct high heat and cook, stirring, until liquid is reduced by half; correct seasoning with salt and pepper. Add grapes and heat through. Ladle grapes and sauce over hens. Serves 6.

Little Birds in Clay

4 20-oz. Cornish game hens	½ tsp. paprika
Salt	¼ tsp. white pepper
¼ c. Calif. dry sherry	¼ tsp. onion powder
Heavy duty foil	¼ tsp. finely-crumbled basil
⅓ c. very soft butter	or oregano
1 T. soy sauce	8 lbs. red or white ceramic clay

Thaw game hens, remove and save giblets for another use. Rinse in cold water, drain and pat dry. Sprinkle inside cavities with salt and tie legs together. Spoon 1 tablespoon sherry into each bird and place each on a large piece of foil. Combine butter with soy, paprika, pepper, onion powder and herbs. Brush generously over birds. Wrap tightly in foil. Shape clay into an oval large enough to enclose each bird and about ¼ inch thick. Wrap around foil covered birds so they are completely enclosed, each one separately. Cut slashes in top of clay. Place birds on shallow baking pan. Bake in a 475- to 500-degree oven 1¼ hours. Remove from oven, knock off clay and remove foil. Serves 4.

Variations

Prepare hens as above, wrapping in foil only. Bake in same oven 1 hour.

Prepare as above but do not wrap. Place in shallow pan and roast at 450 degrees 1 hour, basting with half sherry and half melted butter.

Italian-Style Stuffed Duckling

1 4½- to 5-lb. frozen duckling, defrosted	1 T. cooking oil
¾ tsp. salt	3 c. ½-inch bread cubes
1 clove garlic	½ c. sliced pitted ripe olives
½ lb. pork sausage meat	½ tsp. rosemary
1 c. diced celery	1 tsp. oregano
½ c. coarsely-chopped onion	2 T. sherry
	¼ c. shredded Parmesan cheese

Wash and drain duckling; dry skin gently with paper toweling. Rub body cavity with cut surface of garlic clove. Sprinkle body and neck cavities with salt, using ½ teaspoon. Cook sausage meat, celery and onion in oil until celery is tender but not brown, and meat is crumbly. Drain off excess fat. Add bread cubes, olives, remaining ¼ teaspoon salt, seasonings and sherry; toss gently.

Fill neck and body cavities loosely with stuffing. Skewer neck skin to back, cover opening of body cavity with aluminum foil and tie legs together loosely. Place on rack in shallow roasting pan. Bake in a preheated 325-degree oven until meat on drumsticks is tender, about 2½ hours. Sprinkle cheese over duck during last 15 minutes of roasting. Serves 4.

Lapin aux Pruneaux

1 rabbit	Bouquet garni
2 T. butter	1 tsp. tomato paste
2 med. onions, chopped	2 c. beef bouillon
2 T. flour	¾ c. dry white wine
3 shallots, finely chopped	Salt, pepper
3 cloves garlic, finely chopped	¾ lb. pitted prunes, plumped

Cut rabbit back into 2-inch pieces, then cut up legs. Brown in butter in a wide, flat saute pan. When brown, add onions and brown slightly. Add about 2 tablespoons flour; mix well to coat meat and onion. Add shallots, garlic, bouquet garni, tomato paste, bouillon and wine; season to taste with salt and pepper. Cover and cook gently for 30 minutes; add the prunes and cook another 30 minutes, or until rabbit is quite tender.

Serve the rabbit and prunes in their sauce accompanied by a rice pilaf that has a good dash of nutmeg added to it. Serves 4.

Seafood

In fish cookery, sauce often makes the dish. Filets of Sole Joinville are an excellent example of the fact, and though complicated to prepare, will prove well worth the effort you must expend on them.

Filets of Sole Joinville

8 filets of gray sole

Grease a 9-inch savarin (ring) mold with corn oil margarine. Cut sole filets in half lengthwise. Line mold with filets, arranging them lengthwise across it so that the narrow ends of the filets extend over the inside edge of the mold and the wide ends extend over the outside edge. Place the side from which the skin was removed against the mold and overlap each one a little over the one previously placed in. Fill the center with Salmon Mousse.

Salmon Mousse

1 lb. fresh or frozen salmon	1½ tsp. salt
2 egg whites	⅛ tsp. cayenne pepper
1 c. light cream	

Skin and bone the salmon. (Reserve skin and bones for making sauce.) Run salmon through food chopper into a mixer bowl. Add egg whites and beat well. Slowly add light cream, salt and cayenne and continue beating well. Fill center of filet-lined mold, then fold ends of filets over top of mousse. Cover with a piece of greased waxed paper and tie in place. Set in a shallow pan of hot water and place in a preheated 350-degree oven. Cook 25 to 30 minutes, or until just firm to the touch. Remove from oven, lift pan out of hot water and let stand 5 minutes. Turn out onto a hot, flat serving dish and pour over it the following Joinville Sauce, which is a combination of White Wine and Hollandaise sauces.

White Wine Sauce

¼ c. mixed sliced onion, carrot and celery	2 c. water
1 sprig dill	3 T. corn oil margarine
Few peppercorns	3 T. flour
½ c. dry white wine	Salt and pepper
	½ c. heavy cream

Put reserved skin and bones of salmon into a pan with sliced vegetables, dill, peppercorns and a little salt. Add wine and water, bring to a boil and simmer gently ½ to ¾ hour. Strain. Melt margarine in a small pan, remove from heat and stir in flour. Season with salt and pepper. Stir in 1 cup of the strained fish stock, return to heat and stir until it comes to a boil. Add heavy cream.

Hollandaise Sauce

2 egg yolks	Salt and cayenne pepper
1 tsp. tarragon vinegar	¾ c. corn oil margarine
2 T. heavy cream	2 drops lemon juice

Put egg yolks, vinegar, 2 tablespoons heavy cream, salt and cayenne in a small bowl. Mix well, set in pan of hot water and place over low heat. Beat with a whisk until it thickens, then add, bit by bit, letting each bit melt and combine before adding the next, the margarine. Add lemon juice.

Combine White Wine and Hollandaise sauces to make Joinville Sauce and coat fish mold with it. Put remainder in sauce boat.

Garnishing

½ lb. medium mushrooms	Salt and pepper
2 T. corn oil margarine	1 c. cooked shrimp, peeled, deveined
2 drops lemon juice	

Wash mushrooms in water containing a little lemon juice and drain well. Sauté briskly in margarine, adding lemon juice and a little salt and pepper. Sauté only 2 minutes, then add shrimp and heat all together for a minute, shaking the pan to combine them. Fill center of mold. Decorate top edge of mold with thin slices of truffle. Serves 8 to 10.

Poached Trout, Sauce Genevoise

4 fresh trout, 6 oz. each	4 nice slices truffle
1 T. chopped shallots	1 tsp. beurre manie (flour
½ c. butter	mixed with softened butter)
1 c. whipping cream	4 mushroom caps
1 c. dry white wine	Salt and pepper

Place trout in a well-buttered baking dish. Season with salt and freshly-ground pepper. Moisten with wine. Add mushroom caps. Cover with aluminum foil. Bring to a boil and let simmer gently for 10 minutes. Remove trout. Take skin off both sides. Pass the stock through a fine sieve. Add cream and let boil down gently for 5 minutes. Thicken with beurre manie, stirring constantly with a soft wire whip.

Take sauce off heat. Add remaining butter, piece by piece and very gently. Season to taste. Place fish on a warm platter and top with mushroom caps. Cover with sauce and decorate with truffles. Serve hot but not boiling. (Sauce has a tendency to separate—take care.) Serves 4.

Salmon Poached in Wine

⅓ c. California burgundy	⅛ tsp. celery seed
¾ c. water	1 lb. salmon filets or steaks
½ bay leaf	1 T. butter or margarine
1 sliced green onion	2 tsp. cornstarch
¼ tsp. peppercorns	1 T. chopped parsley
½ tsp. salt	½ c. cooking liquid from salmon

Combine wine, water, bay leaf, onion, peppercorns, salt and celery seed and heat to simmering. Add salmon, cover and cook over very low heat for 10 minutes, or until salmon flakes easily with a fork. (If pieces are thick, turn once as fish cooks.) Remove salmon to heated serving plate. Melt butter and blend in cornstarch and parsley. Stir in ½ cup liquid in which fish was poached and cook, stirring, until mixture boils and is clear and thickened. Pour sauce over salmon and serve at once. Serves 3 or 4.

Saumon Froid Curnonsky

1 whole 6-lb. salmon	¼ tsp. white pepper
½ lb. mushrooms,	3 T. brandy
thinly sliced	1 4/5-qt. bottle
1 T. chopped shallots	Pinot Chardonnay
6 T. soft butter	1 4/5-qt. bottle
1 T. lemon juice	brut champagne
14 oz. filet of sole	1 egg white
1 c. heavy cream	1 T. unflavored gelatin
3 eggs	Thin slices lemon
1½ T. salt	and cucumber

Remove head and fins from salmon. With sharp knife, remove bones, starting along sides of body cavity, then removing back bone and bones above it, being careful not to break skin of back. (Or, have butcher do this for you.) Combine the head and bones with water to cover and simmer to make fish stock while preparing stuffing.

Sauté mushrooms and shallots in 2 tablespoons butter with lemon juice until soft but not brown. Cool. Chop sole coarsely. Combine about ¼ of the sole at a time in blender jar with a scant ¼ cup of the cream and blend until well mixed and smooth. Turn out, and repeat until all of fish is blended.

Turn mushrooms into blender with remaining cream and blend until very finely chopped. Combine with fish. Beat in unbeaten eggs, one at a time, then 1½ teaspoons salt, pepper, brandy and remaining 4 tablespoons butter.

Lay salmon out on a large piece of cheesecloth and spread the sole mixture on bottom half of fish, then fold the other side over the forcemeat. Fold the cheesecloth around fish snugly and set on a trivet. Strain the fish stock into a fish poacher, or large baking pan. Add wine and champagne and remaining tablespoon salt and heat to boiling. Place fish on trivet in liquid. Cover closely. Poach on top of range or in a 350-degree oven for about 1 hour, or until cooked through. Cool slightly, then carefully remove cheesecloth. Chill salmon.

Meanwhile, strain about 3 cups of poaching liquid into a saucepan and heat to simmering. Beat egg white to a fine foam. Stir into simmering broth and cook about 5 minutes, stirring frequently. Moisten a square of muslin and place in a wire strainer. Add fish stock and allow the clear liquid to drip through. When fish is thoroughly chilled, carefully remove skin. Soften gelatin in ¼ cup of the strained fish stock. Heat 1¼ cups stock to boiling and dissolve gelatin in it. Cool until gelatin begins to thicken and jell. Spoon a little of the gelatin at a time over chilled fish. Refrigerate until set.

Warm remaining gelatin slightly, then cool and add another layer to fish. Repeat until fish is nicely glazed. Place overlapping slices of lemon and cucumber along side of fish before adding last layer of gelatin.

Mexican Cilantro Snapper

2 lbs. filets red snapper (or other rockfish)
⅔ c. salad oil
1 T. crumbled dried cilantro
¾ tsp. salt
¼ tsp. crushed dried hot red peppers, about
¼ tsp. crumbled dried oregano
¼ tsp. freshly-ground black pepper, about
2 T. fresh lemon juice
1½ tsp. white wine vinegar
3 T. minced green onion, white only
2 T. finely-chopped fresh parsley
1 large avocado

Wipe fish dry with a damp cloth. Arrange in a single layer in an oiled shallow baking dish. Stir remaining ingredients (except avocado) together with a fork to mix well. Pour ¾ of mixture evenly over fish. Bake in a preheated 350-degree oven just until thickest part of fish flakes when tested with a fork, about 20 minutes. Lift fish onto a warm serving platter; spoon baking juices over it. Peel and slice the avocado lengthwise, thickly, and arrange beside fish filets; spoon reserved quarter of marinade over it. Serves 4.

Squid is one of the finer and more delicate creatures from the sea that an awful lot of people shy away from because they don't know how to treat them. Buy a pound and see what a delight they are.

Okay. Now you've got a pound of squid. Terrific. What do you do with them?

First, you clean them. It's cinchy.

Step one: Off with their heads. Hold the body in one hand and pull the head end. That comes off easily enough, and with it some of the insides, which are discarded.

Next you remove the "shell" or quill, sometimes called the pen (instead of having external armor, like other mollusks, squid have this wrong-side-out arrangement), which is inside. Grasp it firmly, holding the body with the other hand, and pull it out—it's clear and quite pretty—and discard it.

Now squeeze the body, pressing toward the open end to get out any innards remaining. After that, remove the skin (you can rub it off, but it peels off beautifully), revealing the delicate, pearly flesh (fins stay on and skin comes off them, too). Wash thoroughly under cold running water.

Some people discard the whole head, but if you are going to stuff them you'll want to keep the arms to chop for the stuffing. To save them, cut them off behind the head, discard any little hard core in the center and set aside until all are prepared (they look like tiny starfish, sort of, when spread out).

Now, then, squid—stuffed and baked.

Stuffed Squid

1 lb. tiny squid (about 15)

Stuffing

Squid arms	2 T. chopped fresh parsley
4 large mushrooms	4 T. fine dry bread crumbs
1 T. pesto	Salt and pepper to taste
1 T. olive oil	Red wine to moisten

Sauce:

1 T. olive oil	¼ c. dry red wine
1 8-oz. can tomato sauce	Salt and pepper
1 T. pesto	to taste

Clean squid, saving arms. Dry squid and set aside on waxed paper.

Stuffing: Chop arms fine, then add mushrooms and chop. Combine all ingredients and mix well. Use mixture to stuff squid (a salt spoon or baby spoon is the ideal tool); fasten opening with a toothpick and place in an oiled baking dish large enough to hold them in one layer.

Sauce: Combine all ingredients in small saucepan and bring slowly to a boil. Pour over squid and place in a preheated 400-degree oven and bake for 30 minutes. Serve immediately. Serves 3.

Note: They are delicate and may split when cooked. Don't worry about it—just be careful taking them out of the baking dish.

Tuna Puffs

¼ c. butter or margarine	2 tsp. lemon juice
⅓ c. sifted all-purpose flour	2½ c. rich milk
	¼ c. dry sherry
¾ tsp. salt	2 c. cooked peas
⅛ tsp. paprika	1 6½- or 7-oz. can tuna
1 T. finely-chopped onion	Celery Seed Puffs

Measure butter, flour, salt, paprika, onion and lemon juice into top of double boiler. Cook over direct heat until butter is melted and mixture smooth, stirring constantly. Slowly stir in milk. Place over boiling water and continue cooking until mixture is smooth and thickened, about 10 minutes. Add sherry, peas and coarsely-flaked tuna. Heat about 5 minutes longer. Fill baked Celery Seed Puffs with creamed tuna and serve at once.

Celery Seed Puffs: Bring ½ cup water and ¼ cup butter to a boil in a heavy saucepan. Add, all at once, ½ cup sifted all-purpose flour. Stir constantly until mixture clears pan and forms a ball. Remove from heat and cool. Add 2 whole eggs, one at a time, and beat to a smooth paste after each addition. Add 1 teaspoon celery seed and beat until mixture is smooth and velvety. Drop batter by large tablespoonfuls, 2 to 3 inches apart, onto lightly greased and floured baking sheet. Bake in a preheated 425-degree oven for 15 minutes. Reduce temperature to 400 degrees and continue baking 20 minutes longer, or until puffs are dry and golden brown. Slit each puff with a sharp knife and fill with tuna mixture.

Spaghetti with White Clam Sauce

4 dozen cherrystone clams, scrubbed	Salt
¼ c. butter	Freshly-ground pepper
¼ c. olive oil	2 T. salt
⅓ c. chopped parsley	4-6 qts. boiling water
4 cloves garlic, minced	1 lb. spaghetti

Steam clams, one layer at a time, in a covered pot with just a little water. Steam them just until they open, no longer. Force them open the rest of the way with a sharp knife and scrape out meat into a sieve or fine colander placed over a bowl. Strain all juice in shells and pan. Pick over clams to remove any bits of shell. Allow to drain in colander or sieve over juice, then chop coarsely and set aside.

Pour clam juice (there should be 3½ to 4 cups) into heavy saucepan and simmer until reduced to 1½ cups.

In large saucepan over medium heat, cook butter, oil, parsley and garlic 2 minutes, stirring occasionally. Add reduced clam broth and chopped clams; simmer, uncovered, about 3 minutes. Taste and add salt and pepper as needed.

Meanwhile, add 2 tablespoons salt to rapidly boiling water. Gradually add spaghetti so water continues to boil. Cook uncovered, stirring occasionally, until tender. Drain in a colander. Serve in shallow bowls topped with the claim sauce. Serves 4.

Crab Tarts

2 T. butter
2 tsp. minced shallots
   (or green onions)
1 7½-oz. can king crab
1 T. lemon juice
¼ c. minced celery
¼ tsp. Worcestershire

¼ c. finely-diced
   whole scallions
½ c. grated sharp
   cheddar cheese
3 drops Tabasco
¼ tsp. seasoned salt
Miniature Pastry Shells

Cook 2 teaspoons shallots in butter in medium skillet for a minute or two. Add drained crab and lemon juice, celery and scallions. Sauté, stirring for a few minutes, breaking up any large pieces of crab. Remove from heat and stir in grated cheese, Worcestershire and Tabasco sauces and seasoned salt. Spoon into unbaked shells. Bake in a preheated 350-degree oven until pastry is barely browned, about 30 minutes. Cool for a few moments and lift from muffin cups with a small knife tip. Serve at once. Makes 24 tiny tarts.

Miniature Pastry Shells

1 3-oz. package cream cheese
½ c. butter

1 c. flour, unsifted

Blend softened cheese and butter in a bowl with a wooden spoon. Gradually work in flour. Press dough flat in bowl and refrigerate about 30 minutes. With a knife or spatula, mark dough off into 24 equal portions. Roll each portion in a ball, then press over the bottom and up sides of small muffin cups, each about 1¾ inches in diameter. Cover tightly with plastic wrap and refrigerate until ready to use.

Crab Quiche Tarts

1 7½-oz. can Alaska
   king crab
Butter Pastry
3 T. chopped green onion
1 T. chopped parsley
½ c. grated Swiss cheese

2 T. grated Parmesan cheese
2 eggs
1 c. milk
½ tsp. salt
Dash pepper
¼ tsp. fine herbs

Drain and slice crab, reserving 4 leg pieces for garnish. Line 4 5-inch flan pans with pastry. Prick bottoms and sides with fork. Bake at 400 degrees for 10 minutes.

Divide crab, onion, parsley and cheeses evenly among tarts. Beat eggs; add milk and seasonings. Pour over base filling. Garnish with reserved crab and bake at 350 degrees 30 to 40 minutes, or until custard is set. Serves 4.

Butter Pastry

1½ c. flour
½ tsp. salt

½ c. butter
3-4 T. ice water

Mix flour and salt; cut in butter until mixture resembles cornmeal. Add just enough cold water to hold dough together. Shape into a ball. Wrap in waxed paper and refrigerate 1 hour.

Gala Crab Casserole

1 6-oz. package seasoned long
   grain and wild rice mix
⅓ c. chopped green pepper
2 T. sliced green onions
2 T. butter
1 10-oz. can cream of
   shrimp soup

¼ lb. mushrooms, sliced
1 12-oz. package frozen Snow
   crab, partially thawed
1 c. shredded sharp
   cheddar cheese
1 T. chopped pimiento

Cook rice according to package directions. Meanwhile, cook green pepper and onions in butter in a saucepan until almost tender. Stir in mushrooms, cover and cook 3 to 5 minutes. Add soup (undiluted), undrained crab and ½ cup cheese. Heat together until bubbly, stirring occasionally.

Arrange hot cooked rice in a ring around the outer edge of a 2-quart buttered casserole; top with remaining cheese. Pour crab mixture in center; sprinkle pimiento over top. Bake in a preheated 400-degree oven 10 to 15 minutes, until cheese is melted and crab mixture bubbles. Garnish with chopped parsley, if desired. Serves 6.

Emerald Sea Sauce

3 T. soft butter
3 T. flour
2 T. finely-chopped parsley
2 tsp. finely-chopped fresh
   basil *or* ½ teaspoon
   crumbled dried basil
¼ c. finely-chopped onion

1 7½-oz. can chopped
   sea clams
½ c. finely-chopped celery
2 c. sour half and half
¾ tsp. salt
⅛ tsp. white pepper

Cream butter and flour together. Stir in parsley and basil; set aside. Drain liquid from clams into quart saucepan. Add onion and celery; cover and simmer until vegetables are tender-crisp, about 5 minutes. Add drained clams, sour half and half, salt and pepper; heat to simmering. Drop in butter-flour-herb mixture and stir briskly with a wire whip. Cook and stir until sauce thickens. Spoon onto hot cooked linguini or other pasta. Makes about 2½ cups sauce or enough to serve 4 to 6.

Alaskan Crab Bake

1 8-oz. package wide or
   lasagne noodles
2 6-oz. packages frozen Alaska
   king crab, thawed, drained
2 8-oz. cans tomato sauce
   with mushrooms
1 T. chopped parsley

¼ c. chopped green onion
½ tsp. seasoned salt
8 oz. Mozzarella cheese,
   sliced
2 c. Ricotta or cottage cheese
¼ c. grated Parmesan or
   Romano cheese

Cook noodles according to package directions; drain and reserve.

Meanwhile, check crab carefully for any bits of shell, then combine in large skillet with tomato sauce, parsley, onions and seasoned salt; simmer 10 minutes. Spread half the noodles in a 2½-quart shallow baking dish, cover with half the sauce, then with half the Mozzarella slices. Repeat layers in order, using remaining noodles, sauce and Mozzarella. Spread with Ricotta and sprinkle with Parmesan. Bake in a preheated 375-degree oven for 25 to 30 minutes. Let stand about 10 minutes, then cut into portions. Serves 6 to 8.

Crab Puff

1 7½-oz. can Alaska king crab	1½ c. milk
¾ c. grated medium cheddar cheese	1 tsp. Worcestershire
	½ tsp. salt
1 T. lemon juice	⅛ tsp. pepper
6 slices bread	¼ tsp. onion salt
3 eggs	1 T. chopped parsley

Drain and slice canned crab. Combine with cheese and lemon juice. Spread over bread slices. Stack two slices of bread in buttered individual casseroles. Or, place in one large baking dish. Beat eggs. Combine with remaining ingredients. Pour over sandwiches and let stand at least 20 minutes. Bake individual casseroles at 350 degrees for 45 minutes, or until golden and puffy. Large casserole will take about an hour. Serve immediately. Makes 3 sandwiches.

Note: Sandwiches may be covered and refrigerated for several hours or overnight, then baked just before serving.

Sautéed Crab Legs in Butter

Butter	1 large clove garlic, optional
¼ c. chopped parsley	48 crab legs, cooked
¼ c. chopped green onion	¼ c. California sherry
¼ c. chopped mushrooms	Salt and pepper

Melt enough butter to cover bottom of skillet. Sauté parsley, onion, mushrooms and garlic for two minutes. Remove garlic. Add crab legs and sauté for 5 to 6 minutes. Add sherry and cook for one more minute. Season to taste with salt and pepper. Serve immediately. Serves 4.

Superb Baked Crab

3 T. butter or margarine
¼ c. sifted all-purpose flour
1 tsp. seasoned salt
1 c. milk
1½ tsp. instant minced
   onion *or* 2 T. finely-
   chopped raw onion
2 egg yolks

⅓ c. California white
   dinner wine
1 T. fresh lemon juice
1 T. chopped parsley
1 2-oz. can sliced
   mushrooms, drained
¼ c. grated Parmesan cheese
1 lb. cooked crab meat

Melt butter and blend in flour, salt and milk. Add onion and cook and stir until mixture boils and thickens. Stir in wine. Beat egg yolks slightly and stir a spoonful of sauce into them. Combine with remaining sauce and cook over very low heat, stirring constantly, for about 5 minutes longer. Do not allow to boil. Blend in lemon juice, parsley, mushrooms and half the cheese. Add crab meat and mix lightly. Spoon into baking shells or shallow baking dishes, and sprinkle with remaining cheese. Broil about 4 inches from heat until lightly browned on top. Serve at once. Serves 4 to 6 (about 3½ cups creamed crab).

Gouda Crab Meat

1 Gouda cheese, cut in half
2 T. butter or margarine
1 T. grated onion
¼ c. diced green pepper
¼ c. flour
¾ tsp. salt
½ tsp. paprika
¼ tsp. sugar

½ tsp. dry mustard
1 No. 2 can tomatoes
1 7½-oz. can crab meat,
   flaked
¼ c. light cream
1 tsp. lemon juice
   Hot cooked and buttered
   parsley rice

Shred half of Gouda and cut remaining half into wedges. Melt butter, add onion and green pepper and cook slowly about 5 minutes, stirring frequently. Add flour, salt, paprika, sugar and mustard; stir until blended. Add tomatoes; cook, stirring constantly, until thickened. Stir in crab meat, cream, lemon juice and shredded Gouda cheese just before serving and heat thoroughly. Serve in warmer garnished with Gouda wedges. Serve over hot buttered parsley rice.

Crab Legs Sautéed with Snow Peas

(Lon Dow Chow Hai Keem)

1 lb. cooked crab legs and claws	½ tsp. sugar
½ c. dry onions, sliced	¼ tsp. monosodium glutamate
½ c. sliced celery	1 tsp. soy sauce
½ lb. snow peas	½ c. chicken stock
2 T. vegetable oil	1 T. cornstarch
¼ tsp. salt	1 T. water

Crack shells on crab and remove meat carefully without breaking it up. Put the oil in a preheated wok or skillet. Bring to the sizzling point and add the sliced onion, celery and snow peas. Then add salt, sugar, monosodium glutamate and soy sauce. Toss and turn rapidly at high heat for 5 minutes. Add the shelled crab legs and claws and the chicken stock. Cover and cook at medium high heat for 5 minutes. Uncover. Make a paste of the cornstarch and water and add to mixture gradually. Toss and mix until thickened. Serve immediately with steamed or fried rice. Serves 3 or 4.

Grilled Crab Sandwiches

1 lb. crab meat, fresh or frozen, or 3 6½-oz. cans	¼ c. mayonnaise
½ c. shredded cheddar cheese	1 T. lemon juice
	Few drops Tabasco
½ c. chopped black olives	12 slices sandwich bread
⅓ c. chopped parsley	½ c. butter or margarine, melted

Thaw frozen crab; drain. Remove any remaining shell or cartilage. Combine all ingredients except bread and butter. Spread 6 slices bread with crab mixture. Cover with remaining bread. Brush outsides of sandwiches with butter. Place them in a single layer in a hot 12-inch frying pan. Fry at moderate heat for 2 or 3 minutes, or until brown. Turn carefully. Fry 2 to 3 minutes longer, or until nicely browned on both sides. Serves 6.

Crayfish in Court Bouillon

1 gallon water
1 heaping T. whole peppercorns
1 heaping T. whole allspice
6 bay leaves
2 T. whole cloves

1-1½ bottles dry white wine
Handful coarse salt
1 oz. Worcestershire
2 whole onions
4 cloves garlic
Handful chili tepines
48 crayfish

Combine all ingredients but crayfish in large kettle and bring to a boil. When boiling, drop in clean, live crayfish and let solution come back to the boil. Then cook fairly gently for 8 to 10 minutes, until crayfish turn a bright red. Let cool in liquid or remove and chill. Serve as a first course with a little lemon mayonnaise. Serves 6.

Lobster Tails Harlequin

6 frozen rock lobster tails
¼ c. butter or margarine
¼ c. chopped green pepper
¼ c. flour
1 tsp. salt
¼ tsp. pepper
¼ tsp. nutmeg
1¾ c. vegetable broth or water

½ c. heavy cream
½ c. milk
¼ c. sherry
1 3-oz. can ripe olives, pitted, sliced
4 c. hot cooked rice
3 T. butter or margarine
2 T. grated Parmesan cheese

Cook rock lobster tails in boiling salted water until tender. With kitchen scissors, cut around thin transparent undershell. Remove the meat and dice or flake it. Save the cleaned shells. Melt the ¼ cup of butter in a skillet or chafing dish. Add green pepper and cook until tender. Stir in flour, salt, pepper and nutmeg; stir to blend. Gradually stir in broth, then milk and cream and continue to cook over low heat, stirring constantly, until smooth and thickened. Add sherry, olives and lobster meat. Stir to blend. Keep warm over very low heat.

Toss rice with 3 tablespoons butter; pile into cleaned lobster shells (fan out ends of tails for pretty appearance). Top rice with Parmesan cheese. Keep warm in a 250-degree oven until serving time; then, if desired, run under broiler long enough to toast cheese a bit. Serve chafing dish of lobster sauce surrounded by rice in shells. Serves 6.

There are as many versions of the oyster loaf as there are stories about its origin. Here's an excellent one of the former.

Wonderful Oyster Loaf

1 loaf unsliced egg bread	3 8½-oz. cans large whole oysters
¼ lb. butter	½ c. finely-chopped parsley
1 clove garlic, chopped	1 3⅞-oz. can pitted large ripe olives
1 c. flour	3-4 whole dill pickles, sliced lengthwise
¼ tsp. pepper	
¼ tsp. cayenne	

Cut top off bread (about 1 inch deep), lengthwise. Scoop rectangle out of center of bread leaving about an inch on all sides. Save scooped out bread and cut in cubes. Butter inside the edges of loaf and put under broiler until slightly brown.

Sauté garlic in remaining butter. Add bread cubes and cook until golden brown. Remove cubes and set aside; discard garlic. Dip oysters in flour mixed with pepper and cayenne and sauté in butter until nicely browned all over. Fill cavity of loaf with oysters and scatter pickle strips, olives and parsley over oysters. Place top of bread over all, wrap in foil and place in a warm oven for a few minutes.

To serve, cut into slices about an inch thick (makes 8) and accompany with a tossed salad made with the toasted bread cubes and French dressing.

Individual oyster loaves make nice late-night party fare. Either bake or order individual loaves of bread, or use regular bread cut into thick slices; hollow them out to hold oysters and olives, then serve very hot, topped with tartar sauce.

Ripe Olive Oyster Loaves

Ripe Olive Tartar Sauce
4 individual loaves of bread
4 T. butter or margarine,
   melted
20 medium oysters

½ c. flour
2 eggs, beaten
¾ c. corn flake crumbs
16 pitted ripe olives,
   drained

Make up tartar sauce. Slice tops from bread loaves and hollow out insides, leaving a wall slightly less than ½ inch thick. Preheat oven to 350 degrees. Brush insides of loaves and cut surfaces of bread tops with butter. Place on baking sheet and put in oven to toast for about 10 minutes. Pour oil about ½ inch deep in skillet and heat to 375 degrees. Drain oysters well. Roll in flour then dip in egg and coat with crumbs. Fry oysters until golden, turning and cooking about 3 minutes on each side. Drain well. Put olives in the oil and cook a minute, just to heat through. Spread each hot toasted loaf with a tablespoon of tartar sauce and fill with oysters and olives. Top with toasted bread "tops." Serve with additional tartar sauce. Serves 4.

Note: Small loaves of bread are available on special order on some days from many bakeries. *Or*, individual croustades made from unsliced sandwich loaf may be substituted:

Cut the slices about 2½ inches thick. Crusts may be trimmed if desired, but need not be removed. Cut a slice from top, as with individual loaves, and hollow out about 2½-inch section, as above.

Ripe Olive Tartar Sauce

½ c. canned pitted
   ripe olives
¼ c. chopped green pepper
2 T. finely-chopped onion
2 T. chopped capers

2 T. chopped parsley
1 T. tarragon vinegar
1 tsp. prepared mustard
   Dash Tabasco
1 c. mayonnaise

Drain and chop olives; mix with green pepper, onion, capers and parsley. Add vinegar, mustard and Tabasco sauce to mayonnaise and mix well. Stir in olive mixture. Makes about 1¾ cups sauce.

Barbecued Oysters

24 medium oysters in their shells	3 T. finely-chopped fresh dill, parsley or chervil
1 c. butter, melted	Freshly-ground black pepper to taste
2 T. fresh lemon juice	
2 tsp. Worcestershire, optional	2 tsp. horseradish, optional

Combine butter, lemon juice, herbs, pepper and Worcestershire sauce. Keep warm.

Scrub oysters with a brush, removing loose sand and kelp. Place on grill over hot coals for 4 to 5 minutes, or until shells open. (The oysters steam in their own juice.) Remove from grill and carefully detach flat or top portion of the shell. Serve in shell, passing herb butter. Serves 4 to 6.

Oyster Corn Scallop

1½ c. fine cracker crumbs	1 T. finely-chopped green pepper
3 T. butter or margarine, melted	½ pint fresh oysters, coarsely chopped
1 17-oz. can golden cream-style corn	1 2½-oz. jar sliced mushrooms, drained
2 T. finely-chopped onion	

Preheat oven to 350 degrees. Toss cracker crumbs with butter; set aside. Combine corn, onion and pepper. Spread ½ cup crumbs over bottom of greased 10 x 6-inch baking dish. Spoon half corn mixture over crumbs; top with half of oysters and half of mushrooms. Repeat, ending with crackers. Bake at 350 degrees for 30 to 35 minutes. Serves 4.

Note: An 8-ounce can of oysters, drained, may be substituted for fresh oysters.

Coquilles St. Jacques à la Parisienne

8 scallops	Salt
2 shallots, chopped	Pepper
¾ c. white wine	Butter
2 branches parsley	Juice ½ lemon
½ lb. mushrooms	Sauce Velouté

Place scallops in flat, shallow saucepan. Sprinkle with shallots and pour wine over all; put parsley in pan, cover and poach very gently about 10 minutes. Remove from heat and cool. When cool, slice in thirds, crosswise. Set aside.

Wash mushrooms and place in small saucepan. Add cold water to come about ⅓ up around them. Add about 1 tablespoon butter and the lemon juice and salt and white pepper to taste. Bring to boil and boil 2 minutes *only*. Remove from heat and let cool in liquid. When cool, slice and place in mixing bowl. Reserve mushroom liquid and reduce to about half.

Sauce Velouté

2 T. butter	Salt
2 T. flour	Pepper
⅔ c. milk	2 egg yolks
⅓ c. mushroom liquid	2 T. grated Swiss cheese

Melt butter in small saucepan. When hot and bubbly, add flour, stirring until well blended. Add milk and mushroom liquid and cook, stirring constantly, until thick and smooth, about 2 minutes. Off heat, add egg yolks and cheese, stirring to mix well; place back on heat and cook about ½ minute. Add salt and pepper to taste. Sauce should be of medium thickness—if too thick, add a bit more milk.

Assembly

4 scallop shells
4 T. grated Swiss cheese

Mix about half the sauce with the mushrooms, mixing thoroughly and well. Place a good spoonful of this mixture in each scallop shell. Place slices of scallop on top, dividing among shells. Spoon remaining sauce over each, heating it a bit if it has thickened. Sprinkle with cheese. Bake in a 400-degree oven until hot and bubbly. Serves 4.

Note: May be prepared ahead, covered, refrigerated and then baked just before serving.

Skewered Scallops

6 T. mayonnaise
2 T. horseradish
½ tsp. dry mustard
1 lb. fresh or
    frozen scallops
4 T. prepared mustard

4 T. heavy cream
Fine dry bread crumbs
Cherry tomatoes
Green pepper squares
Salt, pepper and paprika
Salad oil

Prepare sauce by combining mayonnaise, horseradish and dry mustard; refrigerate. If fresh scallops are used, wash in cold water and cut, if necessary, into ¾-inch pieces. Combine mustard and heavy cream. Dip scallops in mixture, then in bread crumbs, coating completely. Alternate scallops, tomatoes and green peppers on skewers. Sprinkle with salt, pepper and paprika. Brush scallops and vegetables with salad oil. Broil over medium coals for 10 to 15 minutes, or until scallops are medium brown. Serve with cold sauce. Serves 3 or 4.

Tempura is one of those dishes that uses any number of meats and vegetables. For instance, the dish can consist of butterflied shrimp, scallops, eggplant and zucchini, but then you can add snow peas, sweet potatoes, stringbeans and/or carrots, pieces of chicken.

Tempura Miyako

Raw shrimp or prawns, shelled,
    butterflied, deveined, tails on
Raw scallops, cut in half if large
Fish filets, cut in 1½-inch pieces
Green peppers,
    cut in 1½-inch pieces

Sweet potatoes or carrots, peeled,
    sliced diagonally ¼ inch thick
Eggplant or zucchini, unpeeled,
    sliced ¼ inch thick
Green beans or asparagus tips,
    cut in bite-size pieces

Drain seafoods and vegetables thoroughly on paper towels; arrange on large platter. Pour vegetable oil for frying at least 2 inches deep in electric frying pan, wok or deep, wide frying pan. Heat to 375 degrees.

To fry shrimp: Hold one at a time by the tail and dip into batter. Drain off excess batter slightly and slide shrimp gently into hot oil. Repeat with 3 or 4 more shrimp; fry about 1 minute, turn over and fry a minute longer, or until lightly golden brown.

Dip and fry other ingredients in the same manner. Drain all on paper towels or a wire rack over a pan. Skim off pieces of cooked batter from oil with wire strainer as you go.

Tempura Batter

1 large egg	2 c. sifted cake flour
1¼ c. ice water	

Beat egg thoroughly with wire whisk or hand rotary beater (not electric). Blend in water. Sprinkle all of flour evenly over liquid. Using same beater, stir in flour quickly until all is moistened and large lumps disappear. Batter should be lumpy. Do not stir batter after it is mixed.

Tempura Dipping Sauce

1 c. water	¼ c. mirin
½ c. soy sauce	1 bag dashi-no-moto

Measure water, soy sauce and mirin into saucepan. Add dashi-no-moto. Bring sauce to boil, reduce heat and simmer 1 to 2 minutes. To serve, remove dashi-no-moto and pour sauce into small individual bowls. Serve with tempura.

Mirin is sweet sake—sherry wine may be substituted but it should be sweet.

Dashi is the basic Japanese soup and cooking stock. Dashi-no-moto, roughly translated, means ingredients for the preparation of dashi. They are packaged in ¾-ounce bags similar to tea bags.

Shrimp Iberia

3 T. butter	¼ tsp. salt
1 minced clove garlic	3 T. lime juice
¼ tsp. Tabasco	2 lbs. cooked, shelled shrimp
1½ c. chili sauce	1 c. heavy cream

Melt butter in chafing dish. Add garlic and cook about 5 minutes. Add Tabasco, chili sauce, salt and lime juice; stir in shrimp. Cook, stirring occasionally, until heated through. Gradually stir in heavy cream and heat to serving temperature. Serve over hot cooked rice. Serves 4 to 6.

Note: The original recipe called for ¾ teaspoon Tabasco—experiment and use it to suit your own taste.

Chinese Cilantro Prawns

1½ lbs. large raw prawns	2 T. finely-chopped
6 T. salad oil	fresh parsley
3 T. dry sherry	¼ tsp. freshly-ground
1 large clove garlic,	black pepper, about
minced or mashed	⅛ tsp. crushed dried
1 T. crumbled dried cilantro	red peppers
¾ tsp. salt, about	Hot steamed rice

Shell and devein prawns, leaving tail shells on. Mix remaining ingredients (except rice) in a bowl, add prawns and marinate at room temperature for one hour; turn occasionally. Arrange prawns, with their marinade, in a single layer in a shallow broiling pan. Broil about 6 inches from heat source just until prawns turn pink and lose their translucence, about 4 minutes on each side. Serve on rice. Stir juices to blend and spoon over prawns. Serves 4.

Prawns à la Szechwan

½ lb. raw prawns	2 T. vegetable oil
½ tsp. minced garlic	2 T. sherry
½ tsp. grated ginger root	4 T. catsup
3 whole scallions, sliced thin	Pinch sugar
1 tsp. dried red chili peppers,	1 tsp. cornstarch mixed
chopped *very* fine	with 2 T. water

Heat oil until quite hot in a wok, skillet or chafing dish. Sauté prawns, garlic, ginger, scallions and chili peppers. Cook for a few minutes, then add sherry, catsup and sugar. Add cornstarch mixture and continue to cook, stirring constantly, until prawns are done and sauce is thickened and clear. A few drops of sesame oil may be added.

Deviled Shellfish

¼ c. finely-chopped green pepper
¼ c. finely-chopped onion
1 c. finely-chopped celery
1 tsp. Worcestershire
½ tsp. salt
1 c. mayonnaise

1 c. fresh shrimp *or*
1 7-oz. can shrimp, drained
1 c. fresh crab *or*
1 7-oz. can crab, flaked
2 c. herb-seasoned stuffing, crushed

Stir all ingredients together until blended. Spoon into a 1-quart shallow casserole or 8 ovenproof shells. Bake at 350 degrees for 30 minutes, or until browned. Serves 6 to 8.

Vol-au-Vent is one very large patty shell, really, and it's light and delicate and beautifully flaky because it's made from puff paste.

If you don't want to make your own pastry, use the frozen patty shells. For best results with these, thaw them in the refrigerator overnight. They will then be firm and cold to the touch but pliable.

It is important to note these special instructions:

Stack the patty shells for rolling out; don't place them side by side and never roll them into a ball. Press together with the heel of your hand to flatten slightly before rolling. Edges should be kept aligned to maintain equal distribution of the shortening in the layered dough. Roll the dough out to a uniform thickness, turning it over occasionally to facilitate spreading. Always roll the dough slightly larger than the shape desired. Then trim with a sharp knife. This ensures straight edges and even rising.

Before trimming, turn the dough over one more time, letting it "collect itself" so it won't shrink after cutting. This is especially important if one piece is to be fitted on top of another, as in Vol-au-Vent.

Let the shaped dough rest in the refrigerator before baking. The resting will reduce or eliminate shrinkage, while the chilling will encourage high puffing during baking.

For easier handling, bake the lid of the Vol-au-Vent separately from the shell. Simple decorations will make it look like a crown.

Vol-au-Vent

1½ 10-oz. packages frozen patty
    shells, thawed in refrigerator

1 egg, lightly beaten
1 tsp. cold water

Stack 3 patty shells on a well-floured board or pastry cloth and press them together. Roll into a circle. Place on an ungreased baking sheet and trim to 8 inches in diameter. Moisten edges with water.

Stack the remaining 6 shells and press together with the heel of your hand, taking care to keep edges aligned. Roll into a circle. Turn dough over and trim to 8 inches. Cut a 6-inch circle from the center, using a pot lid as a guide. Fold the outside rim in half and place on top of moistened circle on baking sheet, taking care not to stretch dough. Match edges evenly. Press lightly to seal and moisten rim.

Roll out circle remaining on board (trimmed out dough), turn over and cut as before to form a second rim. Place on top of first, matching edges, and press to seal. With the back edge of a table knife held vertically, make indentations into outside edge of dough every ⅛ inch to create a scalloped effect. Prick bottom with a meat fork. Chill 30 minutes.

Roll out remaining circle, place on baking sheet and trim to 8 inches. This will form the top of the case. Chill. Before baking, brush top of case with a mixture of the egg and water for a shiny glaze. Bake in a 400-degree oven for 25 to 30 minutes; remove top after first 20 minutes, or when well browned. Case may be baked ahead and reheated before filling and serving.

Note: For a decorative effect, stack trimmings, press together and chill. Then roll out to less than ⅛ inch thickness and cut into narrow strips, circles or stars. After brushing top of case with egg glaze, stick on pastry trims, then brush again.

Seafood Newburg

5 T. butter or margarine
1 tsp. paprika
1 lb. peeled cooked shrimp
    (or ½ lb. shrimp, ½ lb. crab)
1 14-oz. can lobster,
    drained (reserve juice)

¼ c. dry sherry
¼ c. flour
Juice from lobster
    plus milk to make 1 c.
1 tsp. salt
Dash pepper

Melt 2 tablespoons butter in medium saucepan, remove from heat and stir in paprika (this amount of paprika gives the dish a nice rosy glow and good flavor—if you're using hot Hungarian paprika, reduce the amount by half). Add shrimp (and crab, if used), lobster and sherry and bring to a boil; cover and simmer one minute.

Melt remaining butter in a small saucepan. Stir in flour and cook together a few minutes. Remove from heat; slowly blend in milk and lobster liquid, stirring. Bring to a boil over low heat, stirring constantly, and simmer one minute. Mixture will be thick. Stir in salt and pepper.

Just before serving, pour hot sauce over hot seafood mixture and stir until blended. Taste for seasonings. Pour into Vol-au-Vent and top with lid. Cut in wedges to serve. Serves 8.

Note: This Newburg is fairly thick, and that's deliberate because it is served in wedges and you don't want it to run all over the plates.

Also, you may substitute 2 pounds of chicken for the seafood if desired.

Scampi

1½ lbs. large raw shrimp	½ tsp. salt
2 T. instant minced garlic	2 tsp. lemon peel
½ lb. butter or margarine	3 T. lemon juice
3 T. parsley flakes	Lemon wedges for garnish

Remove shells from shrimp, leaving on tails; devein and rinse. Mix minced garlic and 2 tablespoons water; let stand 3 to 5 minutes. Melt butter in a 13 x 9 x 2-inch baking pan in oven. Add garlic, parsley and salt; mix well. Arrange shrimp in a single layer in baking pan. Bake in a preheated 400-degree oven 5 minutes. Turn shrimp; sprinkle with lemon peel and juice. Bake 8 to 10 minutes longer. Serve on heated platter; pour garlic butter from baking pan over shrimp. Garnish with lemon wedges. Serves 4 to 6.

Shrimp Creole

⅓ c. shortening
¼ c. flour
½ c. chopped onion plus
2 chopped green onions
½ c. diced green pepper
½ c. sliced celery
¼ c. minced fresh parsley
4 garlic cloves,
chopped

1 c. water
1 8-oz. can tomato sauce
1½ tsp. salt
2 bay leaves
½ tsp. crushed thyme
⅛ tsp. cayenne pepper
1 lemon slice
2 4½-oz. cans shrimp
4 c. cooked rice

Heat shortening in a heavy pan and blend in the flour. Cook over medium-high heat until flour is golden brown, stirring constantly. Add vegetables and cook and stir 2 minutes. Add water, tomato sauce, dry seasonings and lemon. Turn heat low, cover pan closely and simmer 20 minutes, stirring occasionally. Add shrimp and heat. Serve over fluffy rice. Serves 4.

Baked Stuffed Shrimp

1 lb. fresh or frozen shrimp
1 lb. crab meat
2 slices fresh bread, cubed,
crusts removed
2 T. mayonnaise
1 tsp. Worcestershire
1 tsp. prepared mustard

½ tsp. salt
1 small onion, minced
½ green pepper,
finely chopped
½ c. melted butter
or margarine
Few drops Tabasco

Shell uncooked shrimp, leaving tail shells on. Split shrimp down the back and spread apart, butterfly fashion. Combine crab meat, bread cubes, mayonnaise, Tabasco and Worcestershire sauces, mustard and salt. Saute onion and green pepper in 2 tablespoons of the butter until soft; add to crab mixture. Firmly stuff shrimp with mixture. Place shrimp, tail sides up, on a greased shallow baking dish; brush with remaining butter. Bake in a preheated 400-degree oven about 15 to 20 minutes, or until browned.

Vegetables

More and more, it seems, seasonal vegetables are becoming available out of season. This, undoubtedly, is because we are shipping fresh produce from different growing areas all over the continent.

At any rate, there's nothing better than good fresh vegetables, simply cooked, as little as possible, and served nearly plain. When you tire of them that way, you'll want to find ways to vary them.

Artichoke Frito Misto

8 small artichokes, prepared*	8 tomato wedges, floured
3 eggs	8 cauliflower buds, cooked
1½ tsp. garlic salt	crisp-tender, drained
1 tsp. monosodium glutamate	½ lb. whole green beans,
¼ tsp. Tabasco	cooked crisp-tender, drained
3 T. salad oil	1 lb. chicken livers,
1 c. milk	floured
1½ c. flour	Salad oil for frying

Combine and beat eggs, seasonings and oil; add milk. Mix in flour. Remove outer leaves and chokes from artichokes. Dip vegetables and livers in batter. Deep fry in heated oil at 360 degrees for 3 to 8 minutes, turning to brown all sides. Drain on paper towels. Serves 4 to 6.

* To prepare artichokes: Wash each and cut in half. Remove chokes. Place halves in an inch of boiling water and add 2 teaspoons salt. Cover and boil gently for 20 to 40 minutes, or until stems may be pierced easily with a fork. Drain.

Artichokes with Potatoes and Sour Cream

2 6-oz. jars marinated artichoke hearts	2 T. chives (fresh, frozen or freeze-dried)
1 pt. sour cream	6 baking potatoes
2 T. chopped parsley	Salt and pepper

Drain artichoke hearts, reserving marinade for future use as a base for salad dressing. Cut or chop the hearts into small pieces, reserving 6 nice pieces for garnish. Combine artichoke pieces with sour cream, chives and parsley and allow to stand in refrigerator while potatoes are baking. Open baked potatoes, season lightly with salt and pepper and fill with the chilled artichoke mixture. Garnish with reserved bits. Serves 6.

Note: For added skin texture and flavor, sprinkle scrubbed potatoes lightly with salt before baking.

Fonds d'Artichauts
– Pommes de Terre Duchesse

12 artichoke bottoms	Salt and pepper
3 medium potatoes	1 egg yolk
Butter	Cream

Use either canned or frozen artichoke bottoms. If frozen, simmer in boiling salted water about 10 minutes to thaw and cook partially. If canned, rinse and drain.

Place on buttered baking sheet or in a shallow baking dish.

Peel and quarter potatoes. Place in a pan with cold water to cover; salt slightly. Boil until tender. Drain, mash and season with butter, salt and pepper to taste. Add the egg yolk and mix well. If they seem a little stiff, stir in a few drops of cream.

Place mixture in a pastry bag fitted with a "zig-zag" tip. Pipe into artichokes. Bake in a preheated 350-degree oven about 15 minutes, or until heated and slightly browned on top. Serves 6.

Asparagus Omelet

1 15-oz. can white asparagus, drained and chopped	4 eggs, beaten
2 T. chopped onion	¼ tsp. salt
2-3 T. olive oil	1 T. water
	Freshly-ground black pepper

Place olive oil in a 7- or 8-inch skillet or omelet pan, add asparagus and onion and cook over moderate heat until onion is soft. Combine beaten eggs, salt, water and pepper; add, half at a time, to the pan, lifting up with spatula as egg firms. When nearly solid throughout and lightly browned, lift and fold over and slide out onto heated plates. Serves 2 to 4.

Danish Green Beans with Cheese

Select beans that are clean, firm and tender and fairly uniform in size and length. Wash them well in cold water and drain. Rarely do we find green beans today that need "stringing" so don't worry about that.

Cut off only the tip ends of the beans with a sharp knife, using a cutting board. This way you avoid waste.

To cook, use a flat-bottom saucepan with a tight-fitting lid. Don't crowd the beans, but lay them end to end in the pan so they'll be easier to lift out. Use a small amount of salt and only a small amount of water—usually ½ to 1 cup, depending on amount of beans being cooked. Count on two pounds of green beans making six good servings when cooked.

Start beans cooking on high heat and when water is boiling rapidly (don't mistake the steam that rises first as boiling), turn to low heat. Start timing the cooking and allow 18 to 20 minutes to do whole beans crispy tender. Do not lift cover while cooking—get in the habit of timing.

Using a wide spatula or slotted utensil, lift the beans to a warm serving platter. Dribble ¼ cup melted butter over beans and sprinkle with a bit of paprika.

In the meantime, grate 4 ounces of Danish Danbo (or Samsoe or Tybo) cheese. Place in a small pan, which is placed in hot water, and melt just in time to dress the hot green beans. Pour the melted cheese over the beans in a ribbon. Serve immediately.

Swiss Green Beans

½ c. corn flake crumbs
2 T. butter or margarine,
  melted
2 T. flour
1 tsp. salt
¼ tsp. white pepper

¼ tsp. instant minced onion
1 tsp. sugar
1 c. dairy sour cream
4 c. French-cut green beans,
  cooked, drained
2 c. grated Swiss cheese

Mix corn flake crumbs with melted butter. Set aside for topping.

Melt the 2 tablespoons butter in a large saucepan over low heat; stir in flour, salt, pepper, onion and sugar. Add sour cream; stir until smooth. Increase heat to medium and cook until sauce is bubbly and thickened, stirring constantly. Remove from heat. Fold green beans into sour cream sauce; spread in greased 10 x 6½ x 2-inch baking dish. Sprinkle cheese evenly over green bean mixture. Sprinkle crumb topping evenly over cheese. Bake in a preheated 400-degree oven about 20 minutes, or until thoroughly heated. Serves 6.

Italian Snap Beans

1 lb. fresh snap beans
¼ c. olive or salad oil
½ c. diced green pepper
1 tsp. salt
¼ tsp. instant minced garlic

1 T. onion flakes
⅛ tsp. pepper
1 tsp. basil leaves
2 T. water
¼ c. grated Parmesan cheese

Wash beans, drain, cut off tips and cut into 1-inch pieces. Heat oil, add beans, green peppers, salt, garlic and onion. Cover and cook 5 minutes over low heat. Add pepper, basil and hot water. Cook, covered, 20 to 30 minutes, or until beans are tender, watching carefully to prevent burning. Serve hot with Parmesan cheese sprinkled over the top. Serves 4 or 5.

Broccoli, Roman Style

2 lbs. fresh broccoli
1½ c. boiling chicken broth
2 T. olive oil
1 small clove garlic,
  finely minced
½ tsp. salt
  Pinch pepper
1 tomato, diced
2 T. water

1 T. finely-diced
  fresh onion
1 tsp. sugar
¼ tsp. Italian seasoning
¼ tsp. salt
  Pinch pepper
1 tsp. flour
2 T. cold water
¼ c. sliced stuffed olives

Wash and trim broccoli; place in medium-sized saucepan with chicken broth and cook, uncovered, 5 minutes. Add olive oil, garlic, salt and pepper. Cover and cook 10 to 15 minutes longer, or until crisp and tender.

Meanwhile, in a small saucepan, cook tomato, onion, water, sugar, Italian seasoning, salt and pepper over medium heat for 5 minutes. Mix flour with cold water. Stir into tomato sauce. Cook about 2 minutes longer, or until sauce thickens. Add sliced olives and cook only until hot. Arrange broccoli on serving platter. Pour sauce over stems. Serves 6.

French Sprouts and Chestnuts

3 10-oz. packages frozen
  Brussels sprouts
¼ c. butter
¼ c. flour
1 c. chicken broth
1 c. light cream

4 oz. grated Bonbel cheese
1 11-oz. can whole chestnuts,
  drained
  Salt and pepper
4 strips bacon, cubed,
  fried crisp

Cook sprouts in salted boiling water until tender. Drain. Melt butter and stir in flour. Gradually add chicken broth and cream and cook over low heat, stirring constantly, until mixture bubbles and thickens. Add cheese and continue cooking until cheese is melted, then fold in cooked sprouts and chestnuts. Add salt and pepper to taste and serve, topped with the crumbled bacon. Serves 6 to 8.

Cabbage Curry

1 medium head (2 lbs.)
cabbage, shredded
1 T. butter
¼ tsp. ground cumin
1 tsp. salt

½ c. milk
⅛ tsp. cayenne
6 mint leaves (optional)
¼ tsp. (4 or 5) crumbled
saffron stamens

Cover cabbage with salted cold water and let stand 30 minutes. Drain in colander. Melt butter in large saucepan; add drained cabbage, cumin and salt. Cover and cook 10 minutes, stirring often. Add milk, cayenne and mint. Cook uncovered until liquid is almost absorbed, about 5 minutes. Mix in saffron and serve hot. Serves 6.

Red Cabbage and Apples

1 medium head red cabbage,
coarsely shredded
½ c. apple cider vinegar
1 medium onion, sliced
2 tart apples,
peeled and sliced
2 T. butter or margarine

½ tsp. salt
¼ tsp. pepper
1 bay leaf
2 beef bouillon cubes
2 c. boiling water
2 T. currant jelly
1 medium potato, finely grated

Toss cabbage with vinegar. Saute onion and apple in butter in a deep skillet or Dutch oven until golden. Add cabbage, salt, pepper, bay leaf and water in which bouillon cubes have been dissolved. Cover and simmer 30 minutes, or until cabbage is tender. Stir in jelly and potato. Cook, covered, about 5 minutes, or until potato is tender. Serves 8.

Fresh 18-Carrot Dish

18 small fresh carrots
½ tsp. salt
¼ c. butter or margarine

1 lb. fresh mushrooms,
sliced or coarsely chopped
¼ c. chopped fresh parsley

Scrape carrots, wash and cut off ends. Cut each carrot in half lengthwise and cut each length in half crosswise. If pieces are thick, cut again, lengthwise. Add carrots to an inch of boiling water to which the ½ teaspoon salt has been added. Simmer until crisp-tender, about 10 minutes. Drain and keep hot. While carrots are cooking, melt butter in a skillet. Add sliced or chopped mushrooms and cook over low heat, stirring frequently, until tender. Add chopped parsley; toss gently. Arrange carrots on serving dish. Top with mushroom-parsley mixture. Serves 6.

Carrot Soufflé

6 T. butter or margarine	1 T. flour
7 T. flour	1 c. grated raw carrot
1½ c. milk	4 egg yolks
¾ c. egg whites	1 T. finely-minced onion
1½ tsp. salt	¼ tsp. black pepper

Preheat oven to 325 degrees. Set 5-cup casserole in shallow baking pan. Set in oven. Pour boiling water around casserole to a depth of at least 1 inch.

Melt butter, add flour and blend well; cook over low heat until bubbly. Add milk all at once and cook, stirring constantly, until uniformly thickened and smooth. Add salt to egg whites and beat until stiff and glossy but not dry.

Blend the 1 tablespoon flour into carrots and add to beaten egg yolks, onion and pepper, then blend that mixture into hot white sauce. Fold into beaten whites, pouring about ¼ of the mixture in at a time. Pour into hot casserole and bake in preheated oven until fluffy, delicately browned and a knife blade inserted halfway between center and outside edge comes out clean, 60 to 70 minutes. Serves 4.

Baked Fresh Corn Casserole

2 c. fresh corn, cut off cobs	3 eggs, beaten
1 T. flour	1½ tsp. salt
1 T. sugar	⅛ tsp. pepper
1 T. butter	1 c. milk
	½ c. heavy cream

Combine all ingredients. Turn into a buttered 1½-quart casserole. Place in a pan of hot water and bake in a preheated 325-degree oven 1½ hours, or until knife inserted in center comes out clean. Serves 6.

Eggplant Espagnole

1 small eggplant, diced	3 garlic cloves, crushed
⅓ c. olive oil	2 medium tomatoes, diced
1 medium onion, minced	¾ tsp. salt

Be sure to leave the skin on the eggplant, and no soaking is necessary. Combine ingredients, place in center of large sheet of heavy duty foil and fold together with a double fold, crimping edges. Place in coals or on grid of barbecue grill. Cook for at least 1 hour, preferably 2. Serves 4.

Eggplant Palermo

2 large firm eggplants	½ c. butter
Boiling salted water	½ tsp. garlic powder
2 small green peppers	1½ tsp. oregano
2 small fresh tomatoes	1 tsp. sweet basil
2 4½-oz. cans artichoke hearts	2 T. instant minced onion
3 c. thickly-sliced	1 tsp. salt
fresh mushrooms	1 c. Parmesan cheese

Cut eggplant in halves lengthwise; cut ½ inch from edges all around halves. Scoop out centers to form shells. Dice center portion of eggplant and reserve. Parboil shells in boiling salted water until just tender, but shape is retained. Drain and place in baking dish, cut-side up. Cut peppers and tomatoes in chunks. Drain artichoke hearts; cut into halves. Sauté mushrooms in butter with garlic powder. Add diced eggplant and sauté until golden. Stir in oregano, basil, onions and salt, along with peppers, tomatoes and artichokes. Simmer 3 to 4 minutes, until heated through. Stir in ¾ cup Parmesan cheese. Spoon into eggplant shells, mounding filling up quite high. Top with remaining cheese. Bake in a preheated 350-degree oven 20 minutes, until cheese is browned. Serves 8.

Eggplant Parmesan

1 med. eggplant (about 1 lb.)	1 15-oz. can tomato sauce
Flour	½ c. grated Parmesan cheese
2 eggs, slightly beaten	8 oz. Mozzarella cheese,
3-4 T. olive oil	cut in 12 slices

Wash and dry eggplant; do not peel. Cut crosswise about ¼ inch thick, 12 pieces. Sprinkle with salt and place eggplant in a colander. Put a plate on top to weight down. Allow to drain one hour; dry with paper toweling.

Dip eggplant in flour, then in eggs. Fry in olive oil in a large skillet until browned and tender.

Spread a little of the sauce in the bottom of an oblong baking dish (11¾ x 7½ x 2) or similar dish. Put in 6 slices of fried eggplant in a single layer; sprinkle with half the Parmesan cheese and put slices of Mozzarella on each slice of eggplant; add half the tomato sauce. Repeat once again. Cover and refrigerate.

Bring to room temperature before baking. Place, uncovered, in a preheated 350-degree oven for about 25 minutes, or until bubbling. Serves 6.

Patlizan Dolma (Stuffed Eggplant)

6 medium longish eggplants	3 T. chopped parsley
½ c. raw rice	4 oz. tomato sauce
6 medium onions, chopped	1½ c. cold water
1 c. salad oil	Salt and pepper to taste

Wash eggplants and roll on a flat surface with the palm of hand to soften. Cut off stems and cut in half; scoop out the center pulp. Salt pulp and let stand.

Fry onions in oil until light brown. Meanwhile, wash eggplant pulp in deep water so that seeds sink to the bottom; squeeze pulp dry with hands. Add pulp to onions and continue frying a little longer.

Add tomato sauce, rice, parsley, salt and pepper and mix well. Fill eggplant halves with this mixture. Place them in a deep pan, add the water, cover and cook for 1½ hours over low heat. Serves 6.

Braised Belgian Endive

8 hearts of endive	½ tsp. salt
⅓ c. butter	½ c. rich chicken stock

Rinse and trim endive. Place in a heavy saucepan and dot with butter. Sprinkle with salt and pour chicken stock over. Cover tightly, bring quickly to a boil, reduce heat and simmer about 30 minutes, until tender. Serves 4.

Note: If desired, endive may be drained after braising, placed in a buttered baking dish, sprinkled with grated Gruyère cheese and put under the broiler until cheese bubbles and browns lightly.

Poireaux à la Grecque

12 good-sized leeks	Bouquet garni
½ med. onion, finely chopped	1 large tomato, peeled,
2 shallots, finely chopped	seeded and chopped
¼ c. fine olive oil	Salt and pepper
⅓ c. dry white wine	Bouillon
1 tsp. lemon juice	Parsley

Wash leeks well, being sure all sand is removed (this is a tedious but essential step). Cut white part *only* into 2-inch lengths (tough green part should be discarded).

Place onion, shallots, olive oil, wine, lemon juice, bouquet garni, tomato and salt and pepper to taste in a flat aluminum pan. Place the leeks neatly over all. Add bouillon to come ¾ way up around leeks. Cover and cook over low heat about 20 to 25 minutes, or until tender. Be careful not to let liquid simmer too rapidly or leeks will fall apart.

Cool in cooking liquid.

Serve at room temperature, garnished with freshly-chopped parsley. Serves 4.

Stuffed Mushrooms

1 lb. large fresh mushrooms	2 T. fine dry bread crumbs
½ c. olive oil, divided	2 tsp. diced pimiento
¼ c. Duxelles	2 tsp. chopped parsley
2 T. grated cheddar cheese	⅛ tsp. pepper

Rinse, pat dry and remove stems from mushrooms (save stems for making duxelles, soups, stews, etc.). Brush entire cap with ⅓ cup of the oil. Arrange in baking dish, cap side up. Combine Duxelles with remaining ingredients. Stuff into mushrooms. Dribble remaining oil over all. Bake in a preheated 350-degree oven 20 minutes. Makes 14 to 18 stuffed mushrooms.

Duxelles

1 lb. fresh mushrooms	½ tsp. salt
2 T. butter or margarine	⅛ tsp. pepper
¾ c. finely-chopped shallots	Pinch nutmeg

Rinse, pat dry and chop mushrooms finely (makes about 5½ cups). Place in a clean cloth and twist tightly to extract as much liquid as possible. Heat butter in a large skillet. Add shallots, salt, pepper and nutmeg; saute 2 minutes, or until transparent. Add mushrooms and saute over high heat, stirring constantly, about 5 to 8 minutes, or until all moisture from mushrooms has evaporated. Cool thoroughly, cover and refrigerate until ready to use. Keeps well. Makes 1⅔ cups.

Stuffed Mushrooms

12 large mushrooms	2 T. butter
(2-inch diameter)	1 c. fine soft bread crumbs
⅓ c. onion, finely chopped	1 egg yolk
⅓ c. celery, finely chopped	½ tsp. salt
¼ tsp. savory, thyme	⅛ tsp. pepper
or dried dill	Shredded Parmesan cheese

Clean mushrooms and remove stems. Chop stems finely. Cook with onions, celery and savory in the butter until soft but not brown. Off heat, add the bread crumbs, lightly beaten egg yolk and salt and pepper. Put mushroom caps, cavity up, in a shallow buttered baking dish; stuff them with the hot mixture and sprinkle with cheese. Bake in a preheated 350-degree oven for 15 to 20 minutes, or until tops are delicately browned. Serves 6.

Stuffed Mushrooms Piemontese

8 large mushrooms for
   stuffing (about 3½
   inches in diameter)
   Boiling water
¼ lb. chicken livers

1 package brown and
   wild rice mix
¼ c. chopped green onion
2 T. butter
   Salt

Remove stems from mushrooms (save to use another time). Pour sufficient boiling water over mushroom caps to cover. Cover and let stand 10 to 15 minutes. Invert mushrooms on paper toweling to drain well. Prepare rice as package directs, simmering 15 minutes.

Meanwhile, cut chicken livers in eighths and sauté with onion in butter just until livers are tender. Combine with rice. Sprinkle mushroom caps lightly with salt in well-buttered shallow baking pan. Cover loosely with foil. Bake in a preheated 375-degree oven for 15 minutes, or until mushrooms are tender crisp. Serves 4.

Mushrooms Roma

12 ounces tagliarini
   (or other noodles)
½ lb. fresh brown mushrooms
½ c. butter
½ tsp. lemon juice
1 c. whipping cream
¾ c. shredded Parmesan cheese

   Salt
   Ground white pepper
2 T. finely-chopped
   fresh parsley
1 T. finely-chopped
   fresh basil (or
   ½ tsp. basil leaves)

Cook tagliarini in boiling salted water just until barely tender (you will have about 4 cups). Drain well and keep warm. Trim and cut mushrooms in generous slices. Sauté mushrooms in ¼ cup butter with lemon juice about 5 minutes, until golden; remove mushrooms and set aside. Add remaining butter to pan with ½ cup cream. Boil rapidly until large shiny bubbles appear. Reduce heat. Add cooked tagliarini to pan. Gently toss with two forks. Pour on remaining cream, then add the Parmesan cheese in three parts, tossing gently each time. Season with salt and pepper to taste. Add mushrooms, parsley and basil and toss lightly once more. Serves 5 or 6.

Escalloped Onions

6 medium onions	1 tsp. salt
(3 c. sliced)	⅛ tsp. pepper
3 T. butter or margarine	1½ c. rich milk
1 c. diced celery	½ c. pecan halves
2 T. butter or margarine	Paprika
3 T. flour	Parmesan cheese

Wash and peel onions; cut into thin crosswise slices and sauté in 3 tablespoons melted butter in saucepan or skillet. Remove onion slices from pan. Add 2 more tablespoons butter and melt. Blend in flour, salt and pepper. Gradually add milk and cook over low heat until thick and smooth, stirring constantly. While sauce is cooking, cook diced celery, covered, in a small amount of boiling salted water until just tender; drain. Place onions, celery and pecans in alternate layers in a buttered baking dish. Cover with cream sauce, sprinkle generously with grated Parmesan cheese and dust with paprika. Bake in a 350-degree oven until bubbly and hot, about 20 to 30 minutes. Serves 6.

Note: May be made ahead of time, refrigerated, then popped into the oven for the final heating just before serving.

Onion Rice Soufflé

1 c. heavy white sauce*	2 T. minced parsley
4 eggs, separated	¼ tsp. nutmeg
¾ c. cooked rice	¼ tsp. paprika
½ c. drained and minced	½ tsp. basil
boiled onions	

Gradually add white sauce to slightly beaten egg yolks. Blend in rice, onions, parsley and seasonings. Beat egg whites until stiff but not dry. Fold into rice mixture. Pour into an ungreased 2-quart casserole and bake in a preheated 325-degree oven for 45 minutes. Serves 4.

*White Sauce: Melt ¼ cup butter in a saucepan. Stir in ¼ cup flour, then blend in 1 cup milk and ½ teaspoon salt. Cook, stirring constantly, until thickened and smooth.

Sherried Onion Casserole

4 c. sliced onions
3 T. butter
2 T. flour
½ tsp. salt
⅛ tsp. white pepper
  Pinch nutmeg

⅔ c. chicken broth
¼ c. California dry sherry
1½ c. bread cubes
½ c. grated Swiss cheese
2 T. shredded Parmesan
  cheese

Cook onions in butter until soft but not browned (10 to 15 minutes over moderate heat). Blend in flour, salt, pepper and nutmeg. Stir in broth, then sherry. Cook and stir until thickened, about 5 minutes. Turn into a shallow 5-cup baking dish. Top with bread cubes. Sprinkle with Swiss, then Parmesan cheese. Bake in a preheated 425-degree oven until crusty and brown, about 15 minutes. Serves 4.

Baked Potatoes — Dill Sauce

6 medium baked potatoes
1 c. sour cream
½ tsp. beau monde seasoning

¼ tsp. finely-chopped
  dill weed
½ tsp. parsley flakes

Place sour cream in serving bowl. Season with beau monde seasoning, dill and parsley. Makes sauce for 6 medium potatoes.

Fresh Potato Soufflé

3 c. warm mashed
  (unseasoned) potatoes
¼ c. butter
¾ c. finely-grated Swiss
  or Gruyère cheese

3 T. minced chives or scallions
1 tsp. salt
½ tsp. pepper
3 eggs, separated
1 c. heavy cream, whipped

Combine warm mashed potatoes with butter, cheese, chives, salt and pepper. Beat egg yolks lightly; fold into whipped cream, then fold both into potato mixture.

Beat egg whites until stiff; fold into potato mixture. Spoon into a 2½-quart soufflé dish or casserole. Bake in a preheated 350-degree oven for 1 hour. Serves 6.

Creamed New Potatoes and Peas

15-18 small new potatoes
1 10-oz. package frozen peas
   or 1½ to 2 c. fresh peas
3 T. butter
3 T. flour
1½ tsp. salt

¼ tsp. pepper
¼ tsp. paprika
1 T. finely-chopped onion
1 c. milk
1 c. light cream
   Watercress

Boil potatoes until tender; peel. Cook peas until tender. Meanwhile, prepare sauce. Melt butter, blend in flour, salt, pepper, paprika and onion. Add milk and cream; cook, stirring constantly, until smooth and thickened. Add the potatoes and peas and heat thoroughly. Garnish with watercress. Serves 6 to 8.

All-in-One Breakfast Potatoes

6 medium potatoes,
   cooked
6 slices bacon
¼ c. chopped onion
2 T. diced green pepper
   (optional)

1 tsp. salt
¼ tsp. pepper
6 eggs
¼ c. milk

Dice potatoes. Fry bacon in skillet until crisp. Remove bacon, drain and crumble. Remove all but 3 tablespoons bacon fat from skillet. Add potatoes, onion and green pepper. Season with salt and pepper. Cook until potatoes are golden brown, turning occasionally with a spatula.

Beat eggs lightly with milk. Pour over potatoes. Add crumbled bacon. Stir mixture occasionally until eggs have set. Serves 6.

Spinach au Gratin

3 lbs. fresh spinach
1½ tsp. salt
1 egg
3 T. light cream
⅓ c. melted butter

1⅓ c. fine soft bread
   crumbs
¼ tsp. garlic salt
¼ tsp. crumbled basil
1 small avocado

Wash spinach, trim off stems and cook in covered saucepan over low heat with salt for 12 minutes, or until wilted. Drain and chop coarsely. Beat egg lightly with cream and 2 tablespoons butter; combine with spinach in a 9-inch pie plate. Bake in a preheated 350-degree oven for 10 minutes.

Meanwhile, toss crumbs with garlic salt, basil and remaining butter. Cut avocado lengthwise into halves; remove seed and skin. Cut lengthwise into slices; coat with lemon juice. Arrange slices over spinach; sprinkle with crumbs and run under broiler just until crumbs are lightly browned. Serve at once with lemon wedges, if desired. Serves 4 or 5.

Barbecued Squash

2 yellow summer squash, diced	1½ T. minced fresh dill
2 medium onions, chopped	⅓ c. olive oil
½ green pepper, chopped	1 tsp. salt
	Black pepper

Leave peel on squash; combine ingredients and place in the center of a sheet of heavy duty foil and seal, crimping edges. This will be ready to eat in less than half an hour, but tastes far better if it cooks for an hour or longer. Put it in with the charcoal as you prepare your fire for grilling meat. Serves 4.

Skillet Tomatoes

1 pt. cherry tomatoes, about 36	1 large clove garlic, minced
1 T. olive oil	¼ tsp. dried crushed oregano
	Salt

Remove stems from tomatoes; wash, dry and chill. Heat oil in a 10-inch skillet over moderate heat; add tomatoes, garlic and oregano. Cook, shaking the pan, until tomatoes are hot and skins just begin to break—about 3 to 5 minutes. Sprinkle with salt. Serves 4 to 6.

Tomatoes à la Provençal

4 tomatoes, halved
6 cloves garlic, finely
   chopped, *or* 2 T. chopped
   onion or shallots
Olive oil

4 branches parsley,
   finely chopped
Salt
Pepper
Bread crumbs

Heat a little oil in a heavy iron skillet. Fry tomatoes, cut side down, in pan when very hot. Brown quickly, then turn and cook for a few seconds. Remove tomatoes to a flat, oven-proof pan, cut side up, and sprinkle with salt and pepper. Keep warm.

Heat 1 tablespoon oil in a small skillet. Add garlic and cook until tender, but don't let it color at all. Stir well and spoon over tomatoes. Sprinkle a few bread crumbs over tomatoes. Just before serving, sprinkle each one generously with chopped parsley. Serve as a garnish with roasted meats. Serves 4 to 8.

Baked Danish Tomatoes

2 T. butter
¼ c. minced green onion
1 c. grated cheese
   (Tybo, Havarti, Esrom,
   Samsoe, Emmenthal, Blue)
½ c. fine white bread crumbs

1 c. diced cooked or
   canned chicken
1 egg, beaten
2 T. chopped parsley
Salt and pepper
6 medium tomatoes

Melt butter and saute onions in it lightly. Remove from heat. Add ¾ cup of grated cheese, chicken, bread crumbs, egg and parsley. Cut the top third from each tomato and chop. Scoop out pulp. Add both to cheese mixture; mix lightly. Season to taste. Fill tomatoes, mounding them high. Sprinkle with remaining cheese. Arrange on baking sheet and bake in a preheated 375-degree oven about 15 minutes, or until tender and stuffing is browned. Serves 6.

Noodle-Stuffed Tomatoes

1 T. salt
3 qts. boiling water
8 oz. fine egg noodles
2 T. salad oil
1 lb. ground beef chuck
6 beefsteak tomatoes

1 medium onion,
   chopped
½ tsp. basil
Salt to taste
¼ tsp. pepper
2 T. dry sherry

Add 1 tablespoon salt to rapidly boiling water. Gradually add noodles so that water continues to boil. Cook, uncovered, stirring occasionally, until tender. Drain in colander.

Meanwhile, heat oil. Add beef and onion and cook over low heat, stirring occasionally, until beef is lightly browned. Cut slice from top of each tomato. Scoop out pulp, leaving a ½-inch wall on each; reserve shells. Add noodles, tomato pulp, basil, salt, pepper and sherry to beef mixture; mix well. Fill tomato shells with mixture, turning any remaining mixture into a greased shallow baking dish. Top with tomatoes and bake in a preheated 350-degree oven 30 minutes, or until tomatoes are just tender. Serves 6.

Surprise Vegetable Bake

1 10-oz. package frozen chopped spinach *or* broccoli, thawed, drained	1 c. sliced green onions, with tops
3-4 T. butter	6 eggs
6 medium zucchini, thinly sliced	1¼ c. milk
1 clove garlic, minced	1 tsp. salt
	⅛ tsp. pepper
	½ c. Parmesan cheese

Place thoroughly drained spinach or broccoli in well-buttered baking dish (about 9 x 13 x 2 inches). Melt butter in large skillet. Add garlic and zucchini and sauté until squash is slightly soft, about 5 minutes. Add green onions during last few minutes and a bit more butter if needed. Place in baking dish with spinach. Beat eggs slightly; add milk, salt, pepper and cheese and blend thoroughly. Pour over vegetables and stir mixture gently to distribute vegetables. Bake, uncovered, in a preheated 350-degree oven 35 to 40 minutes, or until firm in center and lightly browned around edges. If desired, sprinkle with additional Parmesan cheese. Cut in squares. Serves 6 to 8.

Vegetables in Cheddar Rice Ring

3 c. milk	½ c. chopped parsley
1 c. long grain rice	¼ c. chopped green onion
1½ tsp. salt	2 T. chopped pimiento
3 eggs, beaten	⅛ tsp. pepper
1½ c. grated cheddar cheese	2 T. butter, melted

Combine milk, rice and salt in top of double boiler. Heat to boiling, stirring frequently. Set over boiling water and cook for 30 minutes, stirring now and then. Stir hot rice into beaten eggs. Add all remaining ingredients except butter and mix well. Butter inside of a 4½-cup ring mold. Turn the 2 tablespoons melted butter into bottom of mold; spoon in rice mixture. Set mold in pan containing an inch of hot water. Bake in a preheated 350-degree oven for 30 minutes. Let mold stand 5 minutes, then invert onto serving dish. Fill center with 3 cups hot buttered vegetables. Serves 6.

Casseroles and One-Dish Meals

Casseroles and other creations that make up one-dish meals are popular both for entertaining and for family fare. Both Italian and Spanish (or Mexican) influences are strongly felt in this category.

Carry-Along Casserole

1 8-oz. package
    wide noodles
2 T. butter
2 lbs. ground beef
2 8-oz. cans tomato sauce
2 T. flour

2 c. small curd cottage cheese
1 c. dairy sour cream
1 tsp. salt
½ c. chopped green onions
2 T. chopped green pepper
¼ c. chopped ripe olives

Cook noodles according to package directions. Drain. Melt butter in a skillet, then brown meat in it. Drain excess drippings; stir in tomato sauce and flour; simmer 10 minutes. Mix together cottage cheese, sour cream, salt, onions, green pepper and olives. Place half of noodles in 3-quart baking dish; spread on all the cottage cheese mixture. Top with remaining noodles and cover with ground beef mixture. Bake in a preheated 350-degree oven 30 minutes. Let stand about 10 minutes before serving. Serves 10 to 12.

Note: This casserole may be frozen.

In-From-the-Snow Casserole

1 lb. lean ground beef
2 8-oz. cans tomato sauce
    with cheese
½ c. finely-chopped onion
1 tsp. crushed basil
1 tsp. dried parsley flakes
¾ tsp. salt
½ tsp. crushed oregano

¼ tsp. pepper
2 10-oz. packages frozen
    chopped spinach, cooked,
    well drained
1 pt. cream-style cottage cheese
1 8-oz. package sliced
    Mozzarella or mild
    process cheese

Brown beef in skillet; pour off fat. Stir in tomato sauce, onion, basil, parsley, ½ teaspoon of the salt, oregano and pepper; simmer, uncovered, 10 minutes, stirring occasionally. Combine drained spinach, cottage cheese and remaining ¼ teaspoon salt. Spoon spinach around edge of baking dish (rectangular or oval, about 12 x 8 x 2 inches); pour beef mixture in center. Cut each cheese slice into 3 lengthwise strips; arrange in lattice design over meat. Bake in a preheated 375-degree oven for 20 to 25 minutes. Serves 6 to 8.

Spinach-Hamburger Casserole

2 c. thick white sauce	½ tsp. salt
2 packages frozen spinach	⅛ tsp. pepper
½ c. grated Tillamook cheese	Additional Tillamook for
1 lb. hamburger (ground beef)	sprinkling on top

Cook the frozen spinach, drain and set aside in a colander. Form the meat into four balls, season with salt and pepper and fry until brown on all sides. Add the cheese to the white sauce, heat and mix well until melted and blended. Choose a medium-size casserole and grease it lightly.

Put a layer of spinach in the dish, then place the meat balls on top of it. Spoon part of the cheese sauce over the meat. Cover the meat and sauce with the remaining spinach and top with the rest of the sauce. Sprinkle the top with additional grated cheese and a little paprika, if desired. Bake, uncovered, in a preheated 325-degree oven for 1 hour. Serves 4.

Very Special Beef Cannelloni

⅔ c. chopped onion	1 tsp. salt
2 T. oil	3 T. chopped parsley
1 tsp. mixed Italian herbs	White Sauce *or* Red Sauce
4 c. ground or finely-chopped cooked beef	12 crepes
	Sliced Monterey Jack cheese

Sauté onion in oil with herbs until soft. Combine with beef, salt and parsley. Stir in enough sauce (about a cup) to make beef mixture spreadable. Divide into 12 portions and roll a crepe around each. Pour a thin layer of remaining sauce into a shallow baking dish. Place cannelloni, seam side down, in a single layer in the sauce. Pour on remaining sauce. Cover each with a slice of cheese about the same size. Bake in a preheated 350-degree oven about 15 minutes, until piping hot. Broil a minute or two to brown tops. Serves 6.

Red Sauce: Sauté ⅓ cup chopped onion in 1 tablespoon oil with ½ teaspoon basil until soft but not brown. Stir in 1 teaspoon flour and ½ teaspoon salt. Add 1 8-ounce can tomatoes and 1 15-ounce can tomato sauce with tomato bits. Cook, stirring, until sauce boils and thickens.

White Sauce: Melt ⅓ cup butter and blend in 6 tablespoons flour. Stir in 3 cups milk, 1½ teaspoons salt, ⅛ teaspoon white pepper and a generous dash of nutmeg. Cook, stirring, until sauce boils and thickens.

Crêpes: Beat 3 eggs, ¾ cup sifted flour, 1 cup milk, 3 table-spoons melted butter and ½ teaspoon salt until smooth. Heat a 7- or 8-inch crêpe pan and brush with oil. Use 3 tablespoons batter for each crêpe, tilting pan to spread evenly. Cook over moderate heat until lightly browned on one side. Turn and brown on second side. Makes 12 crêpes.

Moussaka

4 medium eggplants	2-3 eggs, beaten
Salt	½ c. grated cheese
4 T. butter	½ c. bread crumbs
2 lbs. ground beef (or lamb)	6 T. butter
3 onions, chopped	6 T. flour
2 T. tomato paste	3 c. hot milk
¼ c. parsley, chopped	Salt and pepper to taste
½ c. dry red wine	Dash nutmeg
Salt and pepper	4 egg yolks, lightly beaten
½ c. water	Cooking oil
Dash cinnamon	Grated cheese

Remove ½-inch wide strips of peel lengthwise from eggplants, leaving ½ inch of peel between strips. Cut into ½- to ¾-inch slices, sprinkle with salt and let stand between two heavy plates while browning meat and making sauce.

Melt the 4 tablespoons butter in a frying pan and sauté meat and onions in it until meat is browned. Add tomato paste, parsley, wine, salt and pepper and water. Simmer until liquid is absorbed. Cool. Stir in cinnamon, eggs, cheese and half of the bread crumbs.

To make the sauce, melt the 6 tablespoons butter over low heat. Add flour and stir until well blended. Remove from heat and gradually stir in hot milk. Return to heat and cook, stirring, until sauce is thick and smooth. Add salt and pepper to taste and the nutmeg. Combine egg yolks with a little of the hot sauce, then stir egg mixture into the sauce and cook over very low heat for 2 minutes, stirring constantly.

Brown eggplant slices on both sides in hot oil. Grease an oven-proof casserole and sprinkle bottom with remaining bread crumbs, cover with a layer of eggplant slices, then a layer of meat, and continue until all eggplant and meat are used, finishing with a layer of eggplant. Cover with sauce, sprinkle with grated cheese and bake in a preheated 350-degree oven for 1 hour. Serve hot or at room temperature. Serves 10 to 12.

Pasta Fazool

2 lbs. ground beef
¼ c. cooking oil
3 large onions cut in wedges
2 cloves garlic, crushed
½ tsp. nutmeg
1 T. salt
½ tsp. pepper
2 c. canned tomatoes

1 6-oz. can tomato paste
1 1-lb., 12-oz. can red
  or kidney beans, drained
3 c. cooked rigatoni
  or other pasta
¼ c. milk
2 beaten eggs
1 c. grated Parmesan cheese

Heat oil in a large skillet and brown beef in it. Add onions and garlic and cook, stirring, until onions are limp. Add seasonings, tomatoes, tomato paste and beans. Cover; simmer 30 minutes.

Make a well in center of beef mixture and fill with cooked, drained pasta. Mix eggs, milk and cheese and pour over pasta. Bake in a preheated 350-degree oven for 15 minutes until lightly browned and mixture in center is set like a custard. Serves 6.

Italian Tortilla Stacks

1½ lbs. ground beef
1 package spaghetti sauce mix
1 tsp. seasoned salt
1 1-lb. can tomatoes,
   cut in bite-size pieces
1 8-oz. can tomato sauce
½ c. water

1 4-oz. can green chilies,
   seeds removed, chopped
8 corn tortillas
1 lb. ricotta cheese
2 eggs
1 lb. Monterey Jack
   cheese, grated

Brown ground beef until crumbly. Drain fat. Add spaghetti sauce mix, seasoned salt, tomatoes, tomato sauce, water and chilies. Blend thoroughly. Simmer slowly 10 minutes.

Meanwhile, combine ricotta and eggs; blend well. Spread evenly on each tortilla.

Spread 1 cup meat sauce in 12 x 8 x 2-inch baking dish. Place 2 cheese-topped tortillas side by side in the dish. Spread ⅓ cup of meat mixture and ⅓ cup grated cheese over each. Repeat until each stack contains 4 tortillas layered with meat and cheese. Bake in a preheated 350-degree oven for 30 minutes. Let stand 5 minutes before cutting into pie-shaped wedges. Serves 8 to 10.

Mock Ravioli

Meat

1 large clove garlic,
   chopped
2 medium onions, chopped
3 T. salad or olive oil
2 lbs. ground beef

1 8-oz. can tomato sauce
1 6-oz. can tomato paste
1½ c. water
1½ tsp. fines herbs
   Salt and pepper to taste

Spinach

½ c. salad oil
1 pkg. chopped frozen spinach
½ c. chopped parsley
1 c. soft bread crumbs
½ c. grated Parmesan cheese

1 clove garlic, chopped
1 tsp. sage
1 tsp. salt
4 eggs, well beaten
1 lb. butterfly macaroni

Meat: Sauté the onion and garlic until light brown. Add the meat and brown it well. Add remaining ingredients, cover and simmer gently for 2 hours.

Spinach: Mix all ingredients together thoroughly, but do not cook.

Next, cook the macaroni as directed on package. Drain.

Now, grease a large baking dish. In it place a layer of the macaroni, a layer of the spinach mixture and a layer of the meat sauce. Repeat this until all are used, ending with meat sauce. Sprinkle some additional grated Parmesan cheese over top and bake in a preheated 350-degree oven for 30 to 40 minutes. Serves 10.

Sloppy Joes

1 T. salad oil	3 tsp. chili powder
1 lb. ground chuck	1 tsp. salt
1 1-lb. can tomatoes	½ tsp. ground cumin
¼ c. sweet pepper flakes	½ tsp. instant minced garlic
1 T. instant minced onion	Toasted buns or French rolls

Heat oil in large saucepan or Dutch oven. Add meat and cook until lightly browned. Add remaining ingredients except buns. Cover and simmer 25 to 30 minutes. Serve on split toasted buns or rolls. Serves 6.

Cornish Pasties, Updated

2 4½-oz. cans corned beef spread *or* 2 4½-oz. cans deviled ham	3 T. grated onion
	½ tsp. Worcestershire
	⅛ tsp. pepper
1 c. diced cooked potatoes	1 10-oz. package pie crust mix

Combine corned beef spread (or deviled ham), potatoes, onion, Worcestershire sauce and pepper. Prepare pie crust according to package directions and divide into 6 equal parts. Roll each into a six-inch circle on a floured board. Put 3 tablespoons meat mixture in a line across center of each circle. Moisten edges of dough with water, draw opposite edges up over filling and pinch together to completely enclose filling and to form an upright ridge. Place on baking sheet and bake at 400 degrees for 25 to 30 minutes, until browned. Serves 6.

Hot Mexican Rice Ring

2 c. rice	1 4-oz. can chopped green
1 c. shredded Monterey Jack	chili peppers
cheese	1 tsp. pepper
1 tsp. salt	2 c. dairy sour cream

Cook rice according to package directions. Combine with all remaining ingredients. Spoon into an oiled 8-cup ring mold, packing firmly. Bake in a preheated 350-degree oven 30 minutes. Cool a few minutes, loosen around edges with a knife, then cover with a plate and carefully turn upside down and lift off mold. Garnish platter with parsley and red and green chili peppers. Serves 8.

Hot Tamales

2 10-lb. packages corn husks	1 recipe Tamale Filling
1 recipe Corn Meal Mush	Hot pork broth or water
2 T. lard	

Place corn husks in a large basin and add boiling water to cover. Let stand until cool. Take out a few husks at a time and drain well. Spread lower half of each husk (if you have difficulty in spreading one side of the husk, try the other) with approximately 2 tablespoons of the mush, smoothing it over the surface of the husk.

Heat the lard in a large kettle and add the tamale filling. Heat, stirring. Spoon a tablespoon of the filling lengthwise near the center of the mush. Roll the husk like a cigar to enclose the filling. Fold over the "tail" of the husk to enclose one end. Leave the other end open. Continue until all tamales are filled and rolled.

When ready to cook, cover the bottom of a large kettle with wet corn shucks. Place a small solid object in the center, leaving room to arrange the tamales around it. Start arranging the tamales, closed end down (open end up), all around the bottom of the kettle, letting them lean on the solid object. Continue making rings of tamales, layer on top of layer, until all of them are used.

Add hot pork broth or water to the bottom of the kettle to a depth of one inch. Arrange wet shucks on top of the tamales and cover with a damp cloth. Put lid on kettle and cook over gentle heat about three hours. Make sure that there is liquid in the bottom of the kettle at all times to prevent burning. This makes about 60 hot tamales.

Corn Meal Mush

4 c. tamalina or masa harina	2 T. chili powder
¾ c. plus 2 T. lard	2½-3½ c. boiling pork broth
2 T. Red Chili Paste	Salt to taste

Place the tamalina or masa harina (corn meal mixture) in mixing bowl and add the lard and red chili paste and powder. Use fingers and blend well. Gradually add the broth and salt, mixing with a large spoon. When cool enough to handle, mix with the fingers. Add enough broth so that the mush is easily spreadable.

Filling for Hot Tamales

5 lbs. pigs' knuckles	2 T. ground Roasted
3 lbs. pork neck bones	Cumin Seeds
1 bay leaf	4 cloves garlic, finely minced
Salt to taste	1 T. coarsely-ground pepper
1 c. Red Chili Paste	Ground red pepper flakes
¼ c. chili powder	to taste

Place knuckles and neck bones in a kettle and add water to cover. Add bay leaf and salt. Partly cover and bring to a boil. Simmer about 3 hours, or until the meat is fork-tender. Let cool. Spoon meat from kettle. Reserve broth for another recipe. Separate the meat and bones and discard bones. Chop meat, fat and skin until it is medium fine. Do not grind it. Add the remaining ingredients and stir to blend.

Red Chili Paste

3 dried Colorado or ancho chilies
2 c. water, about

Trim off stem ends of the chilies. Split chilies in half and remove seeds. Place split chilies in a saucepan and add water barely to cover. Cover with lid and simmer 20 minutes, or longer, until the skin loosens easily from the pulp. Let cool but do not drain. Scrape the pulp into an electric blender and discard the skins. Add the cooking liquid. Blend thoroughly.

Roasted Cumin Seeds

Pour about 6 tablespoons cumin seeds (a convenient quantity, although more or fewer may be used) into a 9-inch skillet and cook over moderate heat, shaking the skillet and stirring with a pancake turner to distribute and brown the seeds evenly. The seeds will smoke lightly as they roast. Pour the seeds onto a flat surface and roll them fine, while still hot, with a rolling pin.

Tortilla Cheese Pie

1 c. ripe olives	¼ tsp. cinnamon
1½ lbs. ground beef	1 bunch green onions, sliced
1 T. oil	6 tortillas
1¼ tsp. salt	1 10½-oz. can cheddar cheese
½ tsp. pepper	sauce (or 1½ c. cheese sauce)
1 8-oz. can tomato sauce	6 pitted ripe olives
½ tsp. crumbled dried oregano	for garnish

Cut olives into large pieces. Brown beef in skillet with heated oil, stirring with a fork until crumbly. Add salt, pepper, olives, tomato sauce, oregano, cinnamon and onions, and cook a minute or two longer. Remove from heat. Spread tortillas lightly with cheese sauce. Alternate cheese-spread tortillas with meat sauce in a buttered baking dish or pie pan, topping with a tortilla spread with cheese sauce. Skewer the stack with toothpicks. Bake in a preheated 400-degree oven for 20 to 25 minutes, or until hot through and lightly browned on top. Top picks with pitted olives. Cut into pie-shaped wedges to serve. Serves 6.

Burritos al Campo

Tortillas

4 c. all-purpose flour	6 T. shortening
2 tsp. salt	1¼ c. lukewarm water

Filling

2 T. oil	1 onion, finely chopped
3 large sausages (chorizo, Polish, etc.), cut in half, lengthwise	2 firm tomatoes, seeded, chopped
1 4-oz. can green chilies, seeded, chopped	1 1-lb. can refried beans
	½ c. California raisins
	1 c. grated cheddar cheese

Tortillas: Sift flour and salt together into large mixing bowl. Cut in shortening with two knives. Add water and beat until dough forms a ball and cleans sides of bowl. Turn onto floured surface and knead 20 times. Shape into 6 balls and let rest for 15 minutes. Roll out to dinner-plate size and cook in ungreased skillet for about two minutes on each side.

Filling: Heat oil in large skillet. Brown sausages on all sides. Remove sausages and add onion and green chilies to drippings in skillet. Sauté until onions are translucent. Add tomatoes, refried beans and raisins; continue to cook until heated through. Remove from heat and stir in cheddar cheese. Fill each tortilla with some bean mixture and half a sausage. Roll up and secure with picks. Serves 6.

Turkey Tostados

3 c. cooked, chopped turkey	2 avocados, peeled, sliced
3 8-oz. cans tomato sauce with cheese	⅓ c. chopped onion
	Garlic salt
1½ tsp. chili powder	1 head lettuce, shredded
½ tsp. oregano	1 c. shredded sharp cheddar cheese
2 T. butter	
1 9-oz. package tortillas	Radish roses for garnish

Combine turkey, tomato sauce, chili powder and oregano in a saucepan. Simmer, stirring occasionally. Fry tortillas in melted butter until crisp. Drain. Place 6 tortillas on large platter and spoon 2 to 3 tablespoons hot turkey sauce over each and top with avocado slices, onion and garlic salt. Cover with remaining tortillas. Spoon remaining sauce over each. Top with remaining avocado slices; sprinkle with shredded lettuce and cheese. Garnish with radish roses. Serves 6.

Mexican Chili

1 lb. kidney beans	½ tsp. oregano
¼ lb. salt pork, diced	Pinch ground cumin
3 minced cloves garlic	2 c. tomato puree
2 large onions, chopped	3 T. chili powder
1 lb. beef, diced	Salt and pepper
1 lb. pork, diced	to taste

Simmer beans in water to cover (or half-inch more) until not quite cooked. They absorb water as they cook, so add more as needed. Cook salt pork crisp in large skillet or Dutch oven. Add garlic and onion. When wilted, add the pork and beef (shoulder cuts are good) and mix in all other ingredients. Simmer 1½ hours, adding tomato juice or water if necessary from time to time. Taste and correct seasoning, if necessary. Serves 6 to 8.

Baked Lentils

1 lb. washed lentils	2 T. brown sugar
5 c. water	1 tsp. dry mustard
2 tsp. salt	¼ tsp. Worcestershire
½ c. catsup	2 T. minced onion
¼ c. molasses	4 slices bacon cut in thirds

Combine lentils, water and salt in a Dutch oven or other heavy vessel. Bring water to boiling, cover and simmer 30 minutes. Without draining, add catsup, molasses, brown sugar, mustard, Worcestershire sauce and onion. Mix well. Top with the uncooked bacon, cover and bake in a preheated 350-degree oven for 1 hour. Uncover the last few minutes to brown the bacon. Serve with brown bread, relishes and not much else. Serves 6 to 12.

Pilaf

2 T. butter	1 tsp. salt
2 c. cracked wheat	½ tsp. grated lemon rind
1 c. chopped onion	1 c. halved seedless grapes
3½ c. chicken stock	2 T. chopped parsley

Melt butter in a heavy 3-quart saucepan. Add cracked wheat and onion; saute lightly. Remove pan from heat and cool slightly. Add broth, salt and lemon rind. Place over heat and bring to a boil, then cover and cook over low heat for 25 minutes. Add grapes and parsley and mix lightly. Allow to stand in warm place 5 minutes before serving. Serves 6 to 8.

Olive Parsley Rice

¾ c. ripe olives
2 c. cooked rice
1¼ c. grated American cheese
¾ c. chopped parsley

¼ c. melted butter
or margarine
Salt and pepper
2 eggs

Cut olives in large pieces. Combine rice, 1 cup cheese, parsley, olives and butter; mix lightly. Season to taste with salt and pepper. Separate eggs; beat whites stiff then, using same beater, beat yolks lightly. Blend yolks into rice mixture, then fold in stiffly beaten whites. Turn into a 1-quart casserole and top with remaining cheese. Bake in a preheated 350-degree oven 25 to 30 minutes. Serves 4 to 6.

Spaghetti with Clam and Anchovy Sauce

24 cherrystone clams
4-5 T. imported olive oil
3 T. butter
2 shallots, finely chopped
3 or more cloves garlic,
finely chopped
6 anchovy filets
¼ c. finely-chopped parsley

½ tsp. rosemary
½ c. dry white wine
Freshly-ground pepper
to taste
Salt to taste (very little,
clam juice is salty)
½ lb. spaghetti

Open the clams and reserve both clams and juice. Drain clams well and set juice aside. Chop clams finely.

Heat oil, butter and shallots in a saucepan until the shallots are golden brown. Add garlic and anchovies and cook, stirring until anchovies make a paste. Add parsley and rosemary, one cup clam juice, the wine, pepper and salt. Simmer until sauce reduces slightly, about 10 minutes. Add clams and simmer a minute or two longer. Remove from heat.

Cook spaghetti in a large amount of boiling salted water until cooked to the desired degree of doneness. Drain and serve with clam sauce. Serves 6.

Coca de Verdura

4 slices bacon
¼ lb. fresh mushrooms, halved
1 small sweet white onion, sliced
1 10-oz. package frozen chopped spinach, thawed
½ tsp. Italian seasoning

1 8-oz. package refrigerated crescent dinner rolls
1 8-oz. can tomato sauce with cheese
¼ lb. sliced Mozzarella cheese, cut in 1-inch strips

Fry bacon slices until crisp; pour off all but 2 tablespoons drippings. Add mushrooms and onion slices, separated into rings; toss lightly just to coat. Drain spinach thoroughly, pressing between paper towels to remove as much moisture as possible. Unroll roll dough in oblong shape; pat into a 12 x 15-inch oblong on greased baking sheet, building up rim around outer edge. Press dough together at perforations to seal. Prick with fork; brush lightly with drippings and bake in a preheated 450-degree oven for 5 minutes.

Remove from oven and spread with tomato sauce, then sprinkle with Italian seasoning. Arrange spinach and onion rings around outer edge. Place mushroom halves, rounded side up, and cheese strips in alternate diagonal strips over all. Return to oven and continue baking 15 minutes. Garnish with reserved bacon slices. Serves 6.

Manicotti

2 lbs. ricotta or
  cottage cheese
2 eggs
¼ c. grated Romano cheese
¼ lb. sliced ham,
  coarsely chopped
⅛ tsp. nutmeg
⅛ tsp. pepper
1½ tsp. salt
2 tsp. parsley flakes
2 T. sweet pepper flakes
¼ c. onion flakes

¼ tsp. instant minced garlic
⅓ c. water
2 T. olive or salad oil
1 1-lb., 12-oz. can
  whole tomatoes
1 6-oz. can tomato paste
½ tsp. sugar
1½ tsp. Italian seasoning
½ c. water
1 8-oz. package manicotti
  Grated Romano cheese

Combine ricotta, eggs, Romano cheese, ham, nutmeg, pepper, ¾ teaspoon of the salt and parsley flakes. Mix well; set aside.

Mix sweet pepper, onion flakes and garlic with water; let stand 8 minutes for vegetables to soften. Heat oil in a large saucepan. Add softened vegetables and cook over moderate heat until lightly browned. Add tomatoes, tomato paste, remaining ¾ teaspoon salt, pepper, sugar, Italian seasoning and water. Bring to boiling point; reduce heat, cover and simmer about 30 minutes, stirring occasionally. Uncover; cook 10 minutes longer, or until thickened.

Cook manicotti as package directs. Do not overcook. Fill each manicotti with reserved cheese mixture, using a small spatula or teaspoon. Spoon half the sauce over bottom of greased 13 x 9 x 2¼-inch baking pan. Arrange filled manicotti on sauce. Pour remaining sauce over all. Cover tightly with foil. Bake in a preheated 350-degree oven 30 minutes. Remove foil; sprinkle with grated Romano cheese and bake 10 minutes longer, or until hot and bubbly. Serves 6 to 8.

Franks with Cottage Cheese Pancakes

1 lb. frankfurters
1 tsp. caraway seed
2 c. sauerkraut
1 lb. cream-style
  cottage cheese
½ tsp. salt

¼ tsp. pepper
½ tsp. parsley flakes
1 egg
¾ c. sifted all-purpose flour
¼ tsp. baking powder
⅓ c. melted shortening

Cook frankfurters in boiling water 10 minutes. Add caraway seed to undrained kraut and heat. Combine cheese, salt, pepper, parsley and egg in electric blender or with electric mixer. Blend well. Mix in flour and baking powder. Drop ¼ cup batter for each pancake into melted shortening and cook until golden brown on both sides. Serve pancakes with kraut and frankfurters. Serves 4.

Enrollados

6 medium fresh tomatoes	½ tsp. crushed red pepper
2 c. shredded cooked pork	12 corn tortillas
1 c. chopped fresh onion	1 small head lettuce,
1 minced clove garlic	shredded
1½ c. diced cooked potatoes	½ c. fresh onion rings
2 T. butter, margarine	1 T. salad or olive oil
or olive oil	½ tsp. salt
1¼ tsp. salt	¼ tsp. ground oregano
¼ tsp. black pepper	¼ tsp. black pepper

Dice tomatoes and put them through a coarse sieve. Set aside. Cook pork, onion, garlic, potatoes and ⅓ of the tomato puree in butter or oil. Add salt, black pepper and red pepper. Heat tortillas as directed on package and spoon 2 tablespoons of the mixture on each. Roll up and arrange on shredded lettuce.

In the meantime, sauté onion rings in oil. Add remaining tomato pulp and rest of seasonings. Stir and cook 5 minutes. Serve over Enrollados. Serves 6.

Cheese Dumplings

1 lb. dry cottage cheese	2 qts. slightly salted
9 T. flour	boiling water
4 eggs, slightly beaten	2 T. butter
½ tsp. salt	½ c. bread crumbs

Put the cheese in a bowl and break it up with a fork. Add the eggs and stir well. Add flour and salt. Mix until smooth. Form into balls with moist hands. Drop into the boiling water and cook, covered, at a gentle boil for 20 minutes. Melt butter and brown crumbs in it. Roll cooked dumplings in buttered crumbs and serve hot.

Sauces and Such

*S*auces are the mainstay of the repertoires of most good cooks. *Most of the recipes in this book are accompanied by appropriate saucery, but here are a few more for meats, vegetables, salads, etc., as well as some to appeal to the sweet tooth.*

Blender Bearnaise Sauce

1 medium onion, quartered	½ tsp. salt
½ tsp. tarragon	½ tsp. dry mustard
6 parsley sprigs	1 T. lemon juice
2 T. tarragon vinegar	Dash Tabasco
4 egg yolks	¼ lb. butter, melted

Put onion, tarragon, parsley and vinegar into blender container, cover and process at low until chopped. Empty into saucepan and cook until vinegar is evaporated. Set aside.

Put egg yolks, salt, mustard, lemon juice and Tabasco sauce in blender container, cover and begin processing at low (or whip). Immediately remove feeder cap and pour in warm butter in a steady stream until mixture is completely emulsified. Add onion mixture, cover and continue to process only until mixed.

This sauce may be kept warm over hot water until serving time, or refrigerated and then warmed over hot, *not* boiling, water. Makes about 1 cup.

Mayonnaise

1 egg yolk	¾ c. salad oil
1 T. vinegar or lemon juice	Dry mustard

All ingredients must be at room temperature.

Place egg yolk in small mixing bowl. Beat 1 or 2 minutes with a wire whisk. When it is well mixed, add vinegar and a little mustard; whisk another 30 seconds. Add oil a drop at a time and remember—do *not* stop beating until the sauce has thickened. Keep adding oil and beating—switching hands or changing direction to rest, if necessary, but keep going. Stop pouring oil but continue beating every once in a while to be sure egg yolk is absorbing oil.

If sauce becomes too thick, beat in a few more drops of vinegar or lemon juice to thin it. Continue with rest of oil. Makes about 1 cup.

Olive Crumb Sauce

½ c. ripe olives	1 tsp. lemon juice
4-6 T. butter	¼ tsp. salt
3 T. soft bread crumbs	2 T. finely-chopped parsley

Cut olives into wedges. Melt butter in a saucepan. When it begins to brown slightly, stir in bread crumbs. Cook until crumbs are golden. Add olives, lemon juice, salt and parsley. Serve spooned over fresh vegetables. Makes about 1 cup.

Pesto provides the good flavor in Minestrone and spaghetti sauce and is great on almost any pasta.

Pesto

2 c. basil leaves, washed and drained	½ c. olive oil
	Salt and pepper
2-3 cloves garlic, peeled	1 c. freshly-grated Romano
2-3 sprigs fresh parsley	or Parmesan cheese

Chop basil leaves with garlic and parsley. When all are very finely chopped, stir in the olive oil and salt and pepper to taste. Add cheese and mix well.

You can keep this mixture in the refrigerator for a week or even two, or you can freeze it.

Teriyaki Sauce

1 c. soy sauce
¾ c. water
½ c. sweet Sake or vermouth
¾ c. honey

4 large cloves garlic, crushed
1 1-inch piece fresh ginger root, grated

Combine all ingredients, mixing until blended. Use as meat marinade.

Sauce Vinaigrette

¼ tsp. dry mustard
6 T. olive oil
2 T. vinegar
1 tsp. tarragon leaves, crumbled

1 tsp. parsley flakes, crumbled
1 tsp. chives, chopped
¼ tsp. salt
Pinch black pepper

Mix mustard with ¼ teaspoon warm water; let stand 10 minutes. Combine mustard with remaining ingredients, mixing well. Serve cold over chilled vegetables or heat just to boiling point and spoon over hot green beans, asparagus, artichokes or other suitable vegetables. Makes about ¾ cup.

Lemon curd is an old-fashioned sweet that is used as a spread for morning or teatime toast or as dessert sauce for angel or pound cake. It also serves as a filling when pressed between cookies or as a pudding served with lady fingers and whipped cream.

Lemon Curd

1 egg
2 egg yolks
2 tsp. grated lemon peel
6 T. fresh lemon juice

¾ c. sugar
Dash salt
¼ c. butter or margarine, cut in pieces

Beat egg and egg yolks slightly in a heavy saucepan; add remaining ingredients. Cook over low heat, stirring constantly, until thickened and smooth, about 8 to 10 minutes. Chill before using. Keep covered in refrigerator (it lasts for weeks). Makes about 1¼ cups.

Mock Devonshire Cream

3 oz. cream cheese   ½ tsp. salt
¼ c. sugar   ½ pint heavy cream

Whip cream cheese with sugar and salt until light and fluffy. Whip heavy cream and fold into cream cheese mixture. Use as a topping for fruit desserts such as tarts.

Poppy Seed Filling

1 c. poppy seed   ½ c. raisins
½ c. sugar   ½ tsp. cinnamon
1 c. water   1 tsp. grated lemon peel
2 T. honey

Crush poppy seed, about ¼ cup at a time, by rolling between sheets of waxed paper with a rolling pin, or blend ¼ cup at a time in blender. Mix sugar and ½ cup water in a saucepan; bring to boiling point and boil 5 minutes, or until it is the thickness of syrup. Add remaining water and the honey, raisins and cinnamon. Cook 3 minutes. Remove from heat and stir in lemon peel. Cool. Use as filling for sweet rolls and Danish pastries or as a dessert sauce. Makes about 2 cups.

Rhubarb Glaze

2½ c. sliced fresh rhubarb   3 T. cold water
   (1-inch slices)   Grated rind of one lemon
1¼ c. sugar   Few drops red food
2 tsp. unflavored gelatin   coloring

Combine rhubarb and sugar; cook until tender. Soften gelatin in cold water; stir into hot rhubarb mixture. Add lemon rind and food coloring. Chill until the mixture is the consistency of fresh egg white. Spread evenly on top of chilled cheesecake. Cover and chill several hours or overnight.

Strawberry-Pineapple Sauce

2¾ c. sugar
3 T. cornstarch
2 c. pineapple juice
¼ c. lemon juice

¼ c. butter
1½ c. sliced strawberries
1 c. pineapple chunks

Combine sugar and cornstarch. Gradually add pineapple and lemon juices. Cook, stirring constantly, until thick and clear. Add butter; stir until melted. Add sliced strawberries and pineapple chunks. Cook over low heat for a few minutes. Cool and pour into two 1½-pint freezer containers. Snap on lids, date and freeze. When ready to serve, defrost and pour, either hot or cold, over waffles, pancakes, pound cake, ice cream, etc. Makes 3 pints.

Egg Dishes

Omelet parties are neat—especially for brunches or late-evening suppers. What we usually serve are individual tender French omelets, eggy and buttery with an occasional hint of fresh herbs. Sometimes we fill them with chicken livers and/or mushrooms, sometimes we serve them quite plain. Preceded by fresh fruit, and accompanied by hot popovers and sweet butter, they make a delightful meal.

What we offer here, though, is quite another kind of omelet—a hearty job. Its main ingredient is finely-grated Idaho potato and it contains only one egg (cholesterol watchers take note), but serves four. Choose from one of the fillings, toss a big salad, set out fruit and cheese and your meal is ready.

Idaho Half-Moon Omelet

2 c. finely-grated Idaho potato	¼ tsp. pepper
½ c. grated onion	2 T. flour
1 egg	1 T. chopped parsley
¾ tsp. salt	2 T. oil

Drain potatoes well on paper towels. Toss in a bowl with all ingredients except oil. Heat oil in a 12-inch skillet. Spread potato mixture over bottom and fry slowly on one side. Cover half the pancake with one of the fillings and fold as you would a fluffy egg omelet, then cut in wedges. Serves 4.

Indian Filling

¼ c. butter
1 c. diced green pepper
⅔ c. quartered cherry
  tomatoes

2 c. diced smoked ham
1 1-lb. can whole kernel
  corn, drained
Salt, pepper

Melt butter. Add remaining ingredients and cook over low heat, stirring occasionally, about 15 minutes. Makes about 4 cups.

Bolognese Filling

1 c. chopped onions
1 lb. lean ground beef
2 T. flour
¼ c. butter
¼ c. tomato paste
⅔ c. red wine

1 T. sliced pimiento-stuffed
  olives
2 T. grated Parmesan cheese
½ tsp. thyme
½ tsp. garlic powder
Salt, pepper

Sprinkle onions and beef with flour and brown lightly in butter. Add remaining ingredients and cook over low heat for 25 to 30 minutes, stirring occasionally. Makes about 4 cups.

Chicken Liver Filling

1 c. chopped onions
1 lb. chicken livers, cut up
⅓ c. butter
1 c. sliced mushrooms

⅓ c. light cream
1 T. sherry
2 T. chopped parsley
Salt, pepper

Cook onions and livers in butter until brown. Add remaining ingredients and cook over low heat, stirring occasionally, for 25 to 30 minutes. Makes about 4 cups.

Artichoke Soufflé

2 T. butter
2 T. flour
  Salt and pepper
¾ c. milk
4 egg yolks

½ c. chopped cooked
  artichoke pulp (bottoms)
½ c. shredded Swiss
  cheese
5 egg whites

Melt butter, add flour and salt and pepper to taste; then, stirring constantly, milk; cook and stir until thickened. Add egg yolks off heat; beat in well. Add artichoke pulp and cheese.

Beat egg whites with a pinch of salt and a pinch of cream of tartar until stiff but not dry. Beat a third into the cheese mixture, then fold in remaining whites. Turn into a prepared 1-quart soufflé dish and place in a preheated 425-degree oven for 5 minutes. Reduce heat to 375 degrees and bake another 20 minutes. Serve immediately. Serves 4.

Soufflé au Fromage

3 T. butter	½ c. grated Swiss
3 T. flour	cheese
1 c. milk	Salt, pepper and
3 eggs, separated	nutmeg to taste

Butter a 1-quart soufflé mold. Preheat oven to 400 degrees. Melt butter in a saucepan. Add flour and stir with a wire whisk until bubbly, about a minute. Add milk, stirring constantly, and cook until thickened; continue cooking about 2 minutes. Off heat, add egg yolks, cheese and seasonings. Stir to blend thoroughly.

Set aside while beating egg whites until stiff but not dry. If cheese mixture has cooled a little, place back on heat and bring nearly to boil. Turn out into a large mixing bowl. Stir about ¼ of the stiff egg whites into the cheese mixture. Fold in remaining egg whites. Pour into prepared mold, place in oven, turn heat down to 375 degrees and bake 20 minutes. Serve at once. Serves 3.

Variations

Fold ½ cup finely-diced cooked ham *or* ½ cup cooked, drained, finely-chopped spinach into the mixture along with the cheese.

Or, fold 1 cup finely-chopped cooked shrimp into the mixture, omitting the cheese and adding a few drops of lemon juice.

Individual Sherried Cheese Soufflés

3 T. butter or margarine	¼ c. California sherry
4 T. flour	½ tsp. salt
¾ c. milk	½ tsp. Worcestershire
1¼ c. grated cheddar or	3 eggs, separated
Swiss cheese	

Melt butter and stir in flour; add milk and cook, stirring constantly, until mixture is thickened and smooth. Add cheese and sherry; stir over very low heat until cheese is melted; add salt and Worcestershire sauce. Remove from heat and stir in unbeaten egg yolks; pour mixture over the stiffly-beaten egg whites and mix gently but thoroughly. Pour into 4 ungreased individual 1-cup casseroles and bake in a preheated 350-degree oven for 30 minutes, or until set. Serve at once. Serves 4.

'Evap' Cheese Soufflé

1 tall can (1⅔ c.) evaporated milk	¼ tsp. Tabasco
5 T. flour	½ lb. aged cheddar cheese, grated
¾ tsp. salt	5 eggs, separated
½ tsp. dry mustard	

Pour evaporated milk into top of double boiler. Add flour, salt, mustard and Tabasco; beat with a rotary beater until smooth. Place over boiling water and beat until slightly thickened, about 5 minutes. Add cheese to milk mixture and stir occasionally until cheese is melted, about 10 minutes. Beat until smooth. Remove from heat; add egg yolks, one at a time, beating well after each addition.

Wash beater thoroughly and beat egg whites in an ungreased 2-quart casserole until very stiff, but not dry. Gradually fold in cheese mixture. Bake in a preheated 300-degree oven 1 hour. Serve immediately on warmed plates. Serves 6 to 8.

Salmon Soufflé

4 T. butter or margarine	⅛ tsp. pepper
4 T. flour	1 c. grated cheddar cheese
1 c. hot milk	1 7¾-oz. can salmon
1 T. grated onion	3 egg yolks, lightly beaten
¼ tsp. salt	3 egg whites, stiffly beaten

Melt butter in a saucepan; stir in flour and cook, stirring, until mixture is smooth and bubbling. Add milk all at once and stir vigorously over medium heat until sauce is smooth and thickened. Stir in onion, salt, pepper and cheese. Cook, stirring, until cheese is melted. Add egg yolks and stir over low heat for 3 minutes. Remove from heat, stir in salmon liquid from can and let cool slightly. Flake and stir in salmon.

Generously butter an 8-inch deep pie plate. Place in a 400-degree oven until butter is sizzling. Fold egg whites into salmon mixture and pour onto hot plate. Bake in a preheated 400-degree oven about 15 minutes, or until delicately browned. Serves 2 or 3.

There are many versions of this dish, which is alternately known as Mock Soufflé and as Idiot Soufflé—because it's a never-fail dish, simple for even a beginner and popular for many, many years.

Baked Cheese Sandwiches

12 slices bread	2 eggs, beaten
Butter	2 c. rich milk
Prepared mustard	½ c. California dry
Dried dill	white wine
6 slices American cheese	1 tsp. salt
(or more)	½ tsp. Worcestershire

Spread 6 slices of bread lightly with butter and mustard; sprinkle with dill. Place in a 10 x 6 x 2-inch baking dish. Top each slice of bread with cheese, cover with second bread slice. Combine eggs, milk, wine, salt and Worcestershire sauce. Pour over sandwiches, cover and chill in refrigerator 1 hour, or longer. Bake in a preheated 350-degree oven about 45 to 50 minutes. Serve hot. Serves 6.

Quiche Lorraine

Pastry shell, baked for	3 eggs
10 minutes	1½ c. milk
8-10 slices lean bacon	½ tsp. salt
Water	Pinch pepper
Thin Swiss cheese slices	Pinch nutmeg

Cut bacon into 1-inch pieces and simmer for 5 minutes in water to cover. Rinse in cold water and dry on paper towels. Brown lightly in a skillet, drain and place in bottom of pastry shell. Place cheese slices in one layer over bacon.

Heat milk. Beat the eggs, hot milk and seasonings in a mixing bowl until blended. Pour into the pastry shell. Set in upper third of preheated 375-degree oven and bake 25 to 30 minutes, or until it has puffed and is browned. Slide onto a hot platter and serve immediately.

If it is to be held, put on a wire rack to cool. When ready to serve, place in a 350-degree oven for about 5 to 7 minutes, or until warmed.

Variations

You can substitute a cup of flaked crab meat, a cup of sautéed sliced fresh mushrooms or pre-cooked asparagus spears for the bacon—use same way and follow recipe.

Fresh Mushroom Quiche

8 slices bacon, cut crosswise into 1-inch bits
⅓ c. finely-chopped fresh onion
½ lb. fresh mushrooms, coarsely chopped
1 T. flour
4 eggs, lightly beaten

1 c. heavy cream
¾ c. milk
½ tsp. salt
¼ tsp. ground mace
Unbaked 9-inch pastry shell with deep edge
¼ lb. Gruyère cheese, grated

Cook bacon pieces in a large skillet until crisp. Remove bacon and reserve. Remove all but 3 tablespoons fat from pan; reserve remainder. Add onion to skillet; cook over low heat until limp and transparent. Add chopped mushrooms to onion and cook, tossing gently, until mushrooms are tender. Add more bacon fat if necessary. Blend in flour. Let cool a few minutes.

Combine beaten eggs, cream, milk, salt, pepper and mace in a large bowl. Sprinkle crisp bacon over bottom of pie shell. Top with grated cheese and mushroom mixture. Pour egg mixture over all. Bake on lowest shelf in a preheated 425-degree oven 15 minutes; reduce heat to 300 degrees and bake 40 minutes longer, or until custard is set. Serve hot.

California Cheese Custard

4 c. toasted bread cubes	3 c. milk
¾ lb. cheddar cheese,	1 tsp. salt
thinly sliced or grated	Pepper
6 eggs	2 T. butter

Arrange alternate layers of bread cubes and cheese in a buttered 8 x 8 x 2-inch casserole, ending with bread cubes. Beat eggs; add milk, salt and pepper to taste. Pour into casserole over bread and cheese. Dot with butter. Bake in a preheated 325-degree oven 1¼ hours. Serves 4 to 6.

Raisin Custard French Toast

2 egg, separated	2 tsp. sherry *or* 1 tsp.
½ tsp. salt	vanilla
1 T. sugar	6 slices raisin bread
¼ c. cream	Butter or margarine

Beat egg yolks well with salt, sugar and sherry; stir in cream. Beat egg whites until stiff but not dry. Gently fold into first mixture. Turn into shallow pan or dish; quickly dip raisin bread slices on both sides in fluffy custard batter. Sauté in a little butter over moderate heat until golden brown on both sides, turning just once. Serve immediately on heated plates with a sprinkling of powdered sugar and desired topping. Serves 3.

Bombay Raisin Curried Eggs

⅓ c. butter or margarine	2 c. half and half
2 tsp. curry powder	2 tsp. lemon juice
¼ tsp. ginger	¼ tsp. grated lemon rind
½ tsp. salt	1 tart apple, peeled and diced
¼ tsp. garlic salt	10 hard-cooked eggs
¼ c. finely-chopped onion	8 slices Canadian bacon,
1 c. dark seedless raisins	grilled
⅔ c. sifted flour	4 English muffins, split
2 c. chicken broth	and toasted

Heat together butter, curry powder, ginger, salt and garlic salt until bubbly. Add onion and cook slowly until wilted. Add raisins and saute lightly. Blend in flour. Slowly stir in chicken broth and half and half. Cook, stirring, until mixture boils and thickens.

Lower heat and simmer a few minutes longer. Stir in lemon juice and rind and apple. Turn into shallow casserole. Cut a cross in top of 8 of the eggs. Cut a thin slice from bottom of 8 eggs and place upright in hot sauce. Chop remaining eggs and sprinkle in a ring around outside edge.

To serve, place a slice of cooked Canadian bacon on a toasted and buttered English muffin half. Spoon egg and sauce over all. Serves 8.

All Kinds
of Breads

There probably is no more rewarding kitchen experience than baking bread. Once you get the hang of it, bread making isn't "all that much" work. Not only is the product excellent, everyone loves it.

There is no better toast than that made from homemade bread. There is no bread more satisfying to eat—one slice of it is easily equal to two or three (or more) of the air pudding so many of us are used to calling bread.

The house smells wonderful while it is baking, too.

A good pastry cook—who has learned that a light hand is an absolute necessity for turning out tender, flaky pie crust—often has a difficult time grasping the technique of kneading bread, for it is absolutely opposite. Bread must be treated very roughly.

We make bread two ways—one by the mixer method (this requires a big, heavy-duty mixer with a dough hook attachment) and the other by the conventional or old-fashioned hand-knead method.

The first stage takes less than five minutes in the mixer, while the old-fashioned method takes a good 15 minutes. Other than that, and the rather large difference in expenditure of human energy, they are exactly the same—and so is the end result.

Kneading is the trick. When you have added enough flour to your dough so it is manageable, turn it out onto a well-floured board. Sprinkle a little flour over the top and start kneading.

This involves pressing down and away from you with the heels of your hands, then giving the dough a quarter turn, picking up the opposite edge, folding it over again and pressing down and away with the hands.

Keep turning and folding, adding flour as necessary to keep dough from being sticky, until it is smooth and satiny and springs back rather than kneading down into itself any longer.

Bread
(Mixer Method)

1 tall can evaporated milk	4 T. oil or melted
1 milk can hot water	shortening
1 T. sugar	2 c. wheat germ
1 T. salt	7 c. flour
3 yeast cakes	Flour for kneading

Put milk, water, sugar, salt and oil in mixer bowl. Crumble in yeast and stir until dissolved. Add wheat germ and flour. Attach dough hook. Start mixer at speed No. 2 and run for 3 minutes; turn dough over and repeat for ½ minute. Remove dough from bowl, cut in two and let stand for 15 or 20 minutes.

Knead lightly into loaves, place in well-greased bread pans, let rise in warm place until it comes well up above the tops of the pans. Bake in a preheated 400-degree oven for 35 to 45 minutes, until a loaf sounds slightly hollow when tapped. (If using Pyrex pans, set oven at 375 degrees and check after 30 minutes.)

Remove from oven, rub butter over tops of loaves, then turn out of pans on their sides on wire racks to cool.

Bread
(Hand Method)

Exactly same ingredients as for mixer method, except a little more flour may be needed to make dough proper consistency for kneading.

Put milk, water, sugar, salt and oil in mixing bowl. Crumble in yeast and stir until dissolved. Start adding flour, stirring in until a smooth dough is formed (this gets to be rather heavy going). Turn out on a well-floured board and knead until smooth and satiny and air bubbles are gone. Cut dough in two and let stand for 15 or 20 minutes.

Knead lightly into loaves and proceed as for recipe for mixer method.

Note: If you want to leave out the wheat germ, simply substitute 1½ cups flour for it—either white or whole wheat.

Honey Graham Bread

4¾ c. unsifted white flour	2 c. milk
2½ c. unsifted graham flour	½ c. water
1 T. salt	⅓ c. honey
2 packages active dry yeast	¼ c. margarine

Combine white and graham flours. Thoroughly mix 2½ cups flour mixture in a large bowl with the salt and undissolved yeast.

Combine milk, water, honey and margarine in a saucepan. Heat over low heat until liquids are very warm (120 to 130 degrees). Gradually add to dry ingredients and beat 2 minutes at medium speed of electric mixer, scraping bowl occasionally. Stir in enough additional flour mixture to make a soft dough. (If necessary, add additional white flour to obtain desired dough.) Turn out onto lightly-floured board and knead until smooth and elastic, about 8 to 10 minutes. Place in greased bowl, turning to grease top. Cover; let rise in warm place, free from draft, until doubled in bulk, about an hour.

Punch down, let rise again until doubled in bulk, about ½ hour. Punch down; turn out onto lightly-floured board and shape into loaves or pan rolls as follows:

Loaves: Divide into two or three equal pieces, depending on size of loaves desired. Shape each piece into a loaf and place in 3 greased 8½ x 4½ x 2½-inch pans or 2 greased 9 x 5 x 3-inch loaf pans. Cover; let rise in warm place, free from draft, until doubled in bulk, about an hour. Bake in a preheated 350-degree oven for 45 minutes, or until done. Remove from pans and cool on wire racks.

Pan Rolls: Divide in half. Form each half into a 12-inch roll. Cut into 12 equal pieces. Shape each piece into a smooth ball. Place in 2 greased 9-inch round cake pans. Cover; let rise in warm place, free from draft, until doubled in bulk, about 1 hour. Bake in a pre-heated 400-degree oven about 20 minutes, or until done. Remove from pans and cool on wire racks.

Applesauce Date Nut Bread

¾ c. chopped walnuts	1 c. hot applesauce
1 c. cut-up pitted dates	2 eggs
1½ tsp. baking soda	1 tsp. vanilla
½ tsp. salt	1 c. sugar
3 T. shortening	1½ c. sifted all-purpose flour

Mix walnuts, dates, soda and salt with a fork. Add shortening and applesauce; let stand 20 minutes. Heat oven to 350 degrees. Grease a 9 x 5-inch loaf pan. Beat eggs with a fork, beat in vanilla, sugar and flour. Mix in date mixture just until blended; turn into prepared pan. Bake an hour and 5 minutes, or until cake tester inserted in center comes out clean. Cool in pan 10 minutes. Remove to wire rack to finish cooling, then wrap in foil. Store overnight before slicing. This loaf freezes well.

Fresh Blueberry Banana Bread

1 c. fresh blueberries	⅓ c. butter
1¾ c. sifted flour	⅔ c. sugar
2 tsp. baking powder	2 eggs
¼ tsp. baking soda	1 c. mashed ripe
½ tsp. salt	banana

Wash and drain blueberries thoroughly; toss berries with 2 tablespoons flour. Sift together remaining flour, baking powder, soda and salt. Cream butter; gradually beat in sugar until light and fluffy. Beat in eggs, one at a time. Add flour mixture and bananas alternately, in three parts. Stir in blueberries. Spoon into greased 9 x 5 x 3-inch loaf pan. Bake in a preheated 350-degree oven about 50 minutes, or until done.

Cranberry Nut Bread

½ c. light brown sugar
1 egg
1 c. milk
3 c. biscuit mix
¾ c. chopped nuts

1 c. fresh cranberries,
   coarsely chopped
½ tsp. cinnamon
½ tsp. nutmeg

Combine brown sugar, egg and milk. Stir in biscuit mix. Beat well until smooth and fairly thick. Fold in nuts, cranberries and spices. Spoon mixture into a well-greased 9 x 5 x 3-inch loaf pan. Bake in a preheated 350-degree oven for 50 to 60 minutes, or until loaf tests done. Cool in pan 5 minutes. Loosen and turn out on a rack. Cool thoroughly before slicing.

Oatmeal Nut Bread

8½-9½ c. unsifted flour
2 tsp. salt
2 packages dry yeast
1 c. water
½ c. milk
½ c. molasses

½ c. margarine
2 eggs at room
   temperature
2 c. cooked steel-cut or
   old-fashioned oats
1 c. chopped pecans

Thoroughly mix 2 cups flour, salt and undissolved yeast in a large bowl.

Combine water, milk, molasses and margarine in a saucepan. Heat over low heat until liquids are quite warm—margarine does not need to melt completely. Gradually add to dry ingredients and beat 2 minutes at medium speed of electric mixer, scraping bowl occasionally. Add eggs, cooked oats and 1 cup flour. Beat at high speed 2 minutes, scraping bowl occasionally. Stir in enough additional flour to make a stiff dough.

Turn out onto lightly-floured board and knead until smooth and elastic, about 8 to 10 minutes. Place in a greased bowl, turning to grease top. Cover and let rise in a warm place, free from draft, until doubled in bulk, about an hour.

Punch dough down; knead in pecans. Divide into 3 equal pieces. Roll each piece into a 12 x 8-inch rectangle. Beginning at an 8-inch end, roll dough as for jelly roll. Pinch seam to seal. With seam side down, press down ends with heel of hand. Fold underneath. Place, seam side down, in 3 greased 8½ x 4½ x 2½-inch loaf pans. Cover and let rise in a warm place, free from drafts, until doubled in bulk, about an hour.

Bake in a preheated 400-degree oven for 30 minutes, or until done. Remove from pans and cool on wire racks.

Note: If a soft crust is desired, brush tops with soft margarine before turning out of pans.

Orange-Molasses Bread

¾ c. sugar
4 c. sifted all-purpose flour
1 tsp. soda
3 tsp. baking powder
2 tsp. salt

1⅓ c. coarsely-chopped nuts
1 c. evaporated milk
¾ c. orange juice
3 T. melted shortening
¾ c. unsulphured molasses

Sift together sugar, flour, soda, baking powder and salt; add nuts. Combine evaporated milk, orange juice, shortening and molasses. Add to flour mixture all at once; stir just to blend. Turn into a well-greased waxed paper-lined loaf pan 9 x 5 x 3 inches. Bake in a preheated 325-degree oven 1 hour and 15 minutes.

Peach Bread

1¼ c. sugar
½ c. shortening
2 eggs
2 c. Fresh Peach Puree
2 c. unsifted flour
1 tsp. cinnamon

1 tsp. soda
1 tsp. baking powder
¼ tsp. salt
1 tsp. vanilla
1 c. finely-chopped
pecans

Cream sugar and shortening together. Add eggs and mix thoroughly. Add puree and dry ingredients. Mix thoroughly. Add vanilla and pecans and stir until blended. Pour into two 5 x 9-inch loaf pans that have been well greased and floured. Bake in a preheated 325-degree oven for 55 minutes to an hour. Let cool a few minutes before removing from pan.

Fresh Peach Purée

4 lbs. unpeeled fresh
   peaches, sliced
4 tsp. ascorbic acid powder

2 c. sugar
4 pinches salt

Use a fourth ingredients at a time and put in blender. Whiz at high speed about 20 seconds. Repeat. Use as desired or freeze in 1-cup portions. Makes about 2 quarts.

Pineapple Nut Bread

1¾ c. sifted all-purpose
   flour
2 tsp. baking powder
½ tsp. salt
¼ tsp. soda
½ c. raisins

¾ c. chopped walnuts
¾ c. light brown sugar
3 T. soft butter or margarine
2 eggs, unbeaten
1 c. crushed pineapple,
   not drained

Topping

2 T. sugar

½ tsp. cinnamon

First, grease a 9 x 5 x 3-inch pan. Measure first four ingredients into sifter; set aside. Rinse raisins in boiling water to plump them; drain well; set aside with walnuts.

Combine sugar, butter and eggs in mixing bowl; beat until fluffy. Add raisins and nuts.

Sift in about half the flour mixture and stir (don't beat) just until moistened and fairly smooth. Add pineapple with its syrup, then stir in rest of flour. Quickly but gently spoon the heavy batter into prepared pan. Sprinkle with Topping (cinnamon and sugar mixed together). Bake in a preheated 350-degree oven 60 to 70 minutes, or until done. Turn out onto a rack. Slices well even when barely cool.

Baked Walnut Brown Bread

1¼ c. sifted flour
2 tsp. baking powder
¾ tsp. soda
1¼ tsp. salt
1¼ c. graham flour
1 c. chopped walnuts

1 egg
⅓ c. brown sugar
½ c. light molasses
¾ c. buttermilk
3 T. melted shortening

Resift flour with baking powder, soda and salt. Stir in graham flour and walnuts. Beat egg lightly, beat in brown sugar, molasses, buttermilk and shortening. Stir into dry mixture just until all of the flour is moistened. Spoon into three greased one-pound size cans. Bake in a preheated 350-degree oven 45 minutes, or until bread tests done. Let stand 10 minutes, then turn out onto wire rack. Serve warm or cold.

Or: Spoon batter into a 9 x 5 x 3-inch loaf pan and bake in a preheated 350-degree oven for 50 to 55 minutes.

Steamed Brown Bread

1 c. sifted flour
1 tsp. salt
1 tsp. baking powder
1 tsp. baking soda
1 c. whole wheat flour

1 c. cornmeal
¾ c. light molasses
2 c. buttermilk
1 c. chopped pecans
1 c. raisins

Sift flour with salt, baking powder and soda; stir in whole wheat flour and cornmeal. Beat in molasses and buttermilk. Thoroughly mix in pecans and raisins. Pour into 2 greased 1-pound coffee cans. Cover cans tightly with foil. Set in large deep saucepan and steam over low heat for 3 hours, adding more boiling water as necessary to keep it about half way up the cans.

Remove foil from cans and let bread set in cans for about 5 minutes; bread will pull away slightly from sides of cans. Remove bread, slice and serve with sweet butter.

Bread may be stored in freezer. To reheat, steam in foil or slice and toast.

The classic French brioche is a feathery light yeast dough baked in a fluted tin. It's delicious with butter and jam for breakfast or hollowed out and filled with creamed seafood, chicken liver or meat filling for a lunch, brunch or supper entrée.

This version, rich in butter and eggs, may be started one day, refrigerated overnight and shaped and baked the next day.

Brioche

¾ c. milk	5 c. unsifted all-purpose
2 T. sugar	flour
1½ tsp. salt	1 c. soft butter
2 envelopes active dry yeast	5 eggs
¼ c. warm water	Egg Glaze

Scald milk; stir in sugar and salt. Cool to room temperature. Stir together yeast and warm water until dissolved in large bowl of electric mixer. Stir in 2 cups of the flour, and the milk mixture. Mix to blend, then beat in butter. Mix in remaining flour alternately with eggs, adding them one at a time and beating thoroughly after each addition, until dough is soft and sticky. Beat at medium speed until dough is shiny and elastic, about 10 minutes. (If dough becomes too heavy for mixer to handle, pull dough out of bowl with floured hands, then vigorously toss it back into the bowl, continuing until dough is springy and no longer sticky.)

Place dough in buttered bowl, cover lightly and let rise in warm place until doubled in bulk, about 1½ hours. Stir down, then cover with plastic film and refrigerate for about 8 hours or overnight.

For large brioches, divide dough in half. Return unused half to refrigerator. Pinch off about 1/5 of the dough with floured hands. Shape larger portion into a smooth ball, pulling surface of dough to the underside. Place, smooth side up, in a well-buttered 8-inch brioche pan. Roll smaller piece of dough into a teardrop shape.

Cut an X in the center of the larger portion of dough with a sharp knife. Poke down the four points where the X intersects with floured knife tip. Hold the smaller piece of dough by its sides and put it gently, pointed end down, into the hole. Shape remaining half of dough in the same manner in a second pan.

Let dough rise in warm place until doubled, about 2 hours. Brush with glaze and bake in a preheated 350-degree oven for about 45 minutes, until well browned and wooden skewer comes out clean when inserted near center. Cool in pans on wire racks for about 15 minutes, then loosen edges and remove carefully. Makes 2 large or 8 individual brioches.

Egg Glaze: Beat together 1 egg yolk and 1 tablespoon milk.

(To shape individual brioches: Divide chilled dough into 8 portions. Pinch off ¼ of each for topknots. Shape as for large brioches. Place in buttered 4½-inch brioche pans. Shaped dough will rise in about 1½ hours. Bake in preheated 425-degree oven for 20 to 25 minutes.)

Easy Bear Claws

1 1-lb. loaf frozen ready-to-bake bread	⅛ tsp. almond extract
1 c. finely-ground blanched almonds	¼ c. flour
	½ tsp. ground cardamom
¾ c. sifted powdered sugar	¾ c. butter
1 egg, slightly beaten	2 T. shaved or slivered almonds
1½ tsp. lemon juice	

Remove frozen loaf from package. Let thaw at room temperature until soft and pliable—1 to 2 hours.

For filling, whirl almonds in electric blender until very fine or grind in a food grinder. Mix thoroughly with sugar and half the beaten egg (reserve other half for later use in recipe). Blend in lemon juice and almond extract.

Mix flour with cardamom. Cut butter into flour-cardamom mixture. Chill until ready to use.

Roll softened ready-to-bake bread out on well-floured surface to a 12-inch square. Place chilled butter-flour mixture between 2 sheets of waxed paper and roll out to a rectangle 4 x 10 inches. Remove top sheet of paper; invert butter mixture onto half of dough. Remove other sheet of paper. Fold uncovered half of dough over mixture and roll out to a 12-inch square. Fold in thirds. Repeat rolling and folding three times. Roll dough into a 12 x 16-inch rectangle, using more flour as necessary to prevent sticking. Cut in half lengthwise, making two 6 x 16-inch rectangles. Spread almond filling down center of each strip. Fold edges of dough over filling; pat to flatten.

Cut each long roll into 5 rolls. Cut 4 gashes in each roll about ⅔ width of roll. Spread sections apart to form claws. Place on a well-greased baking sheet. Brush tops with remaining half of beaten egg, which has been mixed with 1½ teaspoons water. Sprinkle with shaved or slivered almonds.

Let rise in a warm place until double in size. Bake in a pre-heated 375-degree oven about 15 to 20 minutes, or until golden brown. Glaze while hot with a mixture of 1 cup sifted powdered sugar and 4 teaspoons milk.

Breakfast Cinnamon Twists

1½ c. margarine, softened	2 packages active
2½ tsp. cinnamon	dry yeast
3½-4½ c. unsifted flour	¾ c. milk
½ c. sugar	½ c. water
1½ tsp. salt	¼ c. margarine
2 T. cornstarch	2 eggs at room temperature
1½ tsp. grated lemon rind	½ c. sugar

Thoroughly blend together softened margarine and 2 teaspoons of the cinnamon. Spread on waxed paper in a 10 x 12-inch rectangle. Chill until ready to roll dough.

Thoroughly mix 1¼ cups flour, ½ cup sugar, salt, cornstarch, lemon rind and dry yeast in a large bowl.

Combine milk, water and ¼ cup margarine in a saucepan. Heat over low heat until liquids are warm. Gradually add to dry ingredients and beat 2 minutes at medium speed of electric mixer, scraping bowl occasionally. Add 2 egg yolks, 1 egg white (reserve remaining white) and ¾ cup flour, or enough flour to make a thick batter. Beat at high speed 2 minutes, scraping bowl occasionally. Add enough additional flour to make a stiff batter; stir just until blended. Cover bowl tightly with foil; chill thoroughly, about 1 hour.

Roll chilled dough out on a lightly-floured board to a 12 x 16-inch rectangle. Place chilled margarine slab on ⅔ of dough. Fold uncovered third over middle section; cover with remaining third. Give dough a quarter turn; roll into a 12 x 16-inch rectangle; fold as above. Turn, roll and fold once more; wrap in plastic wrap. Chill thoroughly, about 1 hour. Repeat procedure of 2 rollings, foldings, turnings and chillings two more times.

Divide dough in half on a lightly-floured board. Refrigerate one half hour. Roll half the dough into a 12 x 16-inch rectangle. Cut into 16 strips, ¾ inch wide. To form twist, unfold strip. Grasp ends of strip and, using center of strip as the top, overlap ends several times. Pinch ends together to seal. Place on lightly-greased baking sheets. Repeat with remaining half of dough. Cover loosely with plastic wrap; refrigerate overnight.

Just before baking, brush twists with remaining lightly-beaten egg white. Sprinkle twists with remaining ½ cup sugar and ½ teaspoon cinnamon, which have been blended together. Bake in a preheated 375-degree oven for 15 to 20 minutes, or until done. Remove from baking sheets and place on wire racks. Makes 32 twists, which are best warm.

Danish Cheese Envelopes

1 c. shredded Esrom, Havarti or other Danish cheese
1 egg, separated
¼ c. sour cream
2 tsp. sugar
1 package refrigerator crescent rolls
Sugar for topping

Combine cheese, egg yolk, sour cream and sugar. Unroll dough and flatten gently with rolling pin to close perforations. Cut dough into 8 squares. Put about a tablespoon of cheese mixture in middle of each one. Fold corners in to center and pinch together. Brush each pastry with slightly-beaten egg white and sprinkle with sugar. Bake on a lightly-greased cookie sheet in a preheated 375-degree oven for 12 to 15 minutes, until golden.

Banana Sour Cream Coffee Cake

½ c. shortening
1 c. sugar
2 eggs
1 c. mashed banana
½ tsp. vanilla
½ c. sour cream
1 tsp. baking powder

2 c. sifted all-purpose
  flour
1 tsp. baking soda
¼ tsp. salt
½ c. chopped nuts
¼ c. sugar
½ tsp. cinnamon

Cream shortening and sugar until light and fluffy. Beat in eggs, banana and vanilla. Fold in sour cream. Sift together flour, baking powder, soda and salt. Gently fold into creamed mixture, stirring just to blend.

Mix together nuts, ¼ cup sugar and cinnamon. Sprinkle half of nuts into bottom of a well-greased 6½-cup ring mold or tube pan. Spoon in half the batter. Repeat process.

Bake in a preheated 350-degree oven for 45 minutes, or until cake tester comes out clean. Let stand in pan on rack for 5 minutes; loosen around edges and turn out on plate.

Cheese-Filled Coffee Cake

Dough

2 cakes yeast
½ c. lukewarm water
6 egg yolks
1 c. butter or margarine,
  melted
1 c. dairy sour cream

4½-5 c. sifted all-purpose
  flour
1½ c. quick or old-fashioned
  oats, uncooked
¾ c. sugar
½ tsp. salt

Filling

1 8-oz. package cream
  cheese, softened
½ c. sugar

⅓ c. apricot jam
2 eggs
1 tsp. vanilla

Soften yeast in lukewarm water. (If you use dry yeast, use warm water.) Beat egg yolks until thick and lemon colored. Blend in butter and sour cream; stir in softened yeast. Combine 4 cups flour, oats, sugar and salt in large bowl; gradually add yeast mixture. Stir in enough additional flour to make a soft dough.

Turn out on lightly-floured board and knead until smooth and satiny, about 5 minutes. Round dough into a ball; place in greased bowl, brush lightly with melted shortening; cover and let rise in a warm place until nearly double in size.

Punch down. Knead lightly on floured board or canvas; roll out into an 18-inch circle. Lay dough over greased 3-quart ring mold 10½ inches in diameter; fit dough inside mold, covering center hole and letting dough overhang sides; pour in filling. Turn outer edge of dough over filling. Cut cross in center of dough covering center hole; fold each triangle of dough over toward larger edge of ring; pinch each point to dough in pan to seal tightly.

Let rise until nearly double in size, about 30 minutes. Bake in a preheated 350-degree oven 35 to 40 minutes. Cool 10 minutes; remove from pan. When cool, heat jam and brush over ring. Cut and serve.

Filling: Beat cream cheese until light; blend in sugar. Add eggs, one at a time, beating well after each addition. Stir in vanilla. Use as directed.

Cinnamon Sour Cream Coffee Cake

½ c. soft butter	1 tsp. baking powder
or margarine	½ tsp. soda
1 c. sugar	1 tsp. almond extract
2 eggs	¾ c. chopped almonds
1 c. sour cream	1 tsp. cinnamon
2 c. sifted all-purpose flour	2 T. dark brown sugar

Cream butter and sugar until light and fluffy. Add eggs, one at a time, beating well after each addition. Stir in sour cream. Sift together flour, baking powder and soda and add to creamed mixture. Stir in almond extract.

In a separate bowl, combine almonds, cinnamon and brown sugar. Spoon half of batter into a greased and lightly floured 8-inch tube pan. Sprinkle half of cinnamon mixture on top. Cover with remaining batter and nuts. Bake in a preheated 350-degree oven 1 hour, or until a cake tester inserted in the center comes out clean. Serve warm or cold.

Cranberry Streusel Coffee Cake

1½ c. biscuit mix	⅓ c. brown sugar
½ c. sugar	¾ c. fresh cranberries,
1 egg	coarsely chopped
½ c. milk	½ tsp. nutmeg
2 T. soft shortening	⅓ c. biscuit mix
1 tsp. vanilla	¼ c. butter or margarine
Grated rind of one orange	

Combine 1½ cups biscuit mix, sugar, egg, milk, shortening and vanilla. Beat until very smooth and velvety. Fold in orange rind and cranberries. Spoon batter into a greased and floured 9-inch round cake pan. Combine remaining ingredients and mix with fingers until crumbly. Sprinkle over top of cake. Bake in a preheated 350-degree oven for 35 to 40 minutes, or until cake tests done. Cut into wedges and serve warm.

No-Knead Raisin Bread Ring

⅓ c. sugar	1 package dry yeast
⅓ c. butter, softened	¼ c. warm water
½ tsp. salt	2 eggs, beaten
½ c. boiling water	1 c. seedless raisins
¾ c. evaporated milk	4½ c. sifted flour

Mix sugar, butter and salt together in a large mixing bowl. Add boiling water and stir until butter is melted. Add evaporated milk. Sprinkle yeast on warm water and stir until dissolved. Add to first mixture. Stir in eggs and raisins. Add the flour, a cup at a time, beating until fairly smooth after each addition. Cover and let rise until double in bulk, about 1 to 1½ hours.

Beat batter down, then beat for 2 minutes with a wooden spoon. Turn into a well-greased 10-inch tube pan, smoothing evenly with spoon. Let rise, uncovered, until double in bulk, about 45 minutes. Bake in a preheated 375-degree oven for about 55 minutes. Remove from pan immediately and allow to cool on a rack.

Norwegian Sour Cream Cakes

Batter

1½ c. sifted all-purpose flour	1 tsp. ground cardamom or ginger
½ tsp. salt	3 eggs, well beaten
3 T. sugar	2 c. sour cream

Sauce

1½ c. orange marmalade	2 T. lemon juice
½ c. honey	½ tsp. ground cardamom or ginger
2 T. butter	

Batter: Combine flour, salt, sugar and cardamom; mix well. Beat eggs with sour cream and stir into dry ingredients. Beat with a rotary beater until batter is smooth.

If using a Norwegian plett pan, spoon about a tablespoon of the batter into each circle of preheated pan. Bake until surface of each cake looks set, then turn with a thin-bladed knife and brown other side.

If Norwegian non-electric waffle iron, spoon about ⅔ cup of the batter in center of preheated iron. Spread batter with a spatula, close top and cook until brown on one side. Turn iron and brown on other side. Serves 6.

Sauce: Combine all ingredients in a small saucepan and heat until butter is melted and sauce is warm. Makes 2 cups.

This Make-Your-Own Mix is a big time saver, for you keep a batch of it on hand there are many things in which it may be used—anything, in fact, for which you would use a standard biscuit mix.

Make-Your-Own Mix

9 c. sifted all-purpose flour	4 T. baking powder
1 T. salt	2 c. shortening

Combine sifted flour, salt and baking powder. Stir well. Sift into a large bowl. Add shortening and using a pastry blender, two knives or your fingers, cut and distribute shortening throughout dry ingredients until the mixture resembles coarse cornmeal. The mix is now ready to use or to store in a closed canister on the pantry shelf.

Banana Buttermilk Muffins

1 c. light or dark raisins	2 c. sifted all-purpose flour
1 egg	⅓ c. sugar
½ c. mashed banana	3 tsp. baking powder
½ c. buttermilk	¼ tsp. soda
¼ c. melted shortening	1 tsp. salt

Rinse and drain raisins. Beat egg, add banana, buttermilk, shortening and raisins. Sift together flour, sugar, baking powder, soda and salt. Add to first mixture all at once, stirring only until dry ingredients are moistened. Fill greased muffin pans ⅔ full. Bake in a preheated 400-degree oven 20 to 25 minutes. Serve hot.

Blueberry Muffins

1½ c. unsifted flour, stir before measuring	½ c. milk
2 tsp. baking powder	¼ c. butter, melted and cooled
½ tsp. salt	1 c. fresh blueberries
½ c. sugar	2 T. sugar mixed with
1 large egg	1 tsp. lemon rind

Stir together the flour, baking powder, salt and sugar in a medium mixing bowl, using a fork. In a separate, smaller bowl, combine the egg and milk; add the butter. Make a well in center of dry ingredients; pour in liquid and stir with a fork until dry ingredients are just moistened. Fold in blueberries.

Drop batter into 12 large, buttered muffin-pan cups, filling about ⅔ full. Sprinkle with sugar-lemon mixture. Bake in a preheated 375-degree oven 20 to 25 minutes, until a cake tester comes out clean. Loosen edges and remove. Serve at once.

Wheat Germ Banana Muffins

1½ c. sifted flour	2 eggs, slightly beaten
½ c. sugar	1 c. finely-mashed banana
3 tsp. baking powder	½ c. milk
½ tsp. salt	¼ c. melted shortening
1 c. toasted wheat germ	

Combine flour, sugar, baking powder and salt in sifter; sift into mixing bowl. Stir in wheat germ. Add eggs, banana pulp, milk and shortening. Stir just until dry ingredients are moistened. Fill well-greased large muffin pans ⅔ full. Bake in a preheated 400-degree oven until done and lightly browned, 20 to 25 minutes. Makes a dozen large muffins.

Variation: Add ½ cup chopped pecans to dry ingredients before adding liquids.

King-Size Onion Buns

1 package hot roll mix	1 T. shortening
¾ c. warm (not hot) water	1 c. finely-chopped onion

Saute onion in shortening until tender and golden. Sprinkle yeast over water; stir to dissolve. Add dry mix and onion. Blend well. Let rise in warm place (85 to 90 degrees) until light and doubled in size, 30 to 60 minutes.

Roll out on floured surface to 15 x 10-inch rectangle. Cut into six 5-inch squares. Moisten edges of dough. Shape into round buns, sealing edges firmly. Place sealed side down on well-greased baking sheet. Flatten slightly. Let rise in warm place until light and doubled in size, 30 to 60 minutes. Bake in a preheated 375-degree oven 20 to 25 minutes, until deep golden brown. Makes six 5½- to 6-inch buns, ideal for hamburgers.

Oatmeal Yeast Rolls

¾ c. milk, scalded
1½ tsp. salt
2 T. shortening
2 T. molasses
2 T. brown sugar
1 c. rolled oats,
    quick or regular

1 package dry yeast
⅓ c. warm water
1 egg, beaten
2¾-3 c. sifted all-purpose
    flour

Combine hot milk, salt, shortening, molasses, brown sugar and oats; stir well. Cool to lukewarm. Dissolve yeast in warm water, not hot. Add softened yeast, egg and 1 cup flour; beat until smooth. Gradually add remaining flour, stirring until well mixed. Turn onto a lightly floured board and knead until elastic, about 10 minutes. Place dough in greased bowl; turn and cover with damp towel. Let rise in warm place until it doubles in size. Punch down.

Shape dough into balls of a size to half-fill greased 2½ x 1¼-inch muffin pans. Cover; let rise until double in size. Bake in a preheated 400-degree oven until done, 15 to 18 minutes. Makes 18 rolls.

Easy Spoon Bread

2 c. waterground
    white cornmeal
1 tsp. salt
2 c. boiling water

¼ c. butter, cut up
1½ c. milk
3 large eggs,
    separated

Using a medium mixing bowl, stir together cornmeal, salt, water and butter until butter melts. Add milk; beat with a whisk until smooth. Using a small mixing bowl, beat egg whites until stiff. Beat yolks in another small bowl; stir into cornmeal mixture.

Fold in egg whites; disregard small patches of white that do not fold in. Turn into a buttered 2-quart souffle dish. Bake in a preheated 375-degree oven until puffed and brown, about 1 hour. Serve at once, with lots of butter. Serves 6 to 8.

Good Summer Loafing

1 long loaf sour	1 tsp. paprika
French bread	½ tsp. oregano
½ c. butter	½ tsp. garlic powder
1 8-oz. package cream cheese	8 slices boiled or baked ham
½ c. shredded Parmesan cheese	2 large tomatoes

Slice loaf through the middle lengthwise. Beat together cream cheese, butter, Parmesan cheese, paprika, oregano and garlic powder until well blended. Spread about ⅔ of butter mixture on cut surfaces of bread. Arrange ham slices over butter. Slice tomatoes into thick slices. Place tomato slices over ham, then spoon remaining butter mixture into center of tomato slices. Place under broiler, about 3 inches from heat source, for 4 to 5 minutes, until bread is warmed through and cheese mixture is bubbly and browned. Serves 6 to 8.

Buttermilk Cheese Bread

1 T. dry yeast	1½ c. buttermilk
¼ c. warm water	2 T. salad oil
2 T. sugar	2 tsp. salt
¼ tsp. powdered basil	4½ c. sifted flour
¼ tsp. powdered oregano	⅔ c. grated Parmesan cheese

Soften yeast in warm water with 1 tablespoon sugar, basil and oregano. Let stand until bubbly, about 20 to 25 minutes.

Meanwhile, heat buttermilk to lukewarm. When yeast is bubbly, add buttermilk, remaining tablespoon sugar, oil and salt. Add flour, a cup at a time, beating thoroughly after each addition. The first 3 cups of flour may be added in the electric mixer; add the last 1½ cups flour, and the cheese, mixing in by hand with a spoon.

Turn into well-greased 2-quart casserole. Brush top lightly with melted butter or oil and cover with a clean cloth and let rise in a warm place until doubled, about 1 hour.

Bake below oven center at 350 degrees (preheated oven) for about 55 minutes, or until loaf is well browned and sounds hollow when you tap the crust. Turn out onto wire rack to cool.

Swiss Cheese Bread

2 packages yeast
½ c. warm water
1 c. shredded Swiss cheese
¼ c. oil
2 T. sugar

¾ c. milk, warmed
5 c. sifted all-purpose
flour
3 eggs
Melted butter

Soften yeast in water. Measure cheese, oil, sugar and salt into large bowl. Stir in milk until sugar dissolves. Beat in 1 cup flour until smooth. Blend in yeast and eggs. Stir in enough flour to make a moderately stiff dough. Turn onto a lightly-floured surface and knead until smooth and satiny, about 20 minutes. Shape into ball and place in lightly-greased bowl, turning to grease all sides. Cover and let rise in warm place (80 to 85 degrees) until doubled, about 1½ hours.

Punch down. Divide dough in half; cover and let rest 10 minutes. Shape dough into balls; place in two greased 1½-quart round casseroles. Brush tops with melted butter. Let rise until doubled, about 1 hour. Bake in a preheated 425-degree oven 25 to 30 minutes, or until done. Remove immediately from casseroles and brush with butter. Cool on wire racks before cutting.

Ripe Olive Snack Bread

1½ c. pitted ripe olives
1½ c. sliced onions
2 T. butter or margarine
2 c. packaged biscuit mix

1 medium tomato, peeled
1½ c. shredded Swiss
cheese
3 T. chopped parsley

Preheat oven to 425 degrees. Drain olives; cut in wedges. Melt butter, add onions and cook until tender but not browned. Prepare biscuit mix according to package directions. Knead lightly, then roll into a thin rectangle about 9 x 12 inches on a greased baking sheet. Bake for 5 minutes.

Meanwhile, peel tomato and cut into thin wedges. Remove bread from oven. Spread cooked onions over bread, then sprinkle with ripe olives and cheese. Arrange tomato wedges over top and sprinkle lightly with parsley. Return to oven and bake about 15 minutes longer. Serve hot, cut into squares.

Paula's German Pancake

4 T. butter	½ tsp. salt
½ c. flour	4 eggs
½ c. evaporated milk	

Melt butter in 10-inch oven-proof skillet. Combine flour, milk and salt in mixing bowl. Add eggs, one at a time, whipping after each addition. Pour egg mixture into skillet and cook over medium heat until bottom is golden brown. Loosen from bottom of pan. Make a criss-cross slash with knife through pancake and place in a preheated 400-degree oven. Bake until puffed and golden brown, 12 to 15 minutes. Serve pancake with lemon slices, powdered sugar and syrup. Serves 2, generously.

Swedish Pancakes

2 eggs, beaten	1 c. sifted all-purpose flour
2 c. milk	¼ tsp. salt
2 T. melted butter	¼ tsp. sugar

Combine eggs, milk and butter and beat well. Add sifted dry ingredients gradually, beating constantly during addition. Pour 3 tablespoons batter onto hot griddle for each cake and bake until top is bubbly and edges look cooked. Turn and cook until remaining side is brown. Fill with jelly, preserves or fruit, roll and dust with powdered sugar. Or, if preferred, serve plain with butter and powdered sugar or syrup. Makes about 16 to 18 medium pancakes.

Desserts and Sweets

Cakes

Sachertorte probably is one of the most controversial cakes in the world. Basically, it is a chocolate butter sponge cake that's filled and/or glazed on the top and sides with apricot preserves before it's frosted with bitter-sweet chocolate. The controversy concerns whether or not the original cake was split and filled with apricot preserves.

In this recipe it is not split and filled. However, if you wish to make it that way, simply be sure the cake is cooled completely before you split it.

Sachertorte

¾ c. butter or margarine
1 tsp. vanilla
¾ c. sugar
6 eggs, separated
6 1-oz. squares semi-sweet
   chocolate, melted, cooled
1 c. sifted cake flour
½ c. apricot preserves,
   heated and sieved

⅓ c. toasted filberts,
   ground or grated

Chocolate Glaze
½ c. heavy cream, whipped
1 T. powdered sugar
½ c. toasted filberts,
   chopped

(To toast filberts, spread in a shallow pan and bake in a 400-degree oven 10 to 15 minutes, stirring occasionally.)

Cream butter, vanilla and ½ cup sugar until light and fluffy. Beat in egg yolks, one at a time. Blend in cooled chocolate. Gently stir in flour and ground filberts. Beat egg whites until foamy; gradually add remaining ¼ cup sugar, beating until stiff but not dry. Blend about ¼ of the egg whites into the chocolate mixture, then gently fold in remaining egg whites. Pour batter into a greased 8-inch springform pan. Bake in a preheated 325-degree oven 1 hour and 10 minutes, or until cake tests done. Cool. Remove from pan.

Spread cake with apricot preserves; let stand 1 hour. Frost the top and sides of the cake with Chocolate Glaze. Fold powdered sugar and chopped filberts into whipped cream and serve with the cake.

Chocolate Glaze: Melt 6 1-ounce squares of semi-sweet chocolate (or 1 6-ounce package of semi-sweet chocolate pieces) in top of double boiler over hot water. Remove from heat; stir in 2 tablespoons butter until melted. Add 1 tablespoon hot water and 1 tablespoon light corn syrup. Blend well.

It is important to have all ingredients at room temperature for this recipe.

Apricot Brandy Pound Cake

4¾ c. cake flour	10 eggs
2 c. butter	2 T. apricot brandy
2 c. granulated sugar	

Sift flour once, then measure and sift four times. Cream butter well, adding sugar gradually and creaming until light and fluffy. Add eggs, two at a time, and beat well after each addition. Add brandy. Gradually stir in flour and beat until smooth. Line three standard loaf pans with waxed paper; pour batter into pans and bake in a preheated 300-degree oven an hour and 15 minutes.

Almond-Mace Cake

2 c. sifted all-purpose flour	½ c. butter or margarine
1 tsp. double-acting baking powder	1 c. sugar
	3 eggs
¾ tsp. mace	⅔ c. milk
¼ tsp. salt	Almond-Mace Cream Frosting

Sift together flour and baking powder. Set aside. Add mace and salt to butter and mix well. Gradually cream in sugar. Beat in eggs, one at a time. Add flour mixture alternately with milk. Beat batter ½ minute. Pour into 2 well-greased and lightly-floured 9-inch round layer cake pans and bake in a preheated 350-degree oven for 25 minutes, or until cake tests done. Remove from oven. Cool in pans 10 minutes. Turn out onto wire racks to cool completely. Spread frosting between layers and over top and sides.

Almond-Mace Cream Frosting

⅛ tsp. salt
2 egg whites
¾ c. sugar
½ c. heavy cream, whipped
½ c. heavy cream, whipped
almonds
½ tsp. mace
¼ tsp. almond extract

Add salt to egg whites and beat until they stand in stiff peaks. Gradually beat in sugar. Fold in cream, almonds, mace and almond extract. Spread between cake layers and over top and sides of cake.

Almond Carrot Cake

1 c. slivered almonds
1 8-oz. can crushed pineapple, well drained
2 c. grated carrots
1 c. flaked coconut
1 c. all-purpose flour
1 c. whole wheat flour
1½ c. sugar
1 tsp. baking soda
2 tsp. cinnamon
½ tsp. nutmeg
½ tsp. salt
3 eggs
½ c. salad oil
¾ c. buttermilk
2 tsp. vanilla
Buttermilk Glaze

Combine almonds, pineapple, carrots and coconut. Mix flours, sugar, soda, spices and salt. Beat eggs with oil, buttermilk and vanilla in large mixing bowl. Add flour mixture all at once and stir just until combined. Add almond mixture and mix. Pour into greased and floured 13 x 9 x 2-inch pan. Bake in a preheated 350-degree oven for about 45 minutes, or until pick inserted in center comes out dry.

While cake bakes, prepare glaze. Prick hot baked cake with a fork at about ½-inch intervals. Slowly pour glaze over cake. Serves 16.

Buttermilk Glaze: Combine ⅔ cup sugar, ¼ teaspoon baking soda, ⅓ cup buttermilk, ⅓ cup butter or margarine and ½ teaspoon vanilla in a saucepan. Bring to boil and boil gently 5 minutes.

Walnut Carrot Cake

2 c. sifted all-purpose flour	½ tsp. nutmeg
1 c. granulated sugar	½ tsp. ginger
1 T. cocoa	½ c. soft shortening
1 tsp. salt	2 eggs
1 tsp. baking powder	2 c. finely-grated raw carrot
2 tsp. soda	⅓ c. water
1 tsp. cinnamon	1 c. walnuts, coarsely chopped

Resift flour with sugar, cocoa, salt, baking powder, soda and spices. Add shortening, eggs, carrots and water and blend until moistened. Beat one minute at moderate speed on mixer (or 150 strokes by hand). Stir in walnuts. Turn into greased 9-inch tube pan and bake in a preheated 325-degree oven for about an hour. Let stand 5 minutes, then turn out onto wire rack to cool. Serve plain or with a light sifting of powdered sugar over the top.

Chocolate Pastry Cake Continental

5 squares unsweetened chocolate	½ tsp. salt
½ c. water	½ c. butter
1¼ c. granulated sugar	1 3-oz. package cream cheese
¼ tsp. cinnamon	¼ c. unsifted powdered sugar
2 tsp. vanilla	2 tsp. dark rum
2 c. unsifted all-purpose flour	1 c. whipping cream

Melt chocolate in water in small saucepan over low heat, stirring constantly. Add granulated sugar and cinnamon. Cook and stir until smooth. Remove from heat. Stir in vanilla. Cool.

Combine flour and salt; cut in butter until mixture is the size of peas. Stir in ¾ cup plus 2 tablespoons of the cooled chocolate mixture; divide into four parts. Press or spread each part over the bottom of each of four inverted 8- or 9-inch layer pans to within ¼ inch or so of edges. Bake in a preheated 425-degree oven for 6 to 8 minutes, or until pastry is almost firm. Remove from oven. If pastry has spread over edges of pans, trim with a sharp knife. Cool layers just until firm, about 5 minutes. Then carefully run knife under layers to loosen them from pans. Place on rack to cool thoroughly.

Beat cream cheese until smooth and fluffy. Add powdered sugar. Beat thoroughly. Gradually blend in remaining chocolate mixture; then stir in the rum. Whip cream just until soft peaks form; fold into chocolate mixture. Spread between layers and over top of cake. Chill at least 8 hours, or overnight. Garnish with toasted slivered almonds and candied cherries, if desired. Serves 10 to 12.

Easter Bunny Cake

1¼ c. sifted all-purpose flour	3 egg yolks
1¼ tsp. baking powder	¼ c. sugar
1 tsp. salt	2 tsp. vanilla
1 c. semi-sweet chocolate	½ c. milk
morsels	3 egg whites
⅔ c. shortening	¼ c. sugar

Preheat oven to 325 degrees. Sift together flour, baking powder and salt; set aside. Melt chocolate over hot (not boiling) water. Remove from heat and add shortening and stir until melted. Beat egg yolks until thick and lemon colored. Gradually beat in ¼ cup sugar and vanilla. Stir in chocolate mixture and milk; beat well. Stir in flour mixture. Beat egg whites until stiff but not dry. Gradually beat in ¼ cup sugar and continue beating until stiff and glossy. Fold egg whites into chocolate mixture. Pour into two greased and floured 8-inch round layer cake pans. Bake 25 to 30 minutes. Cool for 10 minutes; remove from pans to racks and cool completely.

From one layer, cut an inner circle that is 5 inches in diameter. This is the head. From the remaining 2-inch (about) rim section, cut four pieces that are 2 inches wide by 3 inches long. These are the bunny's arms and legs. The remainder is for sampling.

From the other layer, cut a 5¼ x 5¼-inch square. This is the body. The four remaining pieces form the ears. Match straight side of one piece with straight side of another to form one ear. Repeat with other two pieces to make second ear.

Place the body of the bunny on a large tray. Put the head just above and touching the body. Arrange arms and legs on either side of the body and add ears to each side of head.

To make frosting easier, put cake in freezer for 15 minutes before frosting. Frost and decorate with candied cherries and marshmallow slices to make eyes, nose and mouth.

Butterscotch-Nut Frosting

1 c. butterscotch flavored morsels	1 c. evaporated milk
	1 c. finely-chopped nuts
1 c. sugar	1 c. flaked coconut

Combine butterscotch morsels, sugar and evaporated milk in a 2-quart saucepan. Bring to a full boil over moderate heat, stirring constantly. Boil 8 minutes, stirring constantly. Remove from heat. Stir in chopped nuts and coconut. Chill until cool enough to spread.

Vermont Gingerbread

¼ c. soft butter	2⅓ c. sifted flour
⅓ c. brown sugar	1 tsp. soda
1 egg	1 tsp. ginger
1 c. maple and cane syrup	1 tsp. cinnamon
1 c. sour cream	1 tsp. salt

Cream butter and sugar; beat in egg. Blend in syrup and sour cream. Sift together flour, soda, spices and salt; blend into first mixture. Pour into a greased and floured 9 x 13-inch baking pan. Bake 30 minutes in a preheated 350-degree oven. Remove from oven and cool 5 minutes before removing from pan. Serve warm, topped with whipped cream sweetened with syrup. Serves 12 to 14.

German Chocolate Cake

1 package sweet cooking	1 tsp. vanilla
chocolate	2½ c. sifted cake flour
½ c. boiling water	1 tsp. soda
½ c. butter or margarine	½ tsp. salt
2 c. sugar	1 c. buttermilk
4 egg yolks, unbeaten	4 egg whites, stiffly beaten

Melt chocolate in ½ cup boiling water; cool. Cream butter and sugar until light and fluffy. Add egg yolks, one at a time, beating after each. Add vanilla and melted chocolate and mix until blended. Sift flour with soda and salt. Add sifted dry ingredients alternately with buttermilk, beating after each addition until batter is smooth. Fold in stiffly beaten egg whites. Pour batter into 3 9-inch layer pans that have been lined on the bottoms with paper. Bake in a preheated 350-degree oven for 35 to 40 minutes. Cool. Frost on top and between layers with Coconut-Pecan Frosting. Do not frost sides of cake.

Coconut-Pecan Frosting: Combine 1 cup evaporated milk or half-and-half, 1 cup sugar, 3 egg yolks, ½ pound margarine and 1 teaspoon vanilla in a saucepan. Cook over medium heat 12 minutes, stirring constantly, until thickened. Add 1 can flaked coconut and 1 cup chopped pecans. Beat until cool and spreadable.

Lemon Cake with Yoghurt

3½ c. sifted all-purpose flour	2 c. sugar
3 tsp. baking powder	5 large eggs, well beaten
2 T. grated fresh lemon rind	1½ c. plain yoghurt
1 c. sweet butter	Vanilla Sugar

Sift together flour and baking powder; set aside. Mix lemon rind with butter. Gradually blend in sugar. Beat in eggs, one at a time. Add flour mixture alternately with yoghurt. Turn into a well-greased and lightly-floured 13 x 9-inch pan. Bake in a preheated 350-degree oven 50 minutes, or until cake tester inserted in center comes out clean. Turn out onto a wire rack to cool. Dust top with Vanilla Sugar.

Vanilla Sugar: Soak a 1-inch ball of cotton in 2 teaspoons pure vanilla extract. Place on a piece of foil, slightly cupped. Store at least one week in a tightly-closed can containing 1 pound of powdered sugar.

Creole Pecan Cake

¾ c. butter	¾ c. milk
2 c. sugar	1 tsp. vanilla
3 egg yolks	6 egg whites
3 c. cake flour	1¼ c. chopped pecans
¼ tsp. salt	1 tsp. cinnamon
2 tsp. baking powder	½ tsp. cloves

Cream butter; gradually add 2 cups sugar. Cream together well. Beat in egg yolks. Sift flour three times, the last time with the salt and baking powder. Add to mixture alternately with milk and vanilla. Fold in stiffly beaten egg whites.

Now, divide dough mixture in half. Add chopped pecans to one half of dough. Add cinnamon and cloves to remaining half. Put nut batter in 2 greased and floured 8-inch round cake pans; spice batter in 2 others. Bake in a preheated 375-degree oven 25 to 30 minutes. Frost when cool.

Boiled Brown Sugar Frosting

4 c. brown sugar	2 egg whites,
½ c. water	stiffly beaten
1 tsp. vanilla	Finely-chopped pecans

Boil sugar with water just past the soft ball stage. Beat this mixture into egg whites. Add vanilla. After frosting, sprinkle top and sides of cake with the pecans.

Poppy Seed Cake Supreme

1 1-lb., 2½-oz. yellow cake mix	4 eggs
1 3¾-oz. package instant French vanilla pudding mix	1 c. dairy sour cream
	½ c. buttery flavor oil
	½ c. cream sherry
	⅓ c. poppy seeds

Combine all ingredients in a large mixing bowl, stirring to blend. Beat at medium speed 5 minutes (700 strokes by hand), scraping sides of bowl frequently. Pour into greased 10-inch bundt pan and bake in a preheated 350-degree oven 1 hour. Cool in pan on rack about 15 minutes. Turn out on cake plate; cool completely before cutting.

Potato Chocolate Cake

1 c. hot mashed potatoes	3½ tsp. baking powder
⅔ c. butter	½ tsp. cinnamon
2 c. sugar	¼ tsp. nutmeg
4 eggs	¼ tsp. cloves
2 squares unsweetened chocolate	¼ tsp. mace
or 3½ T. cocoa	½ c. milk
2 c. sifted all-purpose flour	½ c. chopped walnuts

Prepare unseasoned mashed potatoes. Cream butter with sugar until light and fluffy. Add eggs, one at a time, to creamed mixture, beating well after each addition. If using chocolate, melt over hot water. Add mashed potato and melted chocolate and combine. Sift flour, baking powder and spices together (and cocoa, if used). Add sifted dry ingredients alternately with milk, beating smooth after each addition. Stir in walnuts. Divide batter into two greased and floured 9-inch round cake pans. Bake in a preheated 350-degree oven for 35 to 40 minutes, or until cake tests done. Cool on racks and frost as desired.

Raisin Lemon Cake

¾ c. light or dark raisins	2 c. sifted all-purpose flour
1 large lemon	1 tsp. salt
½ c. water	1 tsp. soda
¼ c. slivered blanched almonds	2 eggs
½ c. shortening	¾ c. milk
1½ c. sugar	Lemon Topping

Rinse and drain raisins. Cut lemon into wedges and remove seeds. Put lemon through food chopper, using fine blade. Combine with water and simmer until tender, about 15 minutes. Add raisins and almonds and cool. Cream shortening with sugar. Sift flour with salt and soda. Add to creamed mixture with eggs and milk. Beat 3 minutes on medium speed of mixer, or 450 strokes by hand. Blend in raisin-lemon mixture. Turn into greased 9-inch square, deep baking dish. Bake in a preheated 325-degree oven 55 to 60 minutes. Spoon on Lemon Topping at once and cool in baking dish.

Lemon Topping

2 T. melted butter or margarine	¼ c. light or dark raisins
1 tsp. grated lemon rind	¼ c. slivered blanched almonds
¼ c. lemon juice	¼ c. sugar

Brush melted butter over cake. Combine lemon rind, juice, raisins and almonds and spoon evenly over cake. Sprinkle with sugar.

Fresh Strawberry Sponge Cake

2¼ c. sifted cake flour	¼ c. shortening
2 tsp. double-acting baking powder	1 c. milk
½ tsp. salt	1 tsp. grated lemon rind
4 eggs	1½ c. whipping cream
1⅓ c. sugar	1 qt. fresh strawberries, sliced and sweetened

Measure sifted flour, add baking powder and salt and sift again. Beat eggs until foamy; gradually add sugar, beating until very thick and light in color. Combine shortening and milk and heat until shortening melts. Then add to egg mixture, mixing quickly. Add flour mixture and lemon rind and beat with egg beater only until smooth.

Pour batter into 3 9-inch layer pans, which have been lined on bottoms with paper. Bake in a preheated 375-degree oven 15 minutes, or until top springs back when touched lightly with finger.

Cool cakes right side up in pans; remove from pans. Whip cream until it holds a shape. Sweeten, if desired. Spread some of the whipped cream and some of the sliced berries between layers and over top of cake. Chill until ready to serve. Serves 12 to 15.

Tomato Spice Cake

1 1-lb., 3-oz. package spice cake mix
1 10½-oz. can condensed tomato soup
¼ c. water

Mix cake as directed on package, substituting soup and water for liquid. (Add eggs, if called for.) Bake as directed on package.

Candied Fruit Frosting

1 6½-oz. package fluffy-type frosting mix
¾ c. candied fruit

Prepare frosting as directed on package. Fold candied fruit into ¾ cup frosting; use as filling between layers of cake. Frost cake with remaining icing.

Shake-Up Pudding Cakes

1 egg	2 tsp. baking powder
½ c. milk	½ tsp. salt
½ c. cooking oil	1 c. seedless raisins
1 c. sifted cake flour	Butterscotch, chocolate
¾ c. sugar	or vanilla pudding
¼ c. unsweetened cocoa	

Measure egg, milk and oil into a 1-quart container with a tight cover. Resift flour with sugar, cocoa, baking powder and salt. Add to container, cover tightly and shake about 40 times, until all of dry mixture is moistened. Add raisins and shake 10 times more. Pour into paper-lined cupcake pans, filling ¾ full. Bake in a preheated 375-degree oven 20 minutes. Makes 8 cupcakes.

Scoop a cone-shaped piece from the top of each cupcake and fill with pudding. After filling, insert cake cone and lightly press down.

Italian Cheese Cake

1 lb. ricotta cheese	1 c. heavy cream, whipped
½ c. sugar	¼ c. finely-chopped
4 T. flour	blanched almonds
¼ tsp. salt	¼ c. white raisins
1 tsp. vanilla	¼ c. diced citron
4 eggs, separated	Special Crust

Make Crust. Beat together cheese, sugar, flour, salt and vanilla. Beat in egg yolks, one at a time. Fold in whipped cream. Beat egg whites until stiff; fold them in, and then the almonds, raisins and citron. Pour into crust.

Bake in a preheated 400-degree oven for 5 minutes; lower heat to 325 and bake until golden brown—about 1 hour and 15 minutes. Cool thoroughly. Sides of cake will be higher than the center.

Serve at room temperature; if held, store in refrigerator, but bring to room temperature before serving. There will be dense layer at bottom holding nuts and fruit and a fluffy layer on top.

Special Crust

Stir together 1 cup sifted flour and ¼ cup sugar. Cut in ½ cup butter until blended, then stir in 1 slightly-beaten egg yolk, 1 tablespoon milk *or* Marsala, and ½ teaspoon vanilla. Gather in a ball and divide in half.

Cover and refrigerate half of the dough. Spread remaining half over bottom of a 9-inch springform pan with sides removed. Bake in a preheated 400-degree oven until golden—about 6 minutes; cool. Attach sides of pan to bottom and pat remainder of dough around sides so it comes up about 2 inches. Fill and bake as directed.

Poppy Seed Cheese Cake

¼ c. graham cracker crumbs	6 large eggs, separated
½ tsp. cinnamon	1 c. dairy sour cream
1¼ c. sugar	1½ tsp. vanilla
3 T. flour	⅛ tsp. salt
3 T. poppy seed	½ tsp. cream of tartar
6 3-oz. packages soft	Powdered sugar,
cream cheese	optional

Mix graham cracker crumbs with cinnamon and sprinkle over bottom and sides of a buttered 9-inch spring form pan; set aside.

Combine ¾ cup of the sugar with flour and poppy seed. Add cream cheese and beat until mixture is fluffy and smooth. Beat egg yolks until light and lemon colored. Blend with the cheese mixture; stir in sour cream and vanilla.

Add salt to egg whites and beat until they are foamy. Add cream of tartar and beat until they stand in soft, stiff peaks. Gradually beat in the remaining ½ cup sugar and fold into first mixture.

Turn into prepared spring form. Place on a rack in a larger pan. Pour in hot water, having it come to the top of the rack, yet not touch the cheese cake pan. Bake in a preheated 325-degree oven 1¾ hours, or until cake is firm in center. Turn off heat and let cake cool in oven 1 hour. Remove from oven. Loosen cake from sides of pan with a spatula, but do not remove pan until ready to serve.

Then, serve on a cake plate (with sides of pan removed). Dust top with powdered sugar, if desired.

No-Bake Cheese Cake

Crumb Mixture

3 T. melted butter or margarine	2 T. sugar
¾ c. graham cracker crumbs	¼ tsp. cinnamon
	¼ tsp. nutmeg

Filling

2 T. unflavored gelatin	1 tsp. vanilla
¾ c. sugar	3 c. creamed cottage cheese
2 egg yolks	2 egg whites
1 c. milk	¼ c. sugar
1 tsp. grated lemon rind	1 c. heavy cream, whipped
1 T. fresh lemon juice	

Crumb Mixture: Combine butter, crumbs, sugar and spices. Press ½ cup of the mixture into an 8- or 9-inch springform pan; reserve remainder for top.

Filling: Combine gelatin and sugar in medium saucepan. Beat egg yolks and milk together; stir into gelatin mixture. Place over low heat; stir constantly until gelatin dissolves and mixture thickens slightly, 3 to 5 minutes. Remove from heat; stir in lemon rind and juice and vanilla.

Sieve or beat cottage cheese on high speed of electric mixer until smooth, 3 to 4 minutes; stir into gelatin mixture. Chill, stirring occasionally, until mixture mounds slightly when dropped from a spoon.

Beat egg whites until stiff but not dry; gradually add ¼ cup sugar and beat until very stiff. Fold into gelatin mixture; fold in whipped cream. Turn into prepared pan and sprinkle with reserved crumb mixture. Chill until firm, 3 to 4 hours, at least. Loosen side of pan with sharp knife; release spring form. Serves 12.

Savarin

Baba

½ c. light or dark
   raisins or currants
¼ c. milk
½ cake compressed yeast
2 eggs
1 T. sugar

1 c. sifted all-purpose
   flour
½ tsp. salt
¼ c. soft butter or margarine
   Golden raisins, candied
    cherries and citron

Syrup

3 c. apricot nectar
1½ c. sugar

2 T. lemon juice
2 T. rum

Baba: Rinse, drain and chop raisins. Scald milk and cool to lukewarm. Soften yeast in milk. Beat eggs lightly; sift flour with sugar and salt. Add eggs and flour to yeast and beat until smooth, about 2 minutes. Let rise in warm place until doubled in bulk, about 45 to 60 minutes. Stir dough down. Add raisins and butter and beat 3 minutes, or until well mixed.

Now, spoon into well-greased 9-inch ring mold, filling pan no more than half full. Let rise in warm place until doubled in bulk, about 30 minutes. Bake in a preheated 450-degree oven 10 to 12 minutes. Cool on rack a minute or two before removing from pan.

Place in a large baking dish so baba sits level and pour hot syrup over it gradually. Let stand in syrup 2 or 3 hours, basting occasionally with the syrup in the dish. Decorate with golden raisins, candied cherries and citron. Serve with whipped cream.

Syrup: Combine apricot nectar and sugar; bring to boil. Cook 10 minutes. Remove from heat; add lemon juice and rum.

Pastries

Our pastries include some made with cream puff dough and some made with puff paste.

Beignets Soufflés

Pâté à Choux

1 c. water	1 c. sifted flour
1 tsp. salt	4 eggs
1 tsp. sugar	Deep fat
¼ lb. sweet butter	Powdered sugar

Heat water with salt, sugar and butter, which has been cut into chunks. Bring to a boil just until butter melts (don't let water boil too long or some will evaporate). Off heat, add flour, all at once, beating with a wooden spoon until dough forms a ball in center of pan. Place back on heat for 20 seconds *only*, stirring the while. Remove from heat and add eggs, two at a time, beating to mix thoroughly.

Drop batter, which should be in bits a little bigger than walnuts but smaller than lemons, into deep, hot fat and cook until light brown on all sides, turning now and then.

If they cook too long, the center begins to ooze out. Don't let this happen. Remove from fat, place on absorbent paper to drain and dust with powdered sugar. Serve with fresh strawberries.

Profiteroles au Chocolat

Cream Puffs

1 c. water	¼ lb. sweet butter
½ tsp. salt	1 c. flour
1 T. sugar	4 eggs and 1 yolk

Heat water with salt, sugar and butter, which has been cut in chunks. Bring to boil just until butter melts. Off heat, add flour, all at once, beating with wooden spoon until dough forms a ball in center of pan. Place on heat for 20 seconds *only*, stirring the while. Remove from heat and add the eggs, two by two, beating well and hard after each addition.

Place dough in pastry bag with 1-inch tip and squeeze 1½-inch dollops onto well-greased and floured baking sheet. Paint with beaten egg yolk. Bake in a preheated 400-degree oven 5 to 7 minutes; turn heat to 375 degrees and bake another 15 minutes, until dry and brown. Cool on rack.

Filling

2 c. whipping cream	Cognac or vanilla
Sugar	

Have cream very cold. Beat until fairly thick, then add sugar and flavoring to taste and continue beating until good peaks form. Use to fill puffs, placing in pastry bag with small tip and forcing some into center of each.

Sauce

¼ lb. semi-sweet cooking chocolate	½-¾ c. water Cognac

Put chocolate, water and a little Cognac in a saucepan, bring slowly to a boil and cook until glossy.

Assembly: Dip filled puffs in chocolate sauce. Place on serving dish, piling to resemble a pyramid. Pour remaining sauce over the top.

Note: These may also be filled with a thick pastry cream (Crème Pâtissière).

Cream Horns and Lady Locks are the same thing, really—just different shapes.

Cream Horns and Lady Locks

1 10-oz. package frozen
patty shells*
Lady lock or cream
horn tubes**

1-1½ c. heavy cream
2-3 T. sugar
¼ tsp. vanilla
Sliced strawberries

*Thaw overnight in refrigerator—shells should be chilled but pliable.

**These are metal forms available at baking supply shops, so-called gourmet cookware shops and cookware sections in many department stores. Buy cream horns no smaller than 4½ inches in length.

Roll out patty shells one at a time on a well-floured board or pastry cloth, forming a circle. Turn dough over and trim to 6 inches in diameter. Using a ruler, make marks from edges every ¾ inch. Starting at the outer edge, cut circle into a continuous strip, ¾ inch wide, using the markings as a guide. Unwind strip, taking care not to stretch, and cut in 2 equal pieces. Wrap each strip around a tube, starting at the narrow end and overlapping edges. Dampen and press lightly to seal. Place tubes on their sides on an ungreased baking sheet, about 3 inches apart. Chill 15 minutes. Bake in a pre-heated 400-degree oven 18 to 20 minutes, or until brown. Remove from tube while still hot, using a gentle twisting motion.

Just before serving, combine the cream, sugar and vanilla. Beat until stiff and fill horns or lady locks with a pastry bag and tip, or an iced tea spoon. Use the larger amounts of cream and sugar for filling the lady locks. Garnish with strawberries. Makes 1 dozen.

Napoléons

1 10-oz. package frozen
patty shells
1 c. powdered sugar
¾ tsp. hot water, or so
1 square unsweetened
chocolate, melted

1 package French vanilla
pudding and pie filling
½ tsp. vanilla
¼ tsp. almond extract

Thaw patty shells in refrigerator overnight. Stack and press together two patty shells on a floured board or pastry cloth. Roll into a rectangle. Turn dough over and trim to 5 x 9 inches. Cut into quarters.

Place one inch apart on an ungreased baking sheet. Prick with a fork at about ¼-inch intervals. Chill. Repeat with remaining shells. Bake in a preheated 400-degree oven 12 to 15 minutes, or until golden brown. Cool.

Meanwhile, prepare cooked pudding, using ½ cup less milk than package directions call for and adding extracts. Cool.

To assemble Napoléons, slit baked rectangles in half, lengthwise. Combine powdered sugar and hot water to make a thin glaze. Spread glaze on the tops of eight slit rectangles. Before glaze dries, use a wooden pick and drizzle melted unsweetened chocolate in thin lines the length of the pastry, about ½ inch apart. Draw pick across lines, alternating from side to side, to give a rippled effect.

Spread about 2 tablespoons pudding on slit side of remaining rectangles and stack two high. Top with frosted rectangles. Store in refrigerator. Serve, if possible, within a few hours. Makes 8 Napoleons.

Palmiers

1 10-oz. package frozen patty shells
  Granulated sugar

Defrost patty shells in refrigerator overnight. Stack and press together three patty shells (leaving remaining three in refrigerator) on a floured board or pastry cloth. Roll out into a rectangle. Turn dough over and trim to 7 x 9 inches. Sprinkle heavily with sugar.

Fold 7-inch edges of rectangle inward, to meet at center. Sprinkle heavily with sugar. Fold in half again to resemble a closed book—2¼ x 7 inches. Sprinkle with sugar and press down firmly. Cut crosswise into ½-inch strips, making 14 strips in all.

Place cut side down on an ungreased baking sheet. Bake in a preheated 400-degree oven 8 to 10 minutes, or until lightly browned. Turn over and bake on the other side for 3 to 5 minutes. Repeat with remaining three patty shells. Makes 28 palm leaves.

Cookies

All kinds of cookies are popular, of course, but bar cookies and most made with fruit are excellent "keepers."

Luscious Apricot Bars

⅔ c. dried apricots
½ c. butter or margarine, softened
¼ c. sugar
1 c. flour
½ tsp. baking powder
¼ tsp. salt

½ c. whole bran cereal
1 c. brown sugar
2 eggs
½ tsp. vanilla
½ c. walnuts, coarsely chopped
¼ c. powdered sugar

Rinse apricots, cover with water; boil 10 minutes. Drain, cool and chop.

In a mixer bowl, combine butter, granulated sugar and half of the sifted flour and beat until smooth. Stir in whole bran cereal and spread mixture in bottom of ungreased 8 x 8 x 2-inch baking pan. Bake in a preheated 350-degree oven for 25 minutes, or until lightly browned.

Meanwhile, sift together remaining ½ cup flour, baking powder and salt. Set aside. Combine brown sugar and eggs in mixer bowl and beat well. Add sifted dry ingredients, vanilla, walnuts and apricots and stir well to mix. Spread this mixture over baked layer in pan. Return to 350-degree oven for 35 minutes, or until lightly browned. Cool and cut into 2 x 1-inch bars. Roll in powdered sugar. Makes 32 bars.

Mrs. Crist's Apple Cookies

½ c. shortening
1 c. sugar
1 egg
1 tsp. vanilla
2 c. flour
2 tsp. baking powder
1 tsp. salt

1 tsp. cinnamon
1 tsp. nutmeg
½ tsp. soda
⅔ c. milk
1½ c. Washington apples, peeled and grated raw
1 c. chopped nuts, optional

Cream shortening and sugar; add egg. Add all dry ingredients alternately with milk. Fold in grated apple and nuts last. Pour into sheet cake or jelly roll pan that has been greased and floured. Spread to edge of pan. Bake in a preheated 325-degree oven for 25 minutes. Cut in squares or bars and roll in powdered sugar.

Molasses Oatmeal Lace Thins

½ c. butter	½ tsp. baking powder
¼ c. milk	½ tsp. salt
¼ c. unsulphured molasses	1 c. sugar
1 tsp. vanilla	1 c. rolled oats
¾ c. sifted all-purpose flour	1 c. finely-chopped nuts

Melt butter in large saucepan. Remove from heat; stir in milk, molasses and vanilla. Sift in flour, baking powder, salt and sugar; mix well. Stir in oats and chopped nuts. Drop by level teaspoonfuls 2 inches apart on greased baking sheets. Bake in a preheated 375-degree oven 6 to 8 minutes. Cool about 1 minute; remove from pan; cool on racks. Makes about 4 dozen.

Crisp Peanut Butter Cookies

1 c. margarine	1 tsp. vanilla
1 c. peanut butter	2½ c. sifted flour
1 c. sugar	1 tsp. baking powder
1 c. brown sugar	1 tsp. soda
2 eggs, beaten	1 tsp. salt

Stir together margarine, peanut butter and sugars until well blended. Beat in eggs and vanilla. Sift together flour, baking powder, soda and salt over sugar mixture. Stir until well blended. If necessary, chill dough until it can be handled easily. Shape into 1-inch balls. Place about 2 inches apart on greased baking sheet. Flatten with floured bottom of a glass or with a floured fork, making criss-cross pattern. Bake in a preheated 350-degree oven 12 to 15 minutes, or until lightly browned. Makes 6 dozen cookies.

Persimmon Cookies

¼ c. butter	2 c. flour
¼ c. lard	¾ tsp. baking powder
¾ c. brown sugar	1 tsp. cinnamon
1 egg	¾ tsp. mace
3 persimmons	½ tsp. ground cloves
Juice of one large lemon	½ tsp. ground ginger
Grated rind of one lemon	½ tsp. salt
¾ tsp. baking soda	1 c. seedless raisins, chopped

Keep persimmons until they are very ripe and soft. Cut fruit in halves and scrape out pulp with a teaspoon. Puree in blender or mash with a fork and pass through a coarse sieve. Add lemon juice and rind and baking soda to fruit.

Cream together butter and lard until light, then gradually add sugar, beating well after each addition. Add egg and beat well. Fold fruit mixture into this. Sift together flour, baking powder and spices and add in small portions, beating well after each addition. Fold in chopped raisins and drop by tablespoons onto a lightly-greased cookie sheet. Bake in a preheated 425-degree oven for 10 minutes, or until cookies are golden brown. Remove to a wire rack and cool.

The little cookies known as Mexican Wedding Cakes really are:

Polvorones

½ c. butter	Pinch salt
2 T. sugar	1 c. flour
1 tsp. vanilla	1 c. finely-chopped nuts

Cream butter and sugar. Add vanilla and salt. Sift flour and measure. Add to butter mixture. Add nuts and blend well. Shape into small balls and place on a lightly-greased baking sheet. Bake in a 400-degree oven for 10 minutes. Cool 3 minutes, then roll immediately in sifted powdered sugar. When cool, again roll in sugar. Makes about 2½ dozen cookies.

Sherry Shortbread Cookies

1 c. soft butter
¾ c. sugar
½ tsp. almond extract
2 tsp. vanilla
½ tsp. grated orange
   or lemon rind

1 egg, well beaten
3 c. sifted all-purpose
   flour
½ tsp. baking powder
1 tsp. salt
¼ c. California sherry

Cream butter, sugar, almond extract, vanilla and rind together until very light and fluffy. Beat in egg. Resift flour with baking powder and salt. Add to creamed mixture alternately with sherry, mixing until well blended. Cover and chill dough several hours or overnight. Roll small portions at a time on a lightly-floured board, about ⅛ inch thick. Cut with shaped cutters. Lift carefully to ungreased baking sheets. Bake in a preheated 425-degree oven just until very lightly browned, about 8 to 10 minutes. Cool before storing in an airtight container. Makes about 5 dozen cookies.

Pies

Probably the most popular pie recipe to appear in years has been this one:

Grasshopper Pie

2 T. butter
14 Hydrox cookies,
   crushed
24 large marshmallows

½ c. milk
4 T. green creme de menthe
2 T. white creme de cacao
1 c. whipping cream

Melt butter and stir into crushed cookies. Press mixture into an 8-inch pie tin and use for crust.

Melt marshmallows in the milk. Stir in creme de menthe and creme de cacao. Whip cream and fold into marshmallow mixture. Pour all into the pie shell and freeze. Serve while still frozen.

Kahlua Black Russian Pie

⅓ c. Kahlua
2 T. unflavored gelatin
½ c. milk, heated
    to boiling

2 eggs
½ c. sugar
⅔ c. vodka
1½ c. whipping cream

Put first three ingredients into blender container; cover and process at "low" until gelatin is dissolved. Remove feeder cap, add eggs, sugar and vodka. Pour into large bowl and chill 15 minutes, or until slightly thickened. Stir occasionally to keep smooth. Whip cream until soft peaks form. Fold gelatin mixture and cream together thoroughly. Pour into crumb crust and chill until set, about 1 hour.

Kahlua Crumb Crust

16 graham crackers *or*
    20 chocolate wafers

¼ c. melted butter
2 T. Kahlua

Break half of crackers or wafers into blender container; cover and process at high speed until crumbed. Empty into 9-inch pie pan and repeat with other half. Add butter and Kahlua to crumbs, mixing well. Press into bottom and sides of pan. Cool at least 30 minutes before filling. Makes 1 9-inch crust.

Pecan Sour Cream Pie

Pastry for
    one-crust pie
1 c. broken pecans
2 tsp. flour
¼ tsp. cinnamon

¼ tsp. cloves
1 c. dairy sour cream
2 eggs
1 c. sugar
½ tsp. grated lemon rind

Prepare pastry for pie shell and line pie plate with it; sprinkle with pecans. Make custard by mixing flour, cinnamon, cloves and a little sour cream, gradually adding balance of sour cream. Stir in well-beaten eggs, sugar and lemon rind. Pour mixture into pie shell and place in a preheated 450-degree oven, lowering temperature control immediately to 325 degrees. Bake until filling is firm, about 40 minutes. Serve either warm or cold, with whipped cream.

Pineapple-Rhubarb Pie

Pastry for two-crust 9-inch pie

Filling

3 T. cornstarch
½ c. brown sugar
¼ tsp. salt

2 c. diced rhubarb
1 20-oz. can crushed
   pineapple

Topping

¼ c. slightly softened
   butter

3 T. flour
3 T. brown sugar

Line a 9-inch pie pan with half of pastry. Combine cornstarch, the ½ cup brown sugar and the salt, toss with rhubarb and crushed pineapple and place in pastry-lined pan. Blend ingredients for Topping and sprinkle over filling. Make a lattice-work top crust and bake the pie in a preheated 425-degree oven for 40 to 45 minutes, until nicely browned.

Pumpkin Ice Cream Pie

1 9- or 10-inch graham
   cracker crumb crust
1 c. mashed, cooked or
   canned pumpkin
½ c. brown sugar

1 T. pumpkin pie spice
1 qt. vanilla ice cream,
   softened
1 c. whipping cream, whipped
16 pecan halves

Put graham cracker crust in freezer to chill. Blend together pumpkin, sugar, salt and pie spice. Fold in softened ice cream. Fill crust and place in freezer to refreeze. Make a border around edge with whipped cream. Garnish with pecan halves.

Sour Cream-Lemon-Berry Pie

2 c. fresh strawberries
1 c. sugar
¼ tsp. salt
3 T. cornstarch
2 eggs
½ c. milk
¼ c. butter

2 tsp. grated
   lemon rind
1 c. sour cream
1 baked, cooled 9-inch
   pie shell
Strawberry or mint leaves
   for decoration

Rinse and hull berries; save 6 for decoration. Slice remaining berries and combine with 1 tablespoon of the sugar; set aside. Mix together remaining sugar, salt and cornstarch in saucepan. Beat eggs, add milk; stir into dry ingredients. Add lemon rind and juice and the butter. Cook and stir over moderate heat until mixture thickens, 5 to 10 minutes. Remove from heat, cool, then chill well. Fold in 1 cup sour cream. Arrange sliced berries in even layer in bottom of pie shell. Top with sour cream filling. Chill several hours. Decorate top with small swirls of sour cream, reserved berries and leaves.

Spiced Cream-Apple Pie

½ c. granulated sugar
½ c. brown sugar
¼ c. flour
¼ tsp. salt
½ tsp. nutmeg
¾ tsp. ginger
⅛ tsp. cloves
6 c. sliced raw pie apples
½ c. heavy cream
1 unbaked 9-inch pie shell
1 T. brown sugar

Combine sugars, flour, salt and spices. Mix well with sliced apples. Turn into the unbaked pie crust. Pour heavy cream over top and sprinkle with the 1 tablespoon brown sugar. Bake in a preheated 400-degree oven 50 to 60 minutes, or until crust has browned and apples have formed a slightly brown glaze over the top. Cool before serving.

Glazed Fresh Strawberry Pie

1 qt. firm, ripe, fresh strawberries
2 T. cornstarch
½ c. water
1 T. fresh lemon juice
¼ tsp. salt
1 c. sugar
¼ tsp. vanilla
9-inch baked pie crust
½ c. heavy cream, whipped
1 T. sugar

Wash and cap strawberries. Mix half the berries with water, cornstarch, lemon juice, salt and sugar; crush. Stir and cook until thick; cool. Turn remaining berries into cold pie shell. Cover with the cold cooked mixture; chill. Sweeten whipped cream with 1 tablespoon sugar and garnish pie as desired with it just before serving.

Golden Summer Pie

3-4 fresh nectarines
¾ c. sugar
¼ tsp. salt
1 T. plain gelatin
3 eggs, separated
½ c. orange juice

2 T. lemon juice
Yellow food coloring
¼ tsp. cream of tartar
½ c. whipping cream
1 baked, cooled 9-inch
pastry shell

Chop enough nectarines to make 2 cups; save remainder for garnish. Combine ½ cup sugar, salt and gelatin in saucepan. Beat egg yolks with orange and lemon juices; stir into gelatin mixture. Cook, stirring constantly, over medium heat until mixture comes just to a boil. Remove from heat and fold in chopped nectarines and a few drops of food coloring, if desired. Chill, stirring occasionally, until partially set.

Beat egg whites until foamy; add cream of tartar and continue beating until soft peaks form. Gradually add remaining ¼ cup sugar and beat until stiff peaks form. Whip cream until thick. Fold egg whites and cream into nectarine mixture; spoon into pastry shell. Garnish with thin nectarine slices and additional cream, if desired. Chill until set. Serves 6 to 8.

Devonshire Apricot Cream Tarts

Pastry for a two-crust pie
4 c. fresh apricots
1 c. sugar
3 T. cornstarch

1 T. lemon juice
2-2½ c. heavy cream patissiere,
or 1 package vanilla
pudding mix

Prepare pastry. Roll out to fit 4 large scallop shells (tart or small pie pan may be used); crimp edges and prick bottoms with tines of a fork. Bake in a preheated 400-degree oven until golden. Cool.

Crush 2 cups of the fruit and blend with sugar and cornstarch in a saucepan. Cook, stirring, until thickened. Add lemon juice and cool. Fold in creme patissiere or prepared vanilla pudding and divide mixture among the 4 shells. Peel and halve remaining apricots and use to garnish tarts, along with:

Mock Devonshire Cream

Whip 3 ounces cream cheese with ¼ cup sugar and ½ teaspoon salt until light and fluffy. Then whip ½ pint heavy cream and fold into cream cheese mixture. Use as topping for tarts.

Other

And then, of course, there are the "other" desserts, ranging from puddings through molds, cold and hot soufflés, jellies and blintzes.

Snow Eggs in Praline Crème

1 qt. milk	3 T. cornstarch
5 eggs	½ tsp. salt
⅛ tsp. salt	½ c. Meloso cream sherry
¼ tsp. cream of tartar	½ c. finely-crushed almond
1 c. sugar, divided	or cashew brittle
¼ tsp. almond extract	

Heat milk in a wide shallow pan. Separate 4 eggs and beat whites with ⅛ teaspoon salt and cream of tartar until nearly stiff. Gradually beat in ¼ cup sugar, adding a tablespoon at a time. Beat in almond extract. Using 2 tablespoons, shape mixture into ovals and drop into pan with hot milk. Poach meringues for 1 minute, then turn over carefully and poach second side for 2 minutes. Remove with slotted spoon and drain on paper towels in flat baking pan.

Thoroughly blend remaining ¾ cup sugar with cornstarch and ½ teaspoon salt in top of double boiler. Stir in hot milk and cook over direct heat, stirring constantly, until mixture boils and thickens. Set off heat. Beat 1 whole egg with the 4 yolks. Stir hot mixture into eggs, then set over hot water and cook about 5 minutes, stirring constantly until thickened. Remove from heat and blend in sherry and about ¾ of the crushed brittle. Chill thoroughly.

Pour into a shallow bowl to serve, and top with poached meringues. Sprinkle meringues with reserved crushed brittle. Serves 8.

If you want to make a trifle absolutely perfectly, you should start with homemade ladyfingers. Of course, you don't have to . . .

Chocolate English Trifle

Ladyfingers

3 egg whites	6 T. sugar
¼ tsp. cream of tartar	1 tsp. vanilla
3 T. sugar	½ c. sifted cake flour
3 egg yolks	⅓ c. powdered sugar

Preheat oven to 300 degrees. Generously grease and flour two baking sheets. Beat egg whites with cream of tartar until foamy. Gradually add 3 tablespoons sugar and beat until stiff peaks form. Using another bowl, beat egg yolks slightly; gradually add 6 tablespoons sugar. Continue beating at medium speed until thick and lemon colored, about 2 minutes; add vanilla.

Place ¼ beaten egg whites on top of yolk mixture and sprinkle with 2 tablespoons flour; carefully fold in with rubber scraper. Repeat this procedure 3 times, folding just until mixture is blended. (Over folding deflates batter.) Drop from a tablespoon onto baking sheets, shaping into oval fingers 3 inches long and 1 inch wide. Just before baking, sift powdered sugar generously over fingers. (Extra sugar on baking sheet will not interfere with baking.) Bake about 18 to 20 minutes, or until edges are lightly browned. Makes 24 to 30 ladyfingers.

Chocolate Filling

⅓ c. sugar
¼ tsp. salt
3 T. cornstarch
2¼ c. milk
1 egg, well beaten

⅔ c. canned chocolate
  flavor syrup
1 T. butter
1 tsp. vanilla

Combine sugar, salt and cornstarch in saucepan; gradually stir in milk, chocolate syrup and egg. Cook over medium heat, stirring constantly, until mixture boils. Continue cooking 1 minute. Remove from heat; blend in butter and vanilla. Pour into bowl; press plastic wrap directly onto filling. Cool to room temperature.

Assembling

24 ladyfingers
  Cooled Chocolate Filling
½ c. apricot preserves
3 T. light rum

½ c. whipping cream
2 T. powdered sugar
¼ c. toasted slivered
  almonds

Combine apricot preserves and 2 tablespoons rum. Spread flat side of each ladyfinger with mixture. Put 8 to 10 ladyfingers together, sandwich style. Arrange on bottom of 1½-quart glass serving bowl or suitable container. Place a vertical layer of single ladyfingers around side of bowl, preserve side facing inward.

Spoon half of cooled chocolate filling into lined dish. Arrange single layer of ladyfingers on filling; sprinkle with 1 tablespoon rum. Top with remaining chocolate filling. Cover; refrigerate several hours. Just before serving, whip cream with powdered sugar until stiff. Decorate top of filling. Garnish with almonds. Serves 10 to 12.

Cinnamon Rhubarb Pudding

4 c. thinly-sliced
  fresh rhubarb
1 c. sugar
1½ tsp. cornstarch
1 tsp. cinnamon

⅛ tsp. salt
2 T. butter or
  margarine
Cottage Pudding Batter
Whipped cream, optional

Turn rhubarb into a buttered 6-cup casserole. Combine sugar, cornstarch, cinnamon and salt; sprinkle over rhubarb. Dot with 2 tablespoons butter. Top with Cottage Pudding Batter.

Cottage Pudding Batter

⅔ c. sugar
⅓ c. shortening
1 large egg
½ tsp. salt

1¼ c. sifted all-purpose
flour
2 tsp. baking powder
¼ c. milk

Gradually blend sugar with shortening. Beat in egg. Sift together flour, salt and baking powder; add alternately with milk. Beat batter ½ minute. Pour over rhubarb, being sure the entire surface is covered. Bake in a preheated 350-degree oven 1½ hours, or until cake tester inserted in center comes out clean. Serve warm or cold, topped with whipped cream, if desired. Serves 6.

Sherried Steamed Carrot Pudding

½ c. shortening
1 c. sugar
2 eggs
1 c. finely-shredded
raw carrot
1 c. fine gingersnap crumbs
2¼ c. sifted all-purpose
flour
½ tsp. soda

1 tsp. salt
1 tsp. baking powder
1 tsp. cinnamon
½ c. milk
½ c. cream sherry
1 c. diced mixed
candied fruits
½ c. raisins
½ c. chopped nuts

Cream shortening, sugar and eggs together. Add carrot and gingersnap crumbs. Resift flour with soda, salt, baking powder and cinnamon. Add to creamed mixture alternately with milk and sherry. Stir in fruits and nuts. Turn into greased and floured molds, filling about ⅔ full. Cover closely with foil, if molds do not have tight-fitting lids. Place in large kettle with boiling water to come to half the depth of the molds. Steam for 1 to 2½ hours, depending on size. Serve warm.

This amount will fill 2 1-quart molds, or any assortment of sizes with that total capacity. Serves 10 to 12.

Note: Steam ahead and reheat by steaming or covered in oven, if desired.

Sherried Angel Custard

12 strips angel food cake	¼ c. sugar
¼ c. sherry	1 T. cornstarch
2 T. strawberry jam	½ tsp. salt
2 c. milk	3 eggs

Sprinkle cake strips with 2 tablespoons of the wine and spread lightly with jam. Arrange in shallow serving bowl. Scald milk in top of double boiler. Blend sugar, cornstarch and salt well. Stir slowly into hot milk and cook and stir until mixture reaches boiling. Blend about ¼ of the mixture into lightly-beaten eggs. Stir egg mixture into remaining milk mixture, place over hot water and cook, stirring constantly, until thickened. Remove from heat and cool to lukewarm. Stir in remaining sherry and pour custard carefully over cake. Chill several hours or overnight. Top with whipped cream and additional jam, if desired. Serves 6.

Eggnog Flan

Eggnog Crust	2 T. finely-chopped
1 T. unflavored gelatin	preserved ginger
¼ c. cold water	½ c. chopped glace cherries
1¾ c. eggnog	Additional whipped cream
⅛ tsp. salt	for garnish
½ tsp. rum extract	Glace cherries and candied
1 c. whipping cream	pineapple for garnish

Bake and cool Eggnog Crust. Soften gelatin in cold water; dissolve over hot water. Warm 1 cup eggnog to below simmering. Stir in salt and dissolved gelatin. Stir in remaining eggnog and rum extract. Cool until mixture begins to thicken and jell. Beat cream until stiff. Fold cream, ginger and chopped cherries into gelatin. Chill again, if necessary, until mixture mounds on a spoon. Turn into baked crust and chill until firm. Garnish with additional whipped cream, cherries and bits of candied pineapple, if desired.

Eggnog Crust: Resift 1 cup sifted flour with 3 tablespoons sugar and ¼ teaspoon salt into mixing bowl. Cut in ¼ cup shortening and 3 tablespoons butter. Add 3 tablespoons eggnog and mix to a stiff dough. Shape into a ball and chill a few minutes. Roll out on lightly-floured board to 13-inch circle. Fit into a 10-inch quiche pan with removable bottom. Prick bottom and sides of shell with tines of fork to allow steam to escape during baking. Bake in a preheated 400-degree oven 15 minutes, until crisp and lightly browned. Cool before filling.

Soufflé au Chocolat

4 oz. semi-sweet	3½ T. sugar
cooking chocolate	3 eggs, separated
1 c. milk	3 T. flour

Butter and sugar a soufflé mold. Melt chocolate with about 2 tablespoons water in small saucepan. Heat milk. Mix egg yolks, flour and sugar together in small mixing bowl. Add about ¼ cup hot milk to egg mixture; beat well, using a wire whisk, and pour back into hot milk. Cook until thickened, about 1 minute, stirring. Off heat, add melted chocolate and mix well.

Beat egg whites until stiff. Fold into chocolate mixture. Pour into prepared soufflé mold and bake in a preheated 375-degree oven about 20 minutes. Serve immediately. Serves 4.

Cold Lemon Soufflé

2 T. unflavored gelatin	1 c. lemon juice
1⅓ c. sugar, divided	½ c. water
½ tsp. salt	1 T. grated lemon rind
8 eggs, separated	

Mix together gelatin, ⅔ cup of the sugar and the salt in top of double boiler. Combine slightly beaten egg yolks, lemon juice and water; add to gelatin mixture. Cook over boiling water, stirring until gelatin dissolves and mixture thickens, about 6 minutes. Add lemon rind. Chill until mixture mounds slightly when dropped from spoon. Beat egg whites until stiff, but not dry. Gradually add remaining ⅔ cup sugar and beat until very stiff. Fold in gelatin mixture. Turn into a 10-cup soufflé dish with a 2-inch collar. Chill until firm.

To make collar, fold waxed paper into several thicknesses 3 inches wide and long enough to go around souffle dish with a generous overlap. Attach to dish with sealing tape, leaving 1 inch of the paper around dish to make a collar 2 inches high.

Pumpkin Mousse

1 8-oz. package cream
   cheese, softened
1¼ c. sugar
1¼ tsp. pumpkin pie spice
½ tsp. salt
1 29-oz. can pumpkin

1 T. unflavored gelatin
¼ c. cold water
2 c. whipping cream, whipped
½ c. slivered almonds,
   toasted
Crumb Crust

Blend cream cheese, sugar, pumpkin pie spice and salt. Add pumpkin and continue beating until thoroughly blended. Sprinkle gelatin over water in a small saucepan. Place over low heat; stir until gelatin is dissolved. Stir into pumpkin mixture; fold in whipped cream. Pour over crust in springform pan. Chill overnight. Remove sides of pan. Garnish sides and top with nuts. Serves 10 to 12.

Crumb Crust: Mix together 1⅓ cups vanilla wafer crumbs, 2 tablespoons sugar and ⅓ cup butter or margarine, melted; press firmly into bottom of 9-inch springform pan.

Fresh Orange Bavarian

3 oranges
1 T. unflavored gelatin
½ c. sugar
⅛ tsp. salt
2 eggs, separated

1¼ c. milk
1 T. fresh lemon juice
½ tsp. vanilla
½ c. heavy cream,
   whipped

Cut oranges in half. Scoop out insides and cut orange sections from membrane. Reserve shells and 1 cup orange sections. Mix gelatin, ¼ cup of the sugar and the salt in top of double boiler. Beat egg yolks and milk together; add to gelatin mixture. Cook over boiling water, stirring constantly, until gelatin is dissolved. Remove from heat and stir in lemon juice and vanilla. Chill mixture until consistency of unbeaten egg white. Beat egg whites until stiff. Beat in remaining ¼ cup sugar. Fold gelatin mixture into stiffly beaten egg whites. Fold 1 cup orange sections and the whipped cream into the gelatin mixture. Turn into reserved orange shells and chill until firm. Serves 6.

Strawberry Bavarian Cream

3 T. unflavored gelatin	2 c. mashed strawberries,
1 c. cold water	juice and pulp
1 c. sugar	2 T. lemon juice
¼ tsp. salt	2 c. heavy cream, whipped

Sprinkle gelatin on cold water in a 2½-quart saucepan to soften. Place over low heat, stirring constantly until dissolved. Remove from heat; add sugar and salt and stir until dissolved. Stir in mashed strawberries and lemon juice. Chill until mixture is the consistency of unbeaten egg white. Fold in heavy cream. Turn mixture into a 2-quart mold; chill until firm. When ready to serve, unmold and garnish with fresh strawberries and mint leaves. Serves 8.

Frozen Nesselrode Mold

¼ c. sugar	1½ tsp. vanilla
1 T. unflavored gelatin	1 tsp. rum extract
Dash salt	½ tsp. almond extract
1½ c. milk, scalded	1 c. heavy cream, whipped
½ c. candied fruits, chopped	and sweetened to taste

Combine sugar, gelatin and salt. Add milk and stir until sugar and gelatin are dissolved. Chill until very thick. Add candied fruits, vanilla and extracts. Fold in whipped cream. Pour into a 1-quart mold and freeze until firm (this will take at least 6 hours, or freeze overnight).

Before serving, allow to stand at room temperature for 10 minutes. Garnish with additional whipped cream, candied fruits and sliced almonds. Serves 6.

Grapes with Sour Cream

2½ c. seedless grapes
⅔ c. sour cream
1 tsp. slivered orange rind

2 T. fresh orange juice
¼ c. light brown sugar

Combine grapes with sour cream, orange rind and juice. Chill for at least an hour to allow flavors to blend. To serve, spoon grapes into serving dishes and sprinkle with brown sugar. Serves 4.

Fresh Melon Sherbet

1 T. gelatin
1½ c. water
4 c. fresh melon cubes

2 tsp. ascorbic acid powder
¾ c. sugar
¼ c. fresh lemon juice

Soften gelatin in ½ cup cold water, then dissolve over hot water. Cool.

Combine remaining cup water, melon cubes and ascorbic acid powder in blender and blend to a smooth puree. Or, force melon through a sieve to puree, and then add water and powder.

Add sugar, lemon juice and cooled liquid gelatin to pureed melon. Continue to blend until very smooth. Turn mixture into a deep ice cube tray or metal pan and freeze until almost firm. Scrape into a chilled bowl and beat until mushy and thick. Return to tray or pan and freeze until firm but spoonable.

Nectarine Rice Ring

2 T. unflavored gelatin
⅓ c. cold water
2¼ c. milk
3 eggs, lightly beaten
½ tsp. salt

2 c. cooked rice
¾ c. sugar
1 tsp. vanilla
1 c. whipping cream
5-6 fresh nectarines

Sprinkle gelatin over water in top of double boiler. Add milk, eggs and salt and set over hot water. Cook, stirring constantly, until gelatin is dissolved and mixture thickens slightly. Remove from heat and stir in rice, ½ cup sugar and vanilla. Cool until mixture begins to thicken. Whip cream and fold into the rice-custard mixture. Turn into lightly-oiled 6½-cup ring mold and chill until firm, several hours or overnight. Unmold onto serving platter. Cut nectarines into thin slices and mix with remaining ¼ cup sugar. Pile into center and around sides of rice mold. Serves 6.

Peaches Praliné

¼ c. brown sugar
¼ c. butter or margarine
¼ c. corn syrup
½ c. sifted all-purpose
    flour

⅛ tsp. salt
¼ c. chopped pecans
    Cream Filling
1 T. finely-ground coffee
8 pecan halves

Cream Filling

1 1-lb., 13-oz. can cling
    peach halves
1 5-oz. package vanilla
    pudding and pie filling

1½ c. milk
2 T. rum *or* ¾ tsp.
    rum extract
1 c. whipping cream

Combine brown sugar, butter and syrup in a saucepan. Heat and stir until butter is melted and ingredients are blended. Remove from heat; stir in flour, salt and chopped pecans. Drop by tablespoonfuls onto baking sheet, two to a sheet. Spread to 3-inch circles. Bake in a preheated 350-degree oven 5 to 6 minutes. Quickly shape baked circles to diameter of 5 to 5½ inches with pancake turner, then lift from baking sheet with turner onto inverted cups. Quickly form into basket shapes. Lift baskets off cups. Repeat procedure until all baskets are formed. (They are made two at a time because that is all you can handle at once—they crisp very quickly.) Just before serving, spoon Cream Filling into praline baskets. Sprinkle with ground coffee. Arrange 2 peach slices and 1 pecan half on top of each basket. Serve immediately. Serves 8.

Cream Filling: Drain peaches, saving 1 cup syrup. Combine syrup, pudding powder and milk in a saucepan. Cook as package directs; stir in rum; chill. Reserve 16 peach slices for garnish; chop remaining slices. Whip cream; fold into pudding with chopped peaches.

Poached Pears with Sabayon Sauce

3 large pears, firm but ripe
1 lemon, cut in half
4 c. water
½ c. plus 6 T. sugar
1 orange

3 egg yolks
1 egg white
¼ c. (about) dry white wine
2 T. Grand Marnier, Cointreau
   or other orange liqueur

Peel pears one at a time and cut each in half. As they are peeled and cut, rub the surface with a cut lemon half. Drop pears immediately into a bowl of cold water.

Combine the 4 cups water with ½ cup of sugar and bring to a boil. Add pear halves and simmer until tender, about 10 to 12 minutes, turning once. Let cool in syrup; drain pears carefully and chill.

Cut skin from orange and slice into thinnest possible strips. Drop these into boiling water and simmer 3 to 4 minutes. Drain and set aside.

Meanwhile, add remaining sugar to a round-bottomed mixing bowl, preferably a copper one. Add the egg yolks and white and beat with a wire whisk. Place the bowl over a double boiler containing hot water and continue beating a few seconds. Add wine, beating constantly, and continue until sauce is three or four times its original volume. Taste for sweetness and beat in more sugar, if desired. If too thick, beat in a little more wine.

Remove sauce from heat and beat in liqueur. Chill. Serve over cold pears sprinkled with orange strips. Serves 6.

After-Dinner Coffee Jelly

4 T. sugar
2 T. unflavored gelatin
6 T. instant coffee powder
6 T. instant cocoa powder
   Dash salt
½ tsp. cinnamon

⅛ tsp. nutmeg
3½ c. boiling water
2 T. brandy (or rum)
1 c. heavy cream, whipped
   and lightly sweetened

Mix sugar, gelatin, coffee powder, cocoa powder, salt, cinnamon and nutmeg in a bowl. Add boiling water, stirring until gelatin is dissolved. Taste—if you prefer it sweeter, add a little more sugar. Stir in brandy and chill. At serving time, break it up with a fork and serve, topped generously with whipped cream. Serves 6.

Dessert Crêpes

1¼ c. flour	1½ c. milk (or more)
½ tsp. salt	1 whole egg plus
1 T. sugar	1 egg yolk

Place flour in bowl, make a well in center and add salt, sugar and eggs. Use a whisk and start blending from center to mix eggs well. Add milk slowly, beating all the while, incorporating all the ingredients. Let rest 2 hours at room temperature.

If batter is too thick (it should just coat the back of a spoon), thin with a little more milk.

Lightly grease crêpe pan and cook crêpes (over medium-high heat), one at a time, using 3 tablespoons batter and tilting pan so it covers bottom. Cook on one side until top is dry, flip and cook 10 seconds on other side. Stack and use as desired.

Note: These freeze very well.

Rose's Blintzes

3 eggs	1 lb. dry cottage
¼ c. flour	cheese
Salt	2 T. sugar
½ c. water	½ c. raisins (rinsed in
Butter	hot water, drained)
2 eggs	Cinnamon

Beat 3 eggs until yolks and whites are combined; gently beat in flour and a dash of salt; gradually beat in water so mixture is smooth after each addition. Heat about 1 teaspoon butter in an 8-inch skillet so surface is well greased and pan is very hot; holding pan above heat and swirling, pour in just enough of the mixture to coat skillet; pour any extra back. Fry quickly on only one side;

dump out on board. Fry remaining pancakes the same way, adding about ½ teaspoon butter to skillet each time. Mix cheese with 2 eggs, sugar, raisins and a dash of cinnamon; place a mound of the cottage cheese mixture in center of each pancake; fold top edge, then side edges over filling; fold bottom edge over. Cover and refrigerate.

When ready to serve, fry stuffed pancakes rapidly in butter, turning to brown both sides. Serve with sour cream. Makes 12 pancakes; serves 6.

Holiday Baking

Late October really is when you should think about Christmas baking chores. Fruit cakes must be aged for from six to eight weeks, so they should be baked then. The rules that follow are quite general and will apply to most of the old-fashioned recipes you may choose or have on file.

Take one day just to check lists of ingredients and buy them. Then in spare time during the next day or so, cut up fruits and nutmeats and store in screw-top jars or plastic containers. The day before baking, prepare the pans (an important step for proper results) and measure out ingredients.

Remember, if you do this in easy steps it won't seem much work at all.

To prepare pans: All sorts of containers may be used—tube or loaf pans, coffee cans, ring molds, casseroles and metal freezer containers, to name a few. You may choose an inexpensive charlotte mold and give it as a gift container.

Pans should be greased well, then lined smoothly with paper (brown wrapping paper, paper bags or heavy bond do nicely—we've been using parchment and it works beautifully), then greased again. Let paper extend up along sides to protect cake from overbaking.

To mix: Fruits and nutmeats should be evenly distributed through the cake, so generally, measure them into a flat pan, sift dry ingredients over the top and toss lightly to mix and coat well.

Add to creamed shortening, sugar and egg mixture alternately with liquid. Spoon batter into pans gently, pushing it carefully into corners and leveling.

(We mix fruit, nuts, jam, brandy and spices, then make the cake batter and mix the two and the results are fine.)

To bake: A shallow pan of water on lowest rack of oven during baking insures moist, tender cakes. The baking time varies according to size, but the oven should always be a slow one, 275 to 300 degrees.

To age: Fruit cakes must be completely cooled before wrapping and storing. Remove from baking pans to cooling racks. If they are not to be ripened with liquor, leave the pan lining papers on until cooled.

When thoroughly cold, wrap in saran, pliofilm or cellophane. Then wrap again in aluminum foil, sealing with double fold and molding foil to cake. Store in airtight containers in a cool place.

If liquor is to be used, remove cakes from oven to cooling racks, top sides up. Pour some brandy (or other liquor—rum, sherry wine, etc.) over the tops of the hot cakes and let sit 15 minutes. Remove from racks, put waxed paper on racks and turn cakes onto them, top sides down. Remove baking paper immediately and pour brandy slowly over warm surfaces.

When liquor has soaked in and cakes are cold, wrap each in a double thickness of cheesecloth or in plastic, then in heavy foil, molding it to the cake. Store in airtight containers in a cool place to age.

To glaze: Fruit cakes should not be glazed or frosted until after they have aged (we often decorate them before baking, however, and do not bother to glaze them). A simple and handsome glaze is made by heating corn syrup to a full, rolling boil, then spreading it over the cakes with a pastry brush.

Whether your favorite fruit cake recipe is short and simple, long and complicated or somewhere in between, these rather general rules should be of help in the holiday baking chores.

Pan Sizes, Baking Times

Fruit cakes may be baked in all sizes and shapes. To estimate baking time, check this list of pan sizes and amounts.

An 8½ x 4½ x 2¾-inch foil loaf pan holds about 4 cups of batter and takes about 2 hours to bake.

A 5½ x 3 x 2½-inch loaf pan holds about 1¾ cups batter and takes about 1½ hours to bake.

A 4½ x 1½-inch round foil pan holds from 1 to 1¼ cups of batter and takes about 1¼ to 1½ hours to bake.

The 3-quart tube pan or mold takes about 2½ quarts of batter and from 2½ to 3 hours or more to bake, depending on tube size.

A 7½-inch ring mold holds 3 cups batter and takes about an hour and 45 minutes to bake.

A 6-ounce juice can will hold ½ cup batter and bake in about 50 minutes.

Cupcake pans measuring 1¾ x ¾ inches each will hold a heaping tablespoon of batter and take about 20 minutes to bake.

Equivalents in Pounds and Cups

When shopping for fruit cake ingredients, it's a good idea to check this list of bulk equivalents.

A pound of raisins, dried apricots, prunes, dried peaches, dried pears or dried figs will measure 3 to 3½ cups.

A pound of fresh California dates or cut up candied fruits and peels will measure 2 cups.

A pound of dried applies will yield 5 cups.

A pound of shelled almonds or Brazil nuts will yield 3 cups and a pound of shelled walnuts or pecans will yield 4 cups.

Fruit cake is a Christmas tradition in many households. The recipe that follows is the one taken from the handwritten loose-leaf cook book that has been handed down in our family for many, many years.

We've tried to simplify the recipe by altering the order a bit, but the ingredients remain the same.

Fruit Cake (Best Recipe)

1 lb. blanched almonds (3 c.)	1 glass jam (blackberry
½ lb. pecans (2 c.)	preferred)
¼ lb. walnuts (1 c.)	4 tsp. cinnamon
1 lb. shredded citron	½ tsp. allspice
½ lb. lemon peel	2 tsp. nutmeg
½ lb. orange peel	½ tsp. cloves
1 c. candied pineapple	1 lb. butter (or margarine)
1 lb. candied cherries	1 lb. brown sugar
2 lbs. seeded raisins	1 c. molasses
1 lb. dry figs (2 c.)	12 eggs
1 lb. pitted dates (2 c.)	1 lb. flour (3½ to 4 c.)
1 lb. currants	2 tsp. salt
1 glass brandy	Whole blanched almonds

Note: We now substitute 4 pounds of the prepared candied fruit for the citron, peels and candied pineapple and cherries in the recipe. A glass of brandy is about ½ cup—more if desired; the glass of jam (which may also be orange marmalade) is an 8- or 10-ounce one, or even larger. The recipe yields about 17 pounds of fruit cake.

Chop nuts and fruits (grind dates and figs—they're very sticky) and combine. Add brandy, jam and spices; mix well. Cream butter, add sugar, molasses and beaten eggs (beaten until foamy), mix thoroughly; add flour and salt and mix to batter consistency. Pour over fruit mixture and combine the two.

A little more flour may be needed, or a little more brandy. What dough there is should be fairly stiff—not runny.

Grease your pans well, line with heavy waxed, brown or parchment paper. Fill the pans three-fourths full and bake in a preheated 275- or 300-degree oven until a straw comes out clean (probably from 2 to 3 hours, depending on sizes). Have a pan of hot water in bottom of oven for moisture during baking.

You can decorate the tops of the cakes with almonds and cherries pressed into them before baking. They will not darken, they will stay on the cakes and you will not have to decorate them after they are cooled.

When done, turn cakes on racks to cool. Pour a little brandy slowly over top of each one. In 15 minutes, invert on waxed paper on racks, remove baking paper and pour more brandy slowly over each one. This must be done gradually, but the warm cake absorbs it much better than a cold one. When cold, wrap and place in airtight containers.

White Fruit Cake

1 c. butter
1¼ c. sugar
3 c. sifted all-purpose flour
¼ tsp. salt
2 tsp. baking powder
1 c. milk
1 tsp. vanilla
½ tsp. almond extract
½ c. chopped candied
  pineapple

1 c. chopped blanched
  almonds
½ c. chopped candied cherries
½ c. chopped mixed
  candied fruit
½ c. chopped dried apricots
1⅓ c. golden raisins
6 egg whites

Closely line a 12-cup bundt pan or ring mold (or two 9 x 5 x 3-inch loaf pans) with foil; grease foil. Cream butter with sugar until fluffy. Sift flour with salt and baking powder; set aside ½ cup.

Combine milk, vanilla and almond extract; add alternately with flour to creamed mixture.

Mix almonds and fruits with reserved ½ cup flour mixture and stir into batter. Beat egg whites until stiff peaks form; fold into batter. Pour into prepared pans and bake in a preheated 275-degree oven for 2½ hours with a shallow pan of water in bottom of oven. Cake is done when a toothpick inserted in center comes out dry. Cool cake 30 minutes; invert from mold. To keep cake moist, wrap while warm in two layers of foil and finish cooling. Makes about 3¾ pounds of cake.

This is a fruit cake that can be made at the last minute.

Quick Almond Fruit Cake with Blueberries

1 1-lb. package blueberry coffee cake mix
½ c. milk
1 egg

⅔ c. slivered almonds
1 c. diced candied lemon peel
⅔ c. diced candied pineapple
⅓ c. quartered candied cherries

Line a 2-pound coffee can or a 5-cup mold with foil, pressing it into corners; grease foil.

Blend cake mix envelope in coffee cake package with ½ cup milk and egg. Beat as package directs. Fold in almonds and candied fruits, then mix in well-drained blueberries from package and the envelope of crumble topping from mix. Spoon batter into foil-lined can. Bake in a 325-degree oven 1 hour, or until pick inserted in center comes out dry. Cool 30 minutes in can, then invert. Wrap cake in more foil to finish cooling. Makes 2½ pounds cake.

Dundee Cake

2¼ c. sifted cake flour
2 tsp. baking powder
¼ tsp. salt
½ tsp. nutmeg
½ tsp. cinnamon
¾ c. butter
1¼ c. sifted powdered sugar
4 eggs
½ c. orange juice

½ c. white raisins
½ c. seedless raisins
1 c. currants
½ c. chopped mixed candied fruit
1 c. finely-slivered almonds
¼ c. finely-chopped almonds
2 T. light corn syrup
2 T. water

Measure sifted flour, add baking powder, salt and spices and sift again.

Cream butter, add sugar gradually and cream until light and fluffy. Add eggs, one at a time, beating well after each addition. Then add flour alternately with orange juice, beginning and ending with flour. Beat after each addition until smooth. (Batter will look somewhat curdled.) Fold in fruit and slivered almonds. Spread batter in well-greased 9-inch tube pan or 3-inch deep 9-inch torte pan. Bake in a preheated 350-degree oven 30 minutes; sprinkle chopped almonds over top of cake. Continue baking 30 to 35 minutes longer, or until cake is done.

Simmer syrup and water together for 1 minute; then brush over top of cake to hold almonds in place and to give a gloss. Cool cake 15 minutes in pan; turn out on rack to finish cooling. When cold, wrap in foil and store at least overnight in refrigerator before serving.

Note: Cake slices best when it is chilled, but tastes best at room temperature. Cake may be wrapped first in cheesecloth that has been soaked in fruit juice or wine, then wrapped in foil and stored in refrigerator for a week or more to mellow flavors and give a moister cake.

Christmas Tree Bread

Dough

1 14½-oz. package hot roll mix	1 T. sugar
	½ tsp. salt
¾ c. warm water	¼ c. softened butter
1 egg	or margarine

Filling

¾ c. pitted prunes	½ tsp. cinnamon
½ c. cooked dried apricots	1 tsp. grated lemon rind
	1 T. lemon juice
½ tsp. nutmeg	¼ c. sugar

Dough: Remove packet of yeast from roll mix and dissolve in warm water. Beat egg in mixing bowl; add yeast, sugar and salt. Gradually stir in the flour, beating well between each addition until smooth dough forms. Grease top; cover with damp cloth and let rise in warm place until doubled in bulk. (Placing bowl in pan of hot water works.) Knead gently on lightly-floured surface and divide in half. Roll each to a 4 x 14-inch rectangle. Let rest 20 minutes or so; dough will relax and hold its shape better if this is done.

Spread dough with butter and filling. Roll up as for jelly roll, starting from long side, tapering at each end. Place on greased cookie sheet. Clip ¼ inch apart with scissors, separating clips as you go by pulling one to left, one to right and one to center. This makes branches of tree. Cover and let rise again in warm place until almost doubled in bulk. Bake in a preheated 375-degree oven about 20 minutes. Cool and drizzle with powdered sugar frosting. Makes two 14-inch trees.

Filling: Cut up prunes and apricots; combine fruits, spices, lemon rind and juice, and sugar. Use as directed.

Miscellaneous

*In any recipe collection worth its salt,
there is a group of recipes that fit no categories in the book.
Technically, they're misfits.
But since they belong, here they are.*

*A lot of Swiss will tell you that their children get their famous
rosy cheeks less from the mountain air than from eating Muesli.*

Bircher Muesli

2 c. quick or old-fashioned
    oats, uncooked
1¾ c. milk
¼ tsp. salt
¼ c. lemon juice
⅓ c. honey

1 c. golden raisins
½ c. chopped, pitted prunes
⅓ c. chopped dried apricots
2 medium apples, cored
    and grated
¾ c. chopped toasted nutmeats

Combine oats, milk and salt. Cover and refrigerate overnight.
Just before serving, add remaining ingredients; mix well. Garnish
with sliced fresh fruit in season and serve with brown sugar and
milk, half and half or cream.

*A*nd then, of course, there's Granola, for which there are several recipes. This is just one of them, called:

Joy in the Morning

3 c. rolled oats	3 T. margarine
¼ c. wheat germ	½ c. brown sugar
½ c. hulled sunflower seeds	¼ tsp. salt
½ c. grated unsweetened coconut	¼ c. water

Mix together the oats, wheat germ, seeds and coconut. Melt together then mix thoroughly into oat mixture the margarine, brown sugar, salt and water. Spread in a shallow baking pan and bake in a 350-degree oven until it smells heavenly—about 10 minutes. Stir once and put back for a few minutes until golden brown.

If desired, you can add chopped nuts, sesame seeds and chopped fresh coconut (instead of grated).

*T*here is brandied fruit and brandied fruit. This is one of the more popular kinds.

Brandied Fruit

To make starter: Drain and slice 2 cups canned peaches. Add 2 cups sugar, stir well. Place in a glass container that *does not* have a tight fitting lid (an apothecary jar is ideal). Stir this mixture once every day for two weeks. It will begin to froth, or work.

Now you have a starter and can begin to add additional fruits —peaches, apricots, pineapple. (Do not use pears or any fresh fruits, especially bananas.) Add to your mixture every two weeks —one cup drained, sliced, canned fruit and one cup sugar every time. After the new fruit and sugar marinate a couple of days, the mixture is ready again. Never let the mixture get lower than one cup in quantity or you will need to start over.

The mixture should never be refrigerated—that would stop the "brandying" process. You can go a month or two before adding more fruit if you wish. It may be more potent that way, but it won't spoil.

And then there is this kind of brandied fruit:

Brandied Cherries

4 c. sweet fresh cherries
3 c. sugar
1 c. brandy

Select large perfect cherries; wash and dry completely. Pit cherries and combine with sugar in large bowl. Cover and let stand 1 hour, stirring every 15 minutes. Pack into crock (or glass container). Add brandy. Cover and let stand in a cool place for four to six months before using. The pot may be replenished with more fruit, sugar and brandy, using the proportions given in the recipe. Stir thoroughly after each addition.

Candied citrus peel is one of the nicest things there is in the whole world, and it's a must to serve during the holidays.

Candied Citrus Peel

1 lb. grapefruit peel
(4 medium to large)
or 1 lb. lemon peel
(12 large)
or 1 lb. orange peel
(about 8 medium)

2 c. sugar
1 c. freshly-squeezed
orange juice
¼ c. light corn syrup
Granulated sugar

Wash fruit. Score peel into quarters; remove sections of peel with fingers. Place peel in large saucepan; add cold salted water to cover, using 2 teaspoons salt for each quart of water. Bring to a full boil; drain immediately and rinse with cold water. Return peel to pan, cover with cold water (no salt). Bring to a boil and cook 20 minutes; rinse in cold water. Pat dry with paper towels. Cut each section of peel into uniform strips, approximately ½ inch wide. Combine 2 cups sugar, orange juice and corn syrup in a saucepan. Boil until thick or candy thermometer registers 228 degrees; add strips of peel. Cook until peel becomes transparent, about 35 to 40 minutes. Drain; spread on waxed paper to cool. Roll in sugar to coat completely. Store in tightly-covered container until ready to serve. Makes about 1 pound.

*I*mported Italian chestnuts usually are in the markets in November. They peel a little more easily than the domestic ones. However, if you don't want to go to the trouble of roasting them, you can boil them in their shells for an hour or so. This way they peel easily and retain their good nutty flavor.

Roasted Chestnuts

Cut a gash in the flat side of each chestnut (makes them easier to peel and keeps them from exploding during cooking). Then put them in a pan with a little bit of oil and bake them in a preheated 450-degree oven for about 20 minutes, shaking the pan once in a while. They should be peeled while hot, so be sure to wear gloves or mitts for the task. If they cool too much, put them back in the oven for a few minutes.

*W*alnuts and dried fruits make ideal sweetmeats to enjoy during the months when fresh fruits are unavailable.

Walnut Stuffed Prunes

½ c. chopped walnuts
½ c. chopped mixed candied
   fruits and peels
1 T. sherry

1 T. honey
24 large, soft, pitted,
   dried prunes

Combine walnuts, candied fruits, sherry and honey. Select soft, tender prunes (or steam prunes 10 to 15 minutes in colander over boiling water; cool). Stuff with walnut mixture.

Walnut Stuffed Brandied Dates

36 pitted fresh dates	2 T. orange juice
¼ c. brandy	36 large walnut halves

Place dates in jar. Add brandy and orange juice. Cover and refrigerate overnight. Turn jar back and forth several times to distribute liquid. Remove from liquid and stuff each date with a walnut half.

A curry dinner without chutney just isn't a curry dinner.

Exotic Pear Chutney

3 lbs. Bartlett pears	1 clove garlic, minced
1 lb. brown sugar	½ tsp. cayenne pepper
1 pt. cider vinegar	2 tsp. salt
1 medium onion, chopped	½ tsp. ground cinnamon
1 c. golden raisins	½ tsp. ground cloves
¼ c. diced preserved ginger	2 tsp. mustard seed

Core and dice, but do not peel, pears. Combine brown sugar and vinegar in a large saucepan and bring to a boil. Add pears and remaining ingredients. Cook slowly, stirring occasionally, until mixture is thick, about 1 hour. Pour into hot, sterilized jars and seal. Or, you may leave jars unsealed and store in the refrigerator for up to four weeks. This makes approximately 5 half-pint jars.

Nectarine Ginger Chutney

4 oz. fresh ginger root	2 medium cloves garlic,
or 2-3 T. ground ginger	minced
1½ c. water	1 c. chopped onion
Salt	½ c. lime juice
3½ lbs. fresh nectarines	1½ T. canned green chili
3½ c. sugar	pepper, chopped
1¼ c. vinegar	1 c. golden or dark
¼ c. Worcestershire	seedless raisins

Pare and coarsely grate or finely chop ginger; cover with water in kettle, add 2 tablespoons salt and cook at a simmer until almost tender, about 20 minutes. (If ground ginger is used, eliminate this step. However, try to use the fresh ginger—it is much, much better.) Slice nectarines into ¼-inch thick slices (they will measure 4 to 4½ cups). Drain ginger, reserving ¼ cup liquid (use ¼ cup water with ground ginger). Mix this ginger liquid with sugar, 2 teaspoons salt, the vinegar, Worcestershire sauce and garlic; bring to boil. Add nectarines, cooked ginger root, onion, lime juice, chopped chili and raisins and cook over medium-low heat to desired thickness, or about 1½ hours. Chutney thickens when cold. Pour into hot sterilized ½-pint glasses, filling them to within ¾ inch of the tops. Melt paraffin over hot water and pour over chutney to seal. Makes 8 half pints.

Chinese Plum Chutney

4 lbs. fresh plums,
halved and pitted
2 qts. vinegar
1½ lbs. brown sugar
1 lb. granulated sugar
¼ lb. ginger root, soaked well
in water, drained
and chopped
½ c. salt

¼ lb. mustard seed, crushed
1 7-oz. can green
chili peppers,
seeded and diced
2 4-oz. cans red pimientos,
seeded and diced
1 small onion, chopped
2 cloves garlic, peeled
and chopped

Cook the plums in 1 quart vinegar until soft. Make a syrup of the other quart of vinegar and the sugars in another kettle. Bring to a boil and cook until syrupy. Add the plum-vinegar mixture and the remaining ingredients and simmer for 1½ hours, stirring frequently until the sauce is as thick as jam and most of the liquid has cooked away. Seal in hot sterilized jars. Makes about 8 half pints.

Pickles, anyone?

Pickled Hot Peppers

2½ lbs. 4- to 5-inch hot peppers
    Boiling water
2 c. distilled white vinegar
2 c. water

1 c. granulated sugar
6 cloves garlic
3 tsp. salad oil
1½ tsp. salt

Wash peppers. Cut off stem end only. Place peppers in bowl; cover with boiling water. Let stand 5 minutes; drain. Combine vinegar, water and sugar in saucepan; boil 5 minutes.

Meanwhile, pack peppers into hot sterilized jars. To each jar add 2 cloves garlic, 1 teaspoon salad oil and ½ tsp. salt. Immediately pour boiling syrup over peppers, one jar at a time, to within ⅛ inch of top, making sure solution covers peppers. Seal each jar at once. Makes 3 pints.

Note: To protect hands, wear rubber gloves throughout preparation.

Pickled Green Peppers

3 lbs. green peppers
    Boiling water
2½ c. distilled white vinegar
2½ c. water

1¼ c. granulated sugar
8 cloves garlic
4 tsp. salad oil
2 tsp. salt

Wash peppers; remove seed pods and white "seams" Cut lengthwise into ¾-inch strips. Place pepper strips in bowl; cover with boiling water and let stand 5 minutes; drain.

Combine vinegar, water and sugar in saucepan; boil 5 minutes. Meanwhile, pack peppers into hot sterilized jars. To each jar add 2 cloves garlic, 1 teaspoon salad oil and ½ teaspoon salt. Immediately pour boiling syrup over peppers, one jar at a time, to within ⅛ inch of top to cover peppers. Seal each jar at once. Makes 4 pints.

Watermelon Pickles

Rind from one large
watermelon, diced
(about 4 quarts)

Brine solution
Pickling syrup
1 lemon, sliced thin

Brine: Add ¼ cup salt and 1 teaspoon ascorbic acid powder to 2 quarts water. Cover rind with this solution and let stand overnight. Drain rind and rinse under cold running water. Add water to cover and bring to a boil. Reduce heat to moderate and cook until rind is almost tender. Drain and let stand.

Pickling syrup: Mix 2 quarts cider vinegar, 2 cups water and 4 pounds sugar (9 cups) in a large kettle. Bring to a boil and add 2 tablespoons whole cloves, 2 tablespoons whole allspice, 1 teaspoon cracked ginger and 3 sticks cinnamon, broken up, all of which have been tied together in a piece of cheesecloth. Add lemon and 2 tablespoons ascorbic acid powder. Bring again to a boil and cook rapidly for 8 to 10 minutes.

Add cooked rind to syrup. Simmer until clear, about 1 hour. Remove spice bag. Pack in hot sterilized jars and seal. Makes about 4 pints.

California Wine Jelly

2 c. California wine
(Burgundy, Sauterne,
Rose, Sherry, Port,
Muscatel or Tokay)

3 c. sugar
½ bottle fruit pectin
Paraffin
5 6-oz. wine glasses

Place wine in top of double boiler over rapidly boiling water; add sugar and mix well. Heat until sugar is completely dissolved, but do not let boil. Remove from heat and stir in fruit pectin. Pour into glasses and immediately seal with paraffin.

Kindergarten teachers and den mothers, as well as their many counterparts, are forever in need of recipes for play clay and playdough, among others, to further the talents of their young charges.

Here, then, a recipe for each.

Playdough

8 c. flour	Vegetable or tempera
2 c. salt	coloring
3 T. vegetable oil	Water

Mix flour, salt, oil and coloring thoroughly and add water to make a soft dough. Store in airtight containers.

Play Clay

2 c. baking soda	1¼ c. cold water
1 c. cornstarch	

Mix soda and cornstarch. Add water and mix until smooth. Bring to a boil and boil one minute, until the consistency of moist mashed potatoes, stirring constantly. Spoon out on a plate. Cover with a damp cloth and cool. Knead and roll out on waxed paper.

Cut out designs with cookie cutters, bottle caps or whatever—or shape by hand. Etch in patterns. Let dry until hard (24 to 48 hours). Mount clips, pins or backing with white glue. Paint with tempera or water colors. Dry. Coat with clear shellac or clear nail polish.

There is no nicer gift to give than a fragrant, old-fashioned Pomander Ball. They're a little tedious to make, but well worth the time and trouble, for they last for years. They give a deliciously spicy scent to both clothes and linen closets.

Pomander Ball

1 thin-skinned orange	3 tsp. cinnamon
1-2 boxes whole cloves	1 sheet saran, about
3 tsp. powdered arrowroot	18 inches square
or acacia	Ribbon for a bow

Wash orange and dry. Start at the stem end and insert row after row of whole cloves, putting them as close together as you can until the orange is completely covered (you may make holes for them with a toothpick or a small nail—it makes the chore a little easier). Then roll in the cinnamon and arrowroot or acacia, which have been mixed together. Wrap in saran and let stand 2 weeks, dust off the powder and then tie up with ribbon as a package, leaving a loop to hang it by.

Potpourri, also known as rose jar, gives off a delightfully fresh and spicy scent and is lovely in any room in the house. You can keep it in a container or sew it up into individual sachet packets for drawers and closets.

Potpourri

Remove petals from opened roses and dry them on sheets of paper. Sprinkle with salt. Add a few other fragrant blossoms, such as garden pinks or heliotropes, and a few herbs, such as rosemary or marjoram. Add a sprinkling of balsam needles and a bit more salt. When all are thoroughly dried, measure out two quarts (rose petals should always predominate) and place in a crockery jar with the following:

¼ oz. cloves
¼ oz. mace
¼ oz. cinnamon
¼ oz. allspice
⅛ oz. crushed coriander

⅛ oz. powdered
    cardamom seeds
Gum benzoin
1 oz. violet sachet

Stir occasionally during a period of two or three weeks and keep the jar covered in between. Then use as desired.

*R*ose petals also are used for making beads. This is a very old-fashioned recipe that has been enjoying fashion again.

Rose Beads

Pick fragrant rose petals and keep them in bags in the refrigerator until you have a good quantity. Now, put the petals through the meat grinder, using a medium or fine blade, catching all the juices, and put the resulting mixture in an iron container with a cover.

Repeat this for 18 to 20 days, each time forcing the mixture through the grinder and replacing it in the iron container. When the pulp gets smooth and holds its shape, make balls by rolling bits the size of large peas.

Stick a large pin through the center of each and stick the pin in a cardboard box to allow to dry. The drying time varies with the weather. Some say in the sun, some say not in the sun.

When done, string, then cover with olive oil in a jar to soak for a week or ten days. Then, put them in a woolen sock and rub them gently for a few days, or until they are shiny. Wipe well and restring on dental floss.

Stamp Pad Ink

Grind up an inch of lead from an indelible pencil and mix it with a teaspoon of glycerin and a teaspoon of water. Let settle for eight to ten hours and it's ready for use.

*H*erbed and spiced wine vinegars make excellent gifts as well as good things for your own table. Be sure to start with good quality. vinegar. These recipes use grapes.

Spiced Vinegar

1½ c. white wine vinegar	2 cinnamon sticks
2 tsp. sugar	6 whole cloves
½ c. grapes	

Combine wine vinegar and sugar in a small saucepan; heat just until sugar is completely dissolved. Place grapes, cloves and cinnamon sticks in a pint bottle and pour in the warmed vinegar. Cork or cap and allow to stand for several days.

Fruited Vinegar

1½ c. white wine vinegar
½ c. grapes
1 small orange rind

1 thin slice fresh pineapple
with shell

Warm the vinegar in a small saucepan. Place grapes, pineapple and orange rind in a pint bottle and pour in the warmed vinegar. Cork or cap and allow to stand for several days.

Rosemary-Grape Vinegar

1½ c. white wine vinegar
1 T. honey

½ c. grapes
2 large sprigs fresh rosemary

Combine wine vinegar and honey in a small saucepan. Heat until honey is dissolved. Place grapes and rosemary in a pint bottle and pour in the vinegar. Cork or cap and allow to mellow for several days.

Dill-Grape Vinegar

1½ c. white wine vinegar
1 T. honey

½ c. grapes
2 sprigs fresh dill

Combine vinegar and honey in a small saucepan and heat until honey is dissolved. Place grapes and dill in a pint bottle and pour in the warmed vinegar. Cork or cap and allow to stand for several days.

All recipes and methods for making yoghurt are pretty much the same, but some people have elaborate yoghurt-making kits and others have devised proofing boxes to keep the mix at the desired 110 degrees.

In fact, about all you need are a Pyrex or ceramic casserole with a cover and an oven you can keep at about 110 degrees.

Plain Yoghurt

1 c. very warm water
¼ c. plain unpasteurized
   commercial yoghurt

1 c. non-instant powdered milk
1 13-oz. can evaporated
   skim milk

Put the water in the blender container (you can put it in a bowl and mix with a wire whisk, if desired), add the powdered milk, commercial yoghurt and evaporated skim milk, whirring slowly all the time. If it seems too thick, add a little water.

Pour mixture into a Pyrex or ceramic casserole that has a top, cover, wrap in a towel (if desired—helps maintain even temperature) and place in the oven heated to 110 degrees. Leave it there for from three to five hours (sometimes it takes longer), until it is set. If you jiggle the container, the mixture is ready if it looks like custard or set gelatin. Refrigerate to chill, then use as desired. Remember to save out a little in a separate container to use as the starter for your next batch.

Note: It is best to use non-instant powdered milk because it yields a thicker, richer product. Also, get unpasteurized commercial yoghurt because pasteurization kills the culture.

Then, there's this method.

Basic Yoghurt

1 qt. milk (slim,
   skim, whole)

2 T. powdered milk
1 T. commercial yoghurt

Combine fresh milk and powdered milk in a heavy pan. Bring slowly to boiling point, stirring. Remove and transfer to a bowl to cool to about 110 degrees, or just above lukewarm.

Blend a little milk with the yoghurt until it is smooth, then add yoghurt mixture to bowl of warm milk. Keep the cultured mixture covered and set in a warm place. When mixture is the consistency of thick cream, refrigerate to chill.

*W*hy not make your own beef jerky? That way, you'll know exactly what's been used in its preparation.

Beef Jerky

1 beef flank steak	Garlic
½ c. soy sauce	Lemon pepper

Have the flank steak well trimmed. Cut it lengthwise (with grain) into long thin strips no more than ¼ inch thick. Toss with soy sauce, then arrange in a single layer on a wire rack on a baking sheet. Sprinkle with garlic salt and lemon pepper. Place a second rack over meat and flip over, removing what is now top rack. Sprinkle again with seasonings, then bake in a very slow (150 to 175 degrees) oven overnight, or about 10 to 12 hours. Store in a covered container.

*P*ersimmons must be very ripe for the best jam. Remove the petals at stem end, wash fruit. Do not peel. Dice into small pieces or put large slices into blender or through strainer, food mill or colander.

Persimmon Jam

(no pectin)

4 c. persimmon pulp	4 c. sugar

Measure pulp into heavy saucepan. Add sugar and stir well. Place on heat and simmer slowly for 20 minutes, stirring constantly. Keep below boiling—just simmer. Pour into hot sterilized glasses and seal. Makes about 4 cups jam.

Persimmon Jam

(pectin)

3 c. prepared fruit
1 c. water
1 pkg. pectin

½ c. lemon juice
6 c. sugar

Measure fruit and water into large kettle. Stir in pectin and lemon juice; bring to a full rolling boil and boil for approximately 30 seconds. Add sugar and again bring to a rolling boil for exactly 4 minutes by the clock. Stir constantly. Remove from heat and pour into hot sterilized containers. Makes about 6 glasses jam.

Almond Paste

8 oz. whole blanched
   almonds
1½ c. sifted powdered sugar

1 egg white
1 tsp. almond extract
¼ tsp. salt

Grind the almonds, ½ cup at a time, in the blender or a food chopper using the fine blade. This will give you between 1½ and 2 cups of ground almonds, which you combine with the sugar, egg white, extract and salt, working to form a stiff paste. Store in an airtight container in the refrigerator.

Blanched Almonds

Put shelled almonds in a bowl, pour boiling water over them and let stand a few minutes. Pour the water off and simply pinch each one between index finger and thumb—the skin will slip right off.

Grenadine Syrup

Ripe pomegranates
Sugar

Red food coloring
(optional)

Peel ripe pomegranates and remove pulp. Put ten parts pulp to 11 parts sugar in a saucepan and let mixture stand for 24 hours. Bring to a boil and strain immediately through a sieve, taking care not to bruise seeds, which would result in an unpleasant flavor. Pour the syrup into hot sterilized bottles and seal them.

If you use the food coloring, add it after bringing the mixture to a boil.

*R*ock candy is something you rarely see any more. This is a very old recipe.

Rock Candy

4 lbs. white sugar
1 qt. water

Gelatin
Gum-arabic

Dissolve the sugar in the water; place this in an enamel kettle over low heat for half an hour; pour into it a small quantity of gelatin and gum-arabic dissolved together; all the impurities that rise to the surface should be skimmed off at once.

Instead of gelatin and gum-arabic, the white of an egg may be used as a (clarifying) substitute with good results. To make the clarifying process still better, strain liquid through a flannel bag.

To make the candy, boil this syrup a few minutes, allow to cool; the crystallization takes place on the sides of the cooking vessel.

Index

APPETIZERS

SOUPS

SALADS

MEAT, BEEF

MEAT, LAMB

MEAT, PORK

MEAT, VEAL

MEAT, VARIETY

POULTRY, CHICKEN

POULTRY, TURKEY

POULTRY, OTHER

SEAFOOD

VEGETABLES

CASSEROLES AND ONE-DISH MEALS

SAUCES AND SUCH

EGG DISHES

ALL KINDS OF BREADS

DESSERTS AND SWEETS, CAKES

DESSERTS AND SWEETS, PASTRIES

DESSERTS AND SWEETS, COOKIES

DESSERTS AND SWEETS, PIES

DESSERTS AND SWEETS, OTHER

DESSERTS AND SWEETS, HOLIDAY BAKING

MISCELLANEOUS

Notes